American
Jihad

American Jihad

Islam After Malcolm X

STEVEN BARBOZA

IMAGE BOOKS
DOUBLEDAY

NEW YORK . LONDON . TORONTO . SYDNEY . AUCKLAND

AN IMAGE BOOK
PUBLISHED BY DOUBLEDAY
a division of Bantam Doubleday Dell Publishing Group, Inc.
1540 Broadway, New York, New York 10036

IMAGE, DOUBLEDAY, and the portrayal of a deer drinking
from a stream are trademarks of Doubleday,
a division of Bantam Doubleday Dell Publishing Group, Inc.

American Jihad was originally published in hardcover by Doubleday in 1994.
The Image Books edition published by special arrangement with Doubleday.

Grateful acknowledgment is made to the following for permission to reprint
material:

Excerpt from *The Autobiography of Malcolm X* by Malcolm X, with the assistance of
Alex Haley. Copyright © 1964 by Alex Haley and Malcolm X, and copyright © 1965 by
Alex Haley and Betty Shabazz. Reprinted by permission of Random House, Inc.
Excerpt from *The Meaning of the Holy Qur'an* by Abdullah Yusuf Ali. Amana
Corporation, Brentwood, Maryland, U.S.A.
Excerpts from "For the Love of Allah," by Idris M. Diaz, the *Philadelphia Inquirer
Magazine,* April 2, 1989.
Lyrics from "Blessed Are Those Who Struggle" and "Get Moving" by Suliaman El Hadi.
Excerpt from *The Fire Next Time* by James Baldwin, © 1962, 1963, copyright renewed.
Published by Vintage Books. Reprinted with permission from the James Baldwin Estate.
Lyrics from "Life's a Test" by Maryum Ali.

The Library of Congress has cataloged the Doubleday edition as follows:
  American jihad : Islam after Malcolm X / by
Steven Barboza.
      p. cm.
    1. Black Muslims—History. 2. Islam—United States—History—20th
century. I. Barboza, Steven.
  BP221.A46 1994
  297′.87′097309045—dc20   93-31469
                                CIP

ISBN 0-385-47694-9
First Image Books Edition: April 1995
10 9 8 7 6 5 4 3 2 1

To Regina Fe, Lillian, and Lillie

Contents

Acknowledgments

To thank those who contributed in some way to the completion of this book would take many pages and I would still unintentionally neglect to name everyone; the list goes on and on. But I would not feel that this book is complete without furnishing at least the short list:

Malaika Adero	Cindy Gilmore
Shamshoodeen Ali	Yvonne Haddad
Nawal Ammar	Carole Hall
Jervis Anderson	Sohail Hashmi
Linda Anderson	Mary Anne Howland
The Barboza Family	Diane Joseph
Jean Barros	The Walter Lewis Family
Sandra Batmangelich	Leonard Muhammad
M Booth & Associates	Sheila Musaji
Karen Borack	Brad Rodney
Marie Brown	Ruben Vargas
Michael Crawford	Mohamed Zakariya

I am especially grateful to my editor, who rescued, polished, and pushed the manuscript toward publication, initiating the whole process in a relatively brief telephone call.

And my wife, Regina: Her generous love, support, comfort, strength, encouragement, and warmth sustained me all along.

There is no God but God,
Muhammad is His Messenger,
God is He.

The *shahada*, the fundamental creed of Islam.

Introduction

Allah's Will in America

I discovered Malcolm X late.

He died in 1965, eight years before I heard his message. Yet for me his words were fresh and new—and they could still strike fear into people's hearts.

Many years before Hollywood got around to putting his life on film, and decades before his X adorned baseball caps, I would hole myself up in a library and listen to recordings of his speeches. They were full of pent-up rage. He lashed out at the white man, whom he called a "blue-eyed devil" and derided as a liar, a drunkard, an adulterer, a thief, a murderer. I marveled at his gall, at the convincing tone of his seditious voice, at the power and conviction with which he said the black man's "natural religion" was Islam.[1] He said the American Negroes' ancestors were, in fact, African Muslims and America wanted to hide this from the Negro because this country actually feared what the Negro could bring himself to do if he set his mind to it. Things could get out of hand.

I wanted to know more, so I visited the Nation of Islam's Boston temple, where I attended a sort of Sunday-school class. There, a well-dressed minister inveighed hard against Christianity, calling it the religion of "death" and saying its symbol, the crucifix, provided clear enough proof of that. Just open your eyes and see how Jesus was nailed to the cross, and how Christians adore the whole idea, he said.

On the streets, I met bow-tied brothers hawking bean pies and *Muhammad Speaks,* the Nation's newspaper. They eagerly preached one on one, and their dignified bearing—it seemed drilled into them—appealed to that

[1] For background information on Islam, refer to page 357.

3

part of me attracted to uniforms and regimentation. They were sharp, respectful, and streetwise—nationalist soldiers molded into a fearless image, that of Malcolm.

Ironically I found them charming. They fired my imagination. They were prepared seemingly to lay down their lives for a sacred-held cause, and as the scholar C. Eric Lincoln pointed out, self-sacrifice was the lifeblood of this movement. And they were always more than willing to carry on for hours, expounding on what they considered to be the treacheries of the white race, rehashing the teachings of their "honorable" spiritual leader, Elijah Muhammad, so their listeners might wake up and come "back to life," to their senses, by understanding a few simple "truths."

Yet they also had the ominous, disciplined look of a firing squad. I sensed there was something secretive, exclusionary, even combative, about them. The slightest perceived offense might tick them off or might be interpreted as a breach of trust. I imagined setting them off in a tirade just by debating some finer point. With their short haircuts and leery, ever-watchful gaze, they seemed ready to fall into rank—poised to bring a karate chop down on my neck. To me they were desperate, indoctrinated men locked in a fierce struggle.

Their version of Islam lacked the spiritual breadth I typically associated with religion. Its focus was shamelessly narrow, politicized and essentially racist. Elijah's Lost-Found Nation in the West was quasi-religious—a cult that appeared to be losing ground since Malcolm's assassination. It was no longer championed by that angry man who'd lured thousands of blacks with his charisma and seductive logic. His death had left a void.

Elijah himself was regarded as messianic and he did inspire the devotion of a large following, but to much of the black community his appeal was basically that of a wizened old man, a venerated entrepreneur with a philosophy of self-help that sounded eminently sensible and levelheaded, that sounded in fact like just the sort of thing I figured black America needed to hear. And heed.

In his teaching he effectively played on blacks' hatred for their conditions and their oppressor, using it as a unifying theme for his dogma and as the foundation upon which to build his community.

His instincts were superb. He worked the black community by crystallizing a clear vision of "the enemy," appealing to blacks' sense of belonging and by taking advantage of the black American's proclivity for joining. As Lincoln pointed out in his book *The Black Muslims in America,* the Negro

Malcolm X in 1963.
PHOTO: ADGER W. COWANS

is compelled to join in order to escape the isolation, the sense of deprivation he experiences as a social outcast. One could very easily become a member of his nationwide community, a positive, spiritually uplifting, intensely pro-black organization.

Still I wasn't convinced of Elijah's "truths" and I certainly didn't want to become one of his angry soldiers.

Then I learned that Elijah had declared his own prophethood and categorically dismissed the existence of life after death, saying this theological concept was ultimately a masterly scheme, a hoax devised to cheat blacks out of what they had earned in this world.

His abolition of the hereafter was heretical and, to me, offensive. It didn't smack of religion in any sense that I had known. In fact, it directly contradicted all I had ever learned about religion that was comforting.

And if I could have found his concept of no hereafter plausible, there was yet another unconscionable story to contend with: Elijah's myth about how the white race was actually an aberration, a race of virtual Frankensteins created by a mad black scientist named Yakub over 6,000 years ago. I also learned that Elijah's followers believed he was divine and thus would never die.

I couldn't decide which story sounded more preposterous. I told myself the Nation was not for me, and like many other black Americans disen-

Muslim sisters at prayer.
PHOTO: ROBERT SENGSTACKE

chanted with him and resolved to repudiate Christianity for all its short-comings, I checked out orthodox Islam.

As Malcolm described it in his gripping autobiography, published after his death, this "other" Islam, this "original" version, better fit my idea of religion. I liked what I learned about it. It was straightforward and unadulterated with racialist, backlash ideology; it stressed deeds more than intentions as the truest test of faith; for a godhead it offered no confusing trinity; and there was no intercessor. With prayer, one had direct access to one's maker. Islam seemed almost perfect. Its one flaw was that Muhammad had enjoined prayer five times a day, and who had time for that.

What finally convinced me to convert was the futility of my own prayers. As a Christian, they made me feel beaten, ignored, betrayed. So, in early 1975, I chose Allah over Jesus.

It was a semiformal ritual, a simple one that ended before I was fully aware it had begun. I walked into a Manhattan mosque, and into the office of an Egyptian imam. He was austere. He took charge of my conversion, mirthlessly administering the *shahada,* the declaration of faith ("I bear witness that there is no god but Allah and that Muhammad is His messenger"), as his equally somber assistant, Muhammad, recorded my name in a ledger. I walked out feeling delivered, telling myself, *insh'Allah* (God willing), someday I will pray in Mecca.

I didn't wear my religion on my sleeve, as many converts do. My approach to Islam took subtler form. Any action I undertook began with a statement of intention, *Bismillah* ("In the name of Allah"); I fasted every Ramadan (the holy month of fasting); and I prayed to Allah daily, feeling no compulsion to broadcast my conversion and thus become the subject of gossip. I'd weave my prayers into my frantic junior executive's schedule, disappearing every so often into a stockroom in J. C. Penney's corporate headquarters, where, barefoot on a flattened-out box and facing the direction I determined Mecca to be in, I whispered Arabic prayers as telephones rang and business buzzed as usual outside the tranquil little universe I'd created for myself.

My conversion was not unusual. I am one of millions of Americans, former Christians and Jews, who have embraced Islam over the last two decades, people who, unlike Muhammad Ali and Kareem Abdul-Jabbar and Malcolm X, have not made news.

Many who converted to Islam (myself included) did so in spite of reading absurd passages like the following from a high school text, a description of Islam that would almost have been amusing if it weren't so dangerously subjective:

> It was started by a wealthy businessman of Arabia called Muhammad. He claimed that he was a prophet. He found followers among other Arabs. He told them that they were picked to rule the world.

Of course, American converts vary greatly in degrees of religiosity. Indeed many today do not practice Islam at all, and some merely borrow what they want from Islam and dismiss the rest, so that now, meeting someone named Khalil or Aisha or Naima or Rasul who is not a practicing Muslim is not altogether uncommon.

One of the mosques I attend has none of the charm of a cozy chapel.[2] It exudes none of the soaring, otherworldly spirit that once inspired great cathedrals. It bears none of the trademarks we usually associate with Islam —no tear-shaped dome, no minaret, no delicate Qur'anic frieze. It's a simple loft in an unassuming building in the maze of lower Manhattan and it's adorned only with a drab carpet, a few posters of arabesque calligraphy, a beat-up desk, a bulletin board, a shoe rack, partitioned areas for men and for women, and a homemade *minbar*—a staired pulpit that looks makeshift enough to have been constructed of leftover paneling and carpeting. The place has the feel of a room where a grass-roots organization meets.

Yet it is here each Friday at lunch hour that hundreds of corporate executives, city employees, diplomats, blue-collar workers, and a few ex-hustlers assemble to answer a muezzin's Arabic summons to prayer. Facing Mecca, the congregation forms neat rows behind the imam, then listens prayerfully to him recite verses from the Qur'an and mimics his every move —standing straight, bowing on cue, standing again, and then prostrating, their noses pressed to the rug.

The mosque is located in a busy downtown district a half block from City Hall. There I meet all types of Muslims—Arabs, Africans, Asians, and many black and white Americans, some who converted because of Malcolm X's influence, some who have never traveled abroad but who nevertheless identify so thoroughly with Prophet Muhammad's *hadith* (traditions) that they wear robes as he did over 1,400 years ago.

[2] In 1993, there were more than 70 to choose from in New York City, more than twice the number a decade earlier. And there are an estimated 800,000 Muslims in the New York metropolitan area.

Reformed sinners praying shoulder to shoulder with those raised to live by Prophet Muhammad's *Sunnah*—all are part of a movement that has spread across America, one paralleling the resurgence of Islam in the Middle East, Africa, and Asia.

As Islam casts its shadow across the geopolitical arena and plays a pivotal role in reshaping the world economic order, it also lives up to its reputation as the fastest-growing[3] of the universal religions. In America it is no longer practiced solely by immigrants or by a mere handful of celebrities; millions pray to Allah daily and gather in large congregations every Friday, the Muslim Sabbath. And this movement stretches from the street corner, where white-robed, skullcapped Muslims sell incense and religious paraphernalia, to the boardroom, where Muslims look and dress no differently from anyone else; from makeshift inner-city mosques to the grand Islamic centers of New York or Chicago or Washington, D.C.; and from black and Hispanic communities to mesas in the Southwest and to lily-white suburbia.

There are more than 200,000 Muslim businesses, 1,200 mosques, 165 Islamic schools, 425 Muslim associations, and 85 Islamic publications. But because Muslims do not yet form a cohesive voting bloc and claim no homogeneous political identity on the local[4] or national level, and because Islam in America approaches the diversity it takes on in other parts of the world, few Americans are aware that Muslims here probably outnumber Jews, making up the second-largest religious group in the nation.[5]

Islam—the word itself means "submission"—is not new to the New World. Evidence suggests that Muslims from Africa and Spain reached America long before Columbus brought Christianity;[6] and it has been said

---

[3] The American Muslim Council estimates the growth rate of the U.S. Muslim community to be 25,000 per year. Some 80 percent of mosques in the U.S. in 1993 were founded within the preceding twelve years.

[4] In 1993, there was one Muslim mayor, in Kountze, Texas, where there were only two Muslim families and a population of 2,700 residents.

[5] According to a report by the American Muslim Council, in 1993 there were between 5 and 8 million Muslims in the U.S. The ethnic percentages are: African American, 42 percent; Indian/Pakistani/Bangladeshi, 24.4 percent; Arabs, 12.4 percent; African, 5.2 percent; Iranians, 3.6 percent; Turkish, 2.4 percent; Southeast Asians, 2 percent; white Americans, 1.6 percent; and others, 6.4 percent. There were some 5,000 Hispanic Muslims. Women accounted for more than 75 percent of European American Muslims. And about 70 percent of Muslims in the U.S. lived in 10 states: California, New York, Illinois, New Jersey, Indiana, Michigan, Virginia, Texas, Ohio, and Maryland.

[6] In *Deeper Roots*, 1990 (Association of Islamic Communities in the Caribbean and Latin America), Abdullah Hakim Quick reports that Arab geographer al-Idrisi (1100–66), in *The*

that perhaps as many as one-fifth of the slaves brought to the Americas were educated in the Maliki[7] principles of Islam. West African Muslims from the Berber-, Fula-, Wolof-, and Mande-speaking tribes and Sudanic Muslims from the Hausa, Fulani, and Yoruba peoples practiced Islam surreptitiously during slavery in North and South America and the West Indies. Muslims were active as missionaries on the island of Hispaniola, where one of the greatest leaders in Haitian history was Machandal, a Muslim slave from Senegal. Arabi led Bush Blacks in eighteenth-century Surinam. Slaves practiced Islam in Venezuela, and in 1910 there were some 100,000 African Muslims in Brazil.

The number of Muslims in America increased dramatically following the liberalization of immigration policies in the 1960s, when a large influx of Muslims arrived from the Third World. But the West has always taken a vivid interest in the religion and the lands it dominated. Scholars estimate that over 60,000 books about Islam and the Orient were published between 1800 and 1950. With few exceptions they focused entirely on Islam abroad. In the 1800s a British "Arabist," an explorer named Richard F. Burton (1821–90; he took the name al-Hajj Abdullah, meaning the Pilgrim Abdullah) reeducated generations of Westerners about Islam, doing so through what amounts to a thousand and one folk tales. He translated the *Arabian Nights,*[8] a collection of erotic and bawdy tales, and a curious means to reintroduce a universal religion to the non-Islamic world. He even went so far as to call Great Britain "at present the greatest Mohammedan empire in the world"—referring, of course, to the large number of Muslims in its colonies.

Interest in Islam now appears at a high point among government leaders principally because of events in the Middle East, where the religion has become a significant factor in shaping political, military, and economic decisions.

With 1.16 billion adherents, or 23.2 percent of humanity,[9] Islam is second only to Christianity (1.6 billion) in the number of followers worldwide, and only 20 percent of them live in the Middle East. Of the trinity of

---

Geography of al-Idrisi, wrote about Muslim sailors who ventured from Lisbon to the Caribbean and were met by native people who could speak Arabic.

[7] One of the four major schools of Islamic jurisprudence. The others are Hanafi, Shafi'i and Hanbali.

[8] The original stories were probably composed in Baghdad in the ninth century.

[9] According to the Institute of Muslim Minority Affairs (1990). The projected world population of Muslims in the year 2000 is expected to be 1.6 billion people, or 26.85 percent, at current growth rates. (Source: *Islamic Horizons,* July–August 1990.)

great monotheistic faiths—which includes Judaism and Christianity—Islam is the youngest and, apparently, the most headstrong and unpredictable. Its role in the modern world should not be underestimated. With other ideologies and philosophies in shambles, Islam alone seems unstoppable. *The Wall Street Journal* reported:

> At a time when Marxism is so debilitated it is being shored up by capitalism, when Christianity lacks much of the missionary fire that once drove it, when Maoism is all but entombed with its founder and when democracy sounds only a muted appeal to much of the world, Islamic fundamentalism stands out as the movement on the march.[10]

As disillusionment with Western values spreads, Islam gains momentum. Each year adherents enter, or reenter, the fold simply by declaring the central tenet of Islam: "There is no god but Allah; Muhammad is His messenger."

Elders, youth, members of the professional class are becoming "born again" believers, many of them renewing their vows and relearning the rudiments of prayer.

On Fridays throughout the Muslim world, life comes to a standstill. Muslims on the job, in shops, and in public squares stop whatever they're doing and face Mecca in prayer.

Congregations have swelled and the annual pilgrimage, required at least once of every Muslim who can afford it, is bigger than ever. Each year, at least two million people converge on Mecca, Islam's spiritual center, temporarily multiplying that city's population by a larger percentage than that of any other major city. There, they perform a five- to seven-day ritual that remains unchanged since the Prophet's time.

Despite this resurgence, myths and misconceptions abound about Islam abetted by the fact that Westerners tend not to differentiate between various sects of Muslims. The American public, for example, knows little about the religious differences between Saudi Arabia's king and Iran's ayatollahs. On the surface, they have much in common. They each wear robes and face Mecca in prayer. The two countries are theocracies and oil-rich members of the Organization of Petroleum Exporting Countries. It matters little to most Americans that Iranian Shiites practice a different brand of Islam from Saudi's Wahhabis. It matters even less that the press, until recently, branded black converts in America "Muslim," reserving the

[10] August 7, 1987.

term "Moslem" for Arabs, Indians, Africans, Indonesians, and others, when American blacks practice the same religion as their Old World brothers and sisters. What is more important from the American perspective is that Islam, whether that of one sect or another, can be construed as a potential threat to world stability. That fact was driven home by the costly Persian Gulf War.[11]

Islam, then, which dominates a region that accounts for 60 percent of the world's proven oil reserves, is perceived by many Americans as a dangerous menace that must be contained, much the same as Communism was during the cold war. And as it has been portrayed in Western media, the religion has taken the form of Islam against all comers; thus, the characteristics that distinguish Islam the religion from Islam the tool of the highly politicized easily become blurred.

Week after week, the television shows us a Middle East embroiled in violence—whole countries, societies, that from here look as if they have switched to self-destruct.

We see the aftermath of "fundamentalist" bombings in Cairo.

We see the Iraqi government singling out Kurds as enemies of the state.

We see Israeli widows wailing over the caskets of victims of terrorist raids.

We learn the PLO was at war with Lebanese Shiites, and realize that not only were Muslims fighting Jews in the Middle East, they were killing each other. Muslim nations turned against Iraq in a war that devastated both Iraq and Kuwait, although the killing fields were restricted for most Americans to smart-bomb and gunsight videotapes.

One newspaper, in a piece about the casual flow of arms from the Eastern bloc, calls Sa'ada "Yemen's answer to Dodge City"—a place where men pop bottle tops with gun barrels, where you can buy grenades in an auto-parts shop, and where you can browse for a machine gun as easily as you can a woven basket.

We think back on Egyptian President Anwar el-Sadat's assassination and can't help but remember that the very word "assassin" is traced back to a

---

[11] As estimated by the Arab Monetary Fund, the cost to Arab states was $676 billion; to Kuwait, $196 billion; to Iraq, $200 billion. The Fund reported in April 1993 that the war wiped out two-thirds of Kuwait's financial surplus, the Fund for Future Generations, which was at $100 billion before the war. Also according to the report, destroyed infrastructure, factories, telecommunications, and roads cost Iraq $256 billion. The Baghdad government was living off savings in 1993, estimated at $30 billion before the war.

secret sect of Muslims who killed Christian leaders during the Crusades, purportedly while high on hashish.

We learn that the Party of God has made a gift to some Islamic country of a machine that more efficiently slices off the right hand of convicted thieves, thereby making it easier to fulfill an edict ordained in the Qur'an.

The media lends to Americans' perception that the World Trade Center bombing was rooted in religion.

To Americans, Islam plays a prominent role in all of this madness. With each successive wave of bad news from the Middle East, it becomes easier to label Muslims the aggressors, to point the finger and become judgmental, to deduce that Islam has gone amuck and seems to be Religion in Reverse, to conjure up old images of Saracens. It then becomes easier to ask: Where is the hand of God in this troubled part of the world?

All of the above contributes to non-Muslim America's fear of the religion. One American, S. Abdullah Schleifer, who converted to Islam and who taught at the American University in Cairo, said he "sees in many Westerners an 'irrational fear' of all things Islamic and an attempt to impose Western values on a different society."

Westerners cringe at the mutilation of girls' genitals in some societies— the removal of the clitoris, called female circumcision—and blame Islam, without realizing that Muslims too cringe; they oppose the practice, saying it is a cultural tradition unsanctioned by Islam and practiced by Christians as well. Westerners also gasp at the *Mutawin,* Saudi Arabia's religious police squad (officially known as the Committee for the Promotion of Virtue and the Prevention of Vice), who patrol the streets in jeeps, shouting, "Cover up!" at women whose strands of hair fall across their face. Finally, Westerners balk at the stories of polygamy—of Muslim wives confronted for the first time by their husbands' younger, more vivacious wives. Westerners interpret these as acts of cruelty, and blame Islam.

The Islamophobia only increased with the death of a Muslim well known and respected in America. The one Muslim leader most familiar to the American public—excluding Khomeini, who was Persian, or Yasir Arafat or Saddam Hussein—was Anwar el-Sadat, who cultivated an image as a "believer President." He became a hero to Americans, and he died a martyr, having set a precedent for the Palestinian-Israeli accord signed in September 1993.

However, to many Arabs his peace treaty with Israel, an avowed enemy, made him no less than a traitor to their cause. He had ultimately forsaken them, and his image of devoutness was seen by many as a political ploy, a lie. He was rumored to have called women dressed in Islamic garb "women in tents."

What has all this to do with the emergence and flourishing of Islamic culture in America? What effect did Malcolm X have on the growth of the religion in America? Will the cry *"Allahu akbar!"* ("God is great!")—heard wherever Muslims are at prayer, or at war—ever shake American society, on American soil? And why are so many Americans converting?

In the black American community Islam spread as a religion, as well as a weapon of protest and a means of self-definition.

In the first half of the twentieth century Islam was spread in America by groups who claimed their own prophets: nonconformist, angry black men, as well as by Ahmadiyyas,[12] whose movement was based in India. Islam attracted America's disenfranchised.

Noble Drew Ali, born in 1886 in North Carolina, was one of the first spiritual leaders to spread the faith, or his reinterpretation of it, to the black masses in America. Based in Newark, New Jersey, his Moorish Science Temple tried to instill self-pride in his followers by convincing them that they were "Asiatics," and requiring them to carry nationality and identity cards indicating that the bearer was a follower of "all the Divine Prophets, Jesus, Mohammed, Buddha, and Confucius." His followers used the name Bey.

Through his spokesman, Malcolm X, Elijah Muhammad was able to reach a wider audience with even more thought-provoking ideas, and his messages on blacks' needs were carried directly—and defiantly—to blacks. The effect was both captivating and mobilizing.

One Islamic scholar outlined how these leaders used Islam as a rallying cry and a means to rethink their own identity, shed turn-the-cheek pacifism, construct communities based on collective rather than individual needs, emphasize men's role as the anchor of the family, cherish wom-

---

[12] The Ahmadiyya denomination was established in India in 1889. Followers, now numbering about 10 million worldwide and an estimated 20,000 in North America, believe its founder, Ghulam Ahmad (1835–1908), was the promised messiah and reformer of Islam. In the early 1920s a missionary, Dr. Mufti Muhammad Sadiq, converted 40 Garveyites in Detroit. His successor, Mohammed Yusuf Khan, of India, continued proselytizing. It has been said that Elijah Muhammad was a uniformed corporal in Garvey's United Negro Improvement Association. During and after the 1940s, many American jazz musicians became Ahmadi Muslims, including Yusef Lateef, Art Blakey, Ahmad Jamal, and Dakota Staton.

anhood, build strong morals, establish healthy lifestyles, and provide economic self-sufficiency.

Today, Islam in America is in a period of dynamic change, with at least 17 distinct groups of black American Muslims—from remnants of the Darul-Islam Tabligh movement, the largest indigenous group of Sunni Muslims, which established 50 branches nationwide, to the African Tijani Sufi order,[13] introduced to Americans by Shaikh Hasan Sese of Senegal, and from the Nubian Islamic Hebrews of Brooklyn to followers of Warith D. Mohammed, Elijah's son.

The changes are apparent. Where Islam was once used by some as a platform from which to espouse racist ideology in the United States, it now promotes brotherhood with few exceptions. And where orthodoxy was once limited principally to immigrants, it has opened its ranks to those born in America. Eighty-five to 90 percent of American converts are black,[14] and the vast majority of both blacks and whites now appear to want an Islam of broader scope, an Islam grounded in history or in the capacity to inspire a sense of personal rebirth rather than an Islam that reflects merely the self-indulgence of some cult personality.

The Islam of Sunnites, of Shiites, of Sufis, and of Minister Louis Farrakhan differ enough to clash, at least on the surface. But all forms now exist in America.

I have worshipped with Sufi orders that strive to annihilate their sense of self, to fade away, or dissolve into God, by means of prayers, meditation, and incantations—jealously guarded secrets handed down over centuries in ceremonies presided over by the groups' masters, most of whom live overseas and visit America occasionally.

I have also seen for myself how American Muslims journeying to Africa to meet sheiks they've adopted as their personal spiritual guides are respected as being wholly Islamic products of a non-Islamic society—which many Africans apparently consider as miraculous a feat as surviving in the belly of a beast.

Some Americans justify their conversions by saying they've come to terms with their past, with their African ancestors, who were Muslim.

---

[13] The Tijaniyya order, founded by Ahmad at-Tijani (1737–1815).

[14] According to Dawud Assad, president of the Council of Masajid (plural of the word "mosque" in Arabic). "I believe that the religion of Islam is part of the genetic memory of African-Americans," Sabir Muhammad, a former seminary student in Atlanta, told *The Wall Street Journal* (October 5, 1990). "We were given [Christianity] on the plantation. There were no Christians brought over on the boat."

Others say that in fact they've been Muslim all along; they just didn't know it or practice the faith. Still others deny that there is any religion but Islam —that Christianity, Judaism, and other faiths are but perversions of the real thing.

I grew up in New Bedford, Massachusetts, the New England seaport town where my grandparents settled after emigrating from the Cape Verde archipelago[15] off West Africa at the start of this century. I was raised Catholic and for one fleeting moment in the fifth or sixth grade I dreamt of becoming a priest. In retrospect I actually considered this no more seriously than I had considered taking up the clarinet or flute, neither of which I play today. It was a passing thought. But faith itself was not. This wasn't something one ordinarily questioned; it was to be inherited without squabble; it was something one was supposed to take for granted, as one does his own name.

I attended religion classes and received the sacraments but was no more religious for having done so than I was for watching television. Building my faith in God was supposed to have evolved through a simple and neat process, extended over the period of my youth, so long as I routinely showed my face in church. But for me and some of my peers, the church aisle came to symbolize more a runway for modeling Easter outfits than a path to the altar, communion, and God's forgiveness.

My links to the old country, at least, were strong and direct. At home I ate island cuisine and heard Crioulo, an Africanized Portuguese, and there were plenty of stories about what life back in the old country was like. All of this implied I was somehow different, yet I was confused about my heritage. I failed to see how it fit into the scheme of things vis-à-vis racism in America.

And then I discovered Malcolm X. He summed up much that was ugly about America, eloquently telling off whites.

But his life showed me something eminently more useful than skillful oratory: what role religion could play as one approached this race-conscious society. He provided an example of how a man could use conviction as a powerful instrument to change the course of life—one's own and others'. His remarkable ability to transform himself from hood to cleaned-up spokesman for the Nation of Islam and then to Sunni Islam—that was his real message.

Robert Penn Warren wrote: "Malcolm X was a latter-day example of an

[15] Reportedly 1 percent Muslim. (Source: *The Minaret*, November–December 1992.)

old-fashioned type of American celebrated in grammar school readers, commencement addresses, and speeches at Rotary Club lunches—the man who 'makes it,' the man who, from humble origins and with meager education, converts—by will, intelligence, and sterling character—his liabilities into assets. Malcolm X was of that breed of American, autodidacts and homemade successes, that has included Benjamin Franklin, Abraham Lincoln, P. T. Barnum, Thomas Alva Edison, Booker T. Washington, Mark Twain, Henry Ford, and the Wright Brothers."

I was to learn that many other converts had discovered Malcolm too, and had grown beyond the point he had reached in the religion—Malcolm ended his spiritual journey in orthodoxy, where many converts began their own, taking their Islamic studies seriously enough to matriculate at universities in Egypt, Saudi Arabia, and elsewhere. Some Muslim converts, leery of the personality cult that developed around Malcolm's revived image—which inspired a $100 million market in X caps, clothing, and paraphernalia—are quick to point out that Malcolm was Sunni Muslim for a relatively short time, and that most of his talks were made while he followed Elijah Muhammad.

Regardless of whether one remembers the angry Malcolm X of earlier days or the equality conscious El-Hajj Malik El-Shabazz, his stamp on the American Islamic landscape is enduring, his influence undeniable. Many Muslim converts were steered toward the religion through his autobiography, as told to Alex Haley. Allah, Muslims say, makes Muslims. How He seems to have done this in the United States in many cases was through Malcolm the Instrument.

Muslims still carry out their obligations for *jihad* ("striving"), with Malcolm long gone, and they do so in a nation that misunderstands them and misconstrues their motives.

The Qur'an forbids aggressive warfare. In the Qur'an, Allah prescribes fighting to preserve freedom of religion, dignity, and conscience. *Jihad,* which merely means "striving," or "struggling," is required of Muslims to defend themselves. *Jihad,* however, has been widely interpreted to signify "fighting," its secondary meaning, as in "holy war" waged against enemies of the *ummah,* the greater Muslim community.

Part of the reason is this: Within centuries after the death of the Prophet, Muslim jurists divided the world not into secular and sacred realms, but into realms of belief and unbelief—the House of Peace and the House of War, or Unbelief. All within the dominion of the Islamic state—including *ummahs* of Christians and Jews—were considered integral parts of the federation, the House of Peace. All outside of it carried the distinct possibility of aggression. Peace, then, had to be "waged." And it was.

By the beginning of the eighth century the *jihad* effort dwindled and Muslims lived side by side with non-Muslims, carrying on diplomatic relations and trade.[16] But Muslims' reputation for sword-bearing had taken root.

Actually, there are several kinds of *jihad*: the first is *jihad bil nafs,* which means "striving within the self." This is considered the greatest *jihad*. The second *jihad* is *jihad fi sabil Allah,* "striving in the path of Allah." This *jihad* is carried out by word or deed—by the tongue, by the pen, or as a last resort, by the hand. Allah forbids Muslims to submit passively to the injustices of others. He gives permission to strive against His enemies:

> Permission (to fight in self-defense) is (now) given to those (Muslims) against whom war is waged (for no reason), because they have been done injustice to, and Allah has indeed might and power to help them;

> Those who have been driven out of their homes without any just cause. Their only fault was that they said, "Our Lord is Allah." If Allah had not repelled some peoples by means of others, cloisters and churches and synagogues and mosques wherein the name of Allah is mentioned very frequently, would have been razed to the ground in large numbers. And Allah will surely help one who helps His cause. Allah is, indeed, All-Powerful, All-Mighty.
>
> Qur'an 22:39–40

Malcolm X's "greater *jihad*" was his striving to turn his life around and mold himself as a Muslim; his "lesser *jihad*" was talking back at white America—which translated as offering blacks a psychological alternative, a perhaps nonpacifist plan for fighting back.

The greater *jihad* is well underway among American converts who seek to transform themselves in the light of Muslim ideals and injunctions in the Qur'an. The stories of some of those *jihads* are included in this book.

My intention was not to write a theological treatise nor to write a book about highly politicized secret societies that operate surreptitiously on the fringes of Islam. This is not a book about "Muslim radicals" or "Islamic

---

[16] Karen Armstrong, *Holy War: The Crusades and Their Impact on Today's World* (New York: Doubleday, 1991), p. 41.

extremists," although the views of subjects I've included sometimes widely diverge from the mainstream. Rather, this work was undertaken principally to feel the pulse of Islamic society in America, to tell what is happening in a community of millions of converts to a religion that is so steeped in myth it remains as mysterious to most Americans as a woman behind a veil.

From the outset I did not intend to be an apologist or to defend the many deeds, or misdeeds, carried out in the name of Islam. Nor have I taken upon myself the role of spokesman for the faith or for the faithful. I have attempted only to document the movement as someone who can bring insight and sensitivity to the subject—a kind of passive sensitivity with which I intended to write about Islam in America from the inside out.

I've included Muslims of many persuasions. But no single book on Islam in America could ever be complete. The community is continually expanding—rapidly—and due to the vast numbers of immigrants who each year bring into play their own cultural influences on the community, Islam in America grows ever more complex. In my opinion, taken as a whole, the Islamic community in America is at least as complicated as any abroad, even in countries where indigenous Muslims predominate.

I decided on the "portrait/interview" format because I think the reader will best learn what these Muslims believe and think by hearing them in their own words. After hundreds of interviews, the cross section of "portrait/interviews" I chose to include I think reflects something of the breadth and complexity of this community but in no way is intended as a definitive representation of it. The Muslims included form but a small piece of a giant mosaic.

The Muslims that follow come from all walks of life, from the grassroots organizations to movers and shakers: a journalist, a rapper, orators, professional athletes, poets, professors, entrepreneurs, ex-convicts, polygamists, mystics, community activists, a comedian, a Pulitzer Prize winner, etc. They are American- and foreign-born. Some are "pre-Malcolm" Muslims. None are bomb throwers. You will learn how they coped with change or refused to; how they struggled to teach or influence non-Muslims; how they abandoned or took on Western ways; how they fought for civil rights; how they live together or apart from one another.

The profiles are grouped into chapters that reflect the various themes which I consider characteristic of each Muslim's *jihad*. Each chapter opens with a verse from the Qur'an.

In many ways, getting this book to print was my own *jihad*. It is my hope that readers will come away with a better understanding of Islam and American Muslims and will seek more material about them and their *jihad*, beginning with the Qur'an itself.

Steven Barboza
New York City

Parting Words

"*Assalaamu alaikum*[1] . . .
Hold it! Hold it! Don't get excited! Let's
cool it, brothers . . ."

—Malcolm X (El-Hajj Malik El-Shabazz),
February 21, 1965

[1] Arabic for "Peace be unto you." For translations of other Islamic terms or phrases, refer to the Glossary.

In the Name of Allah,
the Merciful,
the Compassionate

Chapter One

West Goes East

This day have I perfected your religion for you, completed My favor upon you, and have chosen for you Islam as your religion.

Qur'an 5:3

All Muslims have not taken the same road to their Lord. Many left their families and their sheltered lives to take up the call; many brought the family along with them. For some, the route was full of danger, including the threat of bullets of avowed enemies. Others, dropouts from society, completed crash courses in comparative religion, sipping tea with total strangers in robes and discussing the ills of the world. For still others, Islam presented a means for overcoming suppression, and the Qur'an read like the ultimate handbook on revolution, complete with subversive strategies and moral guidelines to assure success. Islam, for them, provided not only a solution to racism, decadence, imperialism, and commercialism but also a means of dismantling a great devil of a system.

By whichever route they come, many converts find spiritual solace in Islam from the moral vacuum they say exists in the West. Islam offers them a lifeline as the world around them seems to go adrift—even though living as a Muslim means following traditions that seem alien to people around them, like praying in the early watches of the morning, fasting in the daylight hours for a month, or dining without utensils, as the Prophet did. For the convert, internal struggles often persist long after conversion, as they battle for control over their own Western-bred sensibilities.

Be in this world as though you were a stranger or a wayfarer.
—Prophet Muhammad, *Hadith* (Al-Bukhari)[2]

From Al Azhar to Oak Park

Hoda Boyer

*She left for the Arab world, a young white American feminist. She soaked
in the culture and religion like a sponge in the hand of the man she chose as
her spiritual guide. Middle Eastern women also enlightened her about
womanhood. Meanwhile, though partially blind, she nevertheless was able
to drink in the wondrous sights of fabled Cairo, with streets right out of a
centuries-old map she used as a guidebook, with breathtaking mosques for
the praying. She hugged one of the first sheiks she ever met, moved into
poor neighborhoods, ate oranges with the shopkeepers and mosque keepers, and met a family of closet Muslims in Spain. Now she's a Naqsh-
bandiyya Sufi and a poet who "dresses for success." A divorcée, she is
raising two Muslim children in Oak Park, Illinois.*

I had studied Islam in order to develop a background for art history, and I
fell in love with the whole romance of it. I was interested in the Sufi aspect
but I didn't want to be a Muslim and do all that washing and praying and
covering.

I had an introduction to the former dean of the faculty of law at Al
Azhar,[3] a wonderful man. I talked with him and he told me you can't be
Sufi without being Muslim. I met the then grand sheik of Al Azhar. His
secretary gave me private lessons on Islam. After four weeks I officially

---

[2] *Hadith* are traditions and sayings of Prophet Muhammad. *Sahih Bukhari*, the compilation of
9,082 *hadith* by Muhammad Ibn Ismail al-Bukhari (810–70), is widely regarded as the most
authoritative collection.

[3] The most famous university in the Islamic world, in Cairo, constructed 970–72. Also the
world's oldest university, it had a major impact on European universities. Wearing black
academic gowns and dividing universities into undergraduate and graduate facilities were first
done at Al Azhar.

converted. I took the *shahada* by the grand sheik. Of course, the first thing that I did was hug and embrace him. He said, "Well, you know, now that you're Muslim, you really can't hug men anymore." I said, "Oh, okay."

That was 1978, and it was unusual to find a foreign woman who was interested in Islam and had some knowledge about it. I was still actively seeking a Sufi sheik. I went to Damascus, and I met my sheik. When I met him, I was the first foreign follower to come to Damascus. He now has about 10,000 followers. They're Europeans—British, Germans, Swiss, Italian, and he has a big following in Malaysia and Sri Lanka. His original following, which he still has, are Turks and Arabs.

I had gone to the tomb of Ibn 'Arabi.[4] And up the mountain from that tomb is where the sheik lives. Sheik Nazim al-Haqqani lives very simply. I was taken into his house into a reception room. He came out and sat down and drank a glass of water. It sounds silly, but it was clarity flowing into clarity. He smiled at me and said, *"La illaha ill Allah,"*[5] very softly and he didn't say much else for a while, and then he started to chat with me in English.

I stayed with his family there for a couple of weeks, and then he went to Lebanon, and I went on to England. During that couple of weeks, he didn't pressure me. He taught by example. I did a lot of extra prayers because he did it and it seemed to make him and his family happy. His wife was a sheika and gave a *zikr* for about two hundred women in Damascus. I was very impressed by his wife's learning. She had memorized a lot of the Qur'an. She spoke Arabic, Turkish, Russian. She knew the *hadith*.

When I look back on it it's amazing because there I was, this crazy foreigner, and I didn't know all of the Muslim customs and I would just barge into things. But there was this real acceptance and kindness. Occasionally there was a kind of amusement: Isn't this a funny little toy Muslim? Like a cat-dressed-up-in-doll-clothes kind of thing.

But there was this real sympathy too. Nobody beat me over the head with anything. They instructed me very softly.

I told myself I had to bite the bullet and not be a women's libber anymore because I want to have all these mystical experiences. I have to do this thing and be oppressed. In Egypt the sexes do mix, but in Syria and

[4] Muhyi al-Din Ibn 'Arabi (1165–1240), author of *al-Futuhat al-makkiyya* (The Meccan Revelations). His tomb is on Qasiyun mountain, overlooking Damascus from the west.
[5] "There is no god but Allah."

Hoda Boyer.

other countries, you get thrown off with the women. Well, I would be outraged. And then it dawned on me: What am I saying? I'm saying they can't put me off with the women because nothing interesting happens with women; it's the men that the interesting stuff is happening with. Here I am really denigrating women! That didn't dawn on me and wouldn't have dawned on me had I not gone to an Islamic society and been mad and angry and thinking I've being thrown to the women.

Once I picked up a little Arabic, I really enjoyed going to the women's groups and being with the women. In pious Islamic society, there isn't this competition for men. It really makes a difference. I mean, they really are your sisters. If there's any competition, it's piety competition. It's a real nice kind of feeling.

Islam has really done that for me: it's really elevated my feeling that women are important and that being with them is important.

After I went back to Egypt my money ran out, and I became a teacher of English. From then on I never had any problems.

I lived with really poor people, who didn't have sugar, salt, coffee, tea, and had never seen an antibiotic. They lived in materially deprived circumstances, had one outfit of clothes, but had the most elegant and lovely sense of manners and how to act. They had a kind of graciousness that you might think of in the fabled courts of Baghdad. This wonderful sense of awareness and intuitive feeling about people. That's a whole dimension to life that I had not realized existed.

I went on *hajj* in 1980 with a group of Egyptian men and women, and I realized that after that, no matter what, I could never not be Muslim.

I was the only American, so they kept thinking all the time when they looked at the passports that they had somehow gotten an American passport here by mistake.

I lived and ate what they ate, so it wasn't a hardship for me. I was used to living very simply and eating very simply, and was used to the hot weather. A lot of people took me for being Turkish or Syrian. There's an area of southern Turkey and northern Syria where the women have light eyes. I have green eyes. So people thought I was from that area. When they found out I was from America, they were very friendly.

At the Ka'aba, there was this sense of incredible peace and unity— nonduality. At the Prophet's tomb, there was a sense of emotion and ecstasy and elation and love. I wept literally for hours and felt this overwhelming love and kindness emanating from the tomb. I still remember that. It was really something that I hadn't expected. There are two and a half million people there, and all of a sudden there's this wonderful, wonderful feeling. It seemed to be a love and a peace that didn't matter in the slightest whether you were American or Saudi or Persian or black or white. Clearly it was a blessing that was there for anyone who wished to partake of it.

In Egypt, I lived in a magical world. I was always praying in these exquisite mosques and I always lived in the old part of Cairo. It was sort of like an *Arabian Nights* quarter, where you could stand at a crossroads and look in all four directions and not see anything built after the thirteenth century; and where the artisans, like the weavers and the metalsmiths and the cobblers, were all employing the same kinds of tools and the same methods that they would have seven hundred years ago.

I went to the American University and found a book that had a map of Cairo under the Fatimids.[6] The Fatimids were like a *Shi'a* dynasty that ruled from 909 to 1171. That map showed the disposition of the craft guilds along the major streets of Cairo at that time. I found the streets still bearing the same names. I walked along them and, sure enough, in the spot that was marked charcoal makers, there were still charcoal makers. In the

---

[6] The Fatimids founded Cairo in 969 A.D. It is among the world's largest and most densely populated cities, with more than 97,100 people per square mile. By comparison, New York City had 11,480 people per square mile in 1989, according to the U.S. Bureau of the Census.

spot marked coppersmiths, there were still coppersmiths. In the spot marked tent makers, there were still people making canvas tents and carrying bags and feed bags. There was this extraordinary continuity of site use. And you know, Middle Eastern dress hasn't changed since probably the time of Ibrahim.[7] It was like sort of a living museum where everything was magically transported into the past. It was very romantic—an art historian's dream. And it was really easy to forget that anything else existed. It was intoxicating.

The map was in a book called *Fatimid Cairo*. There were photographs of still-extant buildings, and there was a map that had been made at the time that those buildings had been put up. The map showed what buildings were there and which were the ones that had been removed. There's one mosque that has a beautiful wooden railing that's been there since 1200. It's unimpaired because the climate is so dry.

I used to make every prayer in the mosque. Women were readily admitted to the mosques; they were a real essential part of Egyptian life. Middle-class women would come. Women selling oranges in the shops were there. During Ramadan, everybody was in the streets. Women had access to everything.

(That wasn't the case in Sudan. In Sudan, in 1981, I couldn't get into the mosques. And also in Kashmir, I was put in the women's room, which obviously hadn't been opened in about fifteen years; everything was full of dust. The custom there is that it is not suitable for women to come to the mosque. So the area that had been prepared when the mosque was built had never really been used, and you couldn't hear the imam, so you couldn't do the congregational prayer. That would have upset me had I not been in Egypt so long.)

There are all the big mosques that are written up in the art books. But there are so many really exquisite little mosques in what we would call the slums. And most visitors don't really go and look at them.

To a Muslim, the beauty of a mosque is not just its architectural splendor but also the feeling. You go in, you feel so comfortable. There is a blessing that comes where people have prayed over and over for a thousand years. Mosques that have been turned into museums don't give you that feeling.

Very seldom did I see a mosque that I didn't like. My particular favorites were some jewels that were tucked away. Hardly anyone came to them

---

[7] Abraham.

except me and a few other people. Late Mamluk, 1350, and it hasn't been touched! And you'd come in and you'd pray.

When the mosques were built they were endowed. Shops were built around the base of the mosque, and the revenue from those shops continue to support the mosque. Those things are still going. It's really a good system.

In the South of France, the churches have Romanesque capitals. They're very elaborate and have all these wonderful little bounding figures. They also have sort of twisted designs. In fact, those designs often say *Bismillah-ar-Rahman-ar-Rahim.*[8] Perfect Arabic. I was astonished.

The Muslims were stopped in France, but before that the South of France was very Islamic, and whether those people were forced to convert to Christianity or whether they were artisans who were continuing a tradition of which they didn't know the meaning, I don't know. If you don't know Arabic, it just looks like an interesting arabesque design. But if you know Arabic, then oh my gosh, look what that says!

And of course, in Spain that's all over, because the people were forced to convert to Christianity and they continued their work.

When I was in Córdoba,[9] I went to the Great Mosque, which was a tourist spot with this Christian church built in the middle of it. But it's just exquisite. It's a big mosque and it was a day when there weren't very many people in it. It came time to do the prayer, so I just did my prayer there in the mosque. I get up and there's this Spanish guy behind me. I thought, oh my God, what have I done! He comes up and says, *"Assalaamu alaikum."*[10] I say, *"Walaikum salaam."*[11] He takes me to his house and he is one of the mosque keepers. He works for the tourist bureau. He and his family are crypto-Muslims. They've been Muslims since before 1492.[12]

He has pictures of his grandparents wearing Muslim garb inside the house, turbans and things like that. He was so amazed to see someone

[8] In the name of Allah, the Merciful, the Compassionate.

[9] Umayyad capital of Spain. The Great Mosque of Córdoba, one of the finest examples of Moorish architecture, has horseshoe arches, distinctive sculpted columns, red and white stones, and roofing with parallel gables. Construction began in 780 A.D. The mosque became the Cathedral of Córdoba in 1238. Córdoba had 600 mosques in the tenth century. The city was regarded as the medieval world's most cosmopolitan and sophisticated.

[10] "Peace be unto you."

[11] "And unto you be peace."

[12] On January 2, 1492, the African leader abu-Abdullah, known as Boabdil, surrendered to the Spanish, bringing an end to Moorish power and influence in Spain.

praying in the mosque. Now, there are a couple of Sufi communities living there.

In Ramadan they would make extra prayers and things. They certainly weren't in a supportive environment. He said his family would have been tortured. "On the outside we're Christian and we went to church, but on the inside we always kept Islam." They kept the Qur'an in a venerated place, and they had read it, and they marked the passage of Ramadan in some way, for five hundred years.

He was really touched that somebody was praying there, right out in the open.

But it's a mosque. It's prayer time, so pray, right?

He said his family felt like they were guardians of Islam in Córdoba; they were the ones who kept the mosque clean and kept the doors locked. That was something their family had chosen to do, because it enabled them to have a more full experience of Islam, even though it had to be hidden.

As you remember, during the Inquisition,[13] anybody who was even remotely suspicious was likely to be dismembered for the mercy of Christ. So it really wasn't safe, but they felt somehow in keeping up the mosque that they were doing a duty for Islam.

I thought it was nice, because it was an example of how Islam can be hidden in the heart and be kept up all of those years and kind of guarding the tradition and the mosque.

In order for a religion to convert lots of people it has to, to some extent, be cognizant of their native traditions. If it isn't, converting those people isn't going to be successful in the long run, and both Islam and Christianity have been able to absorb some animist elements from indigenous African people, and you see that in Sudan. There are still traditions of people throwing bones to predict the future.

And in Sudan, a woman is not marriageable unless she's had a clitoridectomy. It's just horrible. They have all kinds of infections. Every menstrual period is agony. It is not, however, an Islamic custom. The Christians also do that.

But the people are really solidly Muslim. You talk about fasting in 120-degree heat! Somebody died in Port Sudan when I was there in Ramadan.

---

[13] The Spanish Inquisition was established in 1478 and finally abolished in 1834. During the first two centuries, the Inquisition in Spain resulted in the imprisonment, torture, execution, and exile of some 3 million Muslims and Jews.

The imam got up in the mosque and said, "No, no, no, this is not the intent. For heaven's sake, if you feel that bad, drink water. The intent of this is not to die." So people were literally willing to lay down their life in Ramadan to fast.

In Third World countries, you have lots of people and animals out in the street. America is set up like you're living inside this big machine. America was really hard to get used to. There weren't any Islamic props, any scenery, like a mosque that is just breathtakingly beautiful. The beauty of it seems to open your heart and lift your prayers.

I'm a great believer that the shape of things affects people and that there is a sacred shape to architecture. Mosques have a lot of empty space. There isn't a statue toward which you direct your prayer. There isn't an altar. You're directing your prayer horizontally toward Mecca and vertically toward Allah. And into your own heart. There's this sense of positive space. The mosque is empty so that it can be filled with the spirit of God. There's an Islamic sensibility, whether it's the Taj Mahal or the Sultan Hasan mosque, and mosques are expressions of this.

I miss that, praying in my living room. I live very far from mosques. And the ones here are new. Al Azhar mosque is very old. It was built by the Fatimids. It had some plasterwork by one of the *mihrabs*,[14] and they "beautified" it by removing all of that old plasterwork and putting up these sheets of marbleized plastic, so it looks sort of like the inside of a cheap bathroom. But they were so proud of it. They took all of that old crumbly plaster down, and put up this really neat stuff that you could just tack on and wash. It had these fake marble veins. It was like linoleum. It was really sad.

But that's *my* judgment. And I don't want to be guilty of intellectual colonialism, which is like going over and telling them what's good for them: You should like the old stuff instead of the new stuff. Liking old stuff is kind of a luxury of First World people who have new stuff and have the luxury to sentimentalize. They don't have to live with the difficulties and hardships of that old stuff. Old earthen pots may be beautiful, but carrying them on your head compresses your spine, so that a lot of the women in Sudan and Egypt have spines in bad shape. But if you carry big plastic jugs on your head, it doesn't do that to your spine.

[14] Niche in the center of a front wall inside a mosque. It denotes the direction which Muslims face in prayer—toward the Ka'aba in Mecca.

But I miss the beauty. And sure, I miss the congratulations of people patting me on the back and saying oh how wonderful it is that you became a Muslim. There was always some kind of reinforcement.

Living here once again is sort of like what the Prophet said when he came back from a *jihad*—that he was returning from the lesser *jihad* to the greater one, the greater one being when we fight our egos and our vain desires.

I do believe that God is everywhere and that you can't live without the presence of God. I still feel the presence of God just as strongly in America as I did in Cairo or Damascus or Delhi or wherever.

But the problems that I have are accommodating the Muslim lifestyle, particularly dress, to the contemporary urban American environment. I think it's easier for immigrants to dress Islamically than it is for people who are obviously American.

It's much harder for Americans to wear the kind of clothes that immigrant women wear, because people regard that as, well, part of their culture. That's natural for them. But for Americans it's immediately visible that it's not part of traditional American life. These people are dressed as Muslims. Well, Muslims are not Christians, so they've obviously rejected Christianity. And currently Muslims don't do very well in the world press. These are the people that are blowing up airplanes. You hear all of the negative things that terrorism brings in its wake.

It's been pointed out many times that it's much easier to be a Buddhist or a Hindu and dress like one in America than it is to be a Muslim. Because we never really had that much contact with Buddhists and Hindus, but because of the Crusades and the ebb and flow between Europe and the Middle East, there's a lot of antipathy toward Muslims. It's age-old.

Even with all the negativity, Islam is the fastest-growing religion in Europe and America. So I feel like it's the wave of the future. And I'm pleased to be part of it.

My sheik emphasizes that it's very important to follow the *shari'ah*, because that's the way we submit our behavior to God. Assimilation in the Jewish sense of the word is really out of the question. But I think flexibility is possible. What I do is cover my hair with a hat often, rather than with a scarf. That way I don't feel like I attract undue attention.

Yesterday I saw a woman in Dunkin' Donuts. An American woman and her husband and she was fully veiled. I don't think she could have caused any more distraction. People couldn't have scrutinized her any more fully. It was as if she were wearing a bikini to come in to buy doughnuts.

For those sisters who can carry that, that's wonderful. My personal feeling is that if you're going to dress in a way that calls a lot of attention to yourself, you're defeating the purpose of *hijab*.[15] So I dress in what I like to think of as an American *Sunnah*. It's what I call Muslim dress for success: suits—because I have baggy jackets and long skirts and hats and scarves.

I used to go to a shop and buy things, and the clerk was always so nice to me, and I would have my children with me. There were times when she looked like she was almost going to cry. I couldn't understand what was the matter. We talked about our lives. I told her I was divorced. She said, "Oh, how sad." I said, "Well, yeah, but lots of people are divorced." Finally she said to me, "Have you thought about making provisions for your children? Just in case?"

I said, "In case of what?"

She didn't want to say. She's looking all around, and she finally says, "Are you in a cancer support group?"

I said, "No," and then I realized.

Many women who have breast cancer have radiation therapy that makes their hair fall out, and they wear scarves. I know a couple of cancer sufferers who are Christian who look exactly like Muslims because they don't have any hair and they cover their heads with scarves.

I explained that I cover like this because I'm Muslim, and that's part of our religion; it's not because I have cancer.

It's kind of comical yet sad. I try to wear scarves and leave a little hair sticking out to show that I do have hair.

---

[15] Veiling or concealing.

Then We made you heirs in the land after them,
to see how ye would behave!

Qur'an 10:14

Allah at Harvard

Ali S. Asani

"Where else but in America could you get the imam of the Sunni
mosque taking a course on Islam at a Western university—a secular
institution—taught by a Shi'a?"

Asani is professor of the practice of Indo-Muslim languages and culture at
Harvard University. He estimates that only six or seven professors teaching
Islam in religion departments at major universities are actually Muslim.
Born in Kenya of South Asian ancestry, Asani immigrated to the U.S. in
1973.

I had a graduate student who was working on a postcolonial literature
project for the English department, and he came to me for help in interpret-
ing texts in Orientalism. For helping him out, he invited me out for dinner.
We had a wonderful time and a wonderful intellectual conversation. And
then somewhere in the middle of the dinner, he said, "I hope this doesn't
offend you, but I can't figure one thing out." I said, "What is it?" He said,
"Well, how is it that somebody who is a professor at a big university like
Harvard, who is an intellectual, who's obviously very rational, and intelligent—how can you at the same time believe in a religion that espouses
jihad and holy war and terrorism?"

I had to explain that if you open up an Arabic dictionary, you're going
to find neither the word "holy" nor the word "war" under the definition of
jihad. The term itself comes from the consonants *j, h, d*. And if you look at

the root meaning, it means "to strive, to struggle." So you could say, there's *jihad,* and then there's *jihad.* To struggle to get out of bed in the morning—that's a *jihad.* If you're struggling through a snowstorm to come to work, that's a *jihad.* So it's a term that has a specific grammatical meaning, and in the religious context, it's taken on certain meanings.

Unfortunately sometimes Muslims play up to this. They start using terms like *jihad* very loosely, as part of their political ideology. And I think a beautiful religious concept has gotten distorted.

I came to realize a couple of years ago is how centrally this concept of *jihad* has been associated with Islam. It has such a negative connotation in the American mind.

As far as I see as a Muslim, the Gulf War had nothing to do with Islam, absolutely nothing. It was a war of aggression. It was not caused by religion. It was power politics. Yet everybody perceived it to be somehow related to the religion. They immediately think the reason behind this set of events is Islam.

Not only is that a very naive way of analyzing society, in a way it's also very denigrating. It implies that Muslims are not like other human beings. The only thing that makes them tick is their religion. They are not influenced by politics or economics or sociological factors, nothing. They live in this vacuum, and the only thing that matters is religion.

People don't realize that you can reverse this kind of analysis. Hitler considered himself to be a devout Christian. He thought he was doing the "Christian thing." But the fact that Hitler was Christian doesn't matter, because of course what he was doing was evil, and there's an attempt to distance the faith, Christianity, from the actions of the man—because, you know, it's unacceptable Christian behavior.

Arabs conquered North Africa and went all the way into Spain. They ruled Spain for seven centuries. Then you had the Turks much later on who were a threat to Eastern Europe. So I think Europe was always conscious of the fact that there were these groups who were Muslim coming at them from both sides. And of course, people were part of these conquests just for territory, as the normal growth of empires. The early Arab conquests of North Africa were not wars of conversion. They were political wars. But yet, people associated it with the "Islamic army." Here again, they think that the only motivation for the Arabs and the Turks is religion, not realizing that Arab empires are like any other empires. They bring their ways with them. They have political motives. They want wealth just like European empires wanted the same things. If you're given the opportunity to expand, you expand.

But I think there is this perception that there are these societies that follow faith that seems to be aggressive and seems to be anti-Western. And yet when you take the history of Arabs in Spain, you find that by and large you don't get people being forced to convert to Islam. In fact, Jews and Muslims and Christians coexisted. And then the moment you had the Catholics take over, the Muslims and the Jews were targeted.

In this history of conflict and antagonism, the dichotomy thrives on stereotypes. What stereotypes do is help you to mask the humanity of the others. So if you think of them as barbaric, you don't think of them as human beings. And if you think that Muslim societies are different from other societies, because the only thing that makes them tick is religion, what that's saying is they're a different breed of human beings, as Muslims. They don't have the same kinds of feelings as normal human beings do. And hence, you can get away with treating them the way you want.

In the eighteenth, nineteenth, and early twentieth centuries, when you had European nations actually ruling parts of the Islamic world, the whole

Ali S. Asani.
PHOTO: JOE WRINN

power structure changed. And there you had the British look down on their native populations. The French who ruled Muslim populations in West Africa thought their job was in fact to civilize these people. So there is this notion that Islam is primitive because it was connected with subject populations. This is the same problem that you find facing Muslims in Europe today. In France, the immigrant Arab populations from North Africa, or the Turks in Germany, are often regarded as primitives.

The kinds of things that are happening to Islam and Muslims in America are not happening in any other part of the world. Because America is a nation of immigrants, you have Muslims from many different parts of the world and different cultures coming here and making America their home. Muslims with different interpretations of Islam must confront each other and reconcile their differences.

This is an era in which the question is being asked: What does it mean to be Muslim? When you use Islam as a political ideology, then you get into defining who a Muslim is, what Muslim behavior is, and what Muslim behavior is not. And when you get into something like that, you are running the danger of going against the basic teachings of the faith.

The Qur'an says there is no compulsion in religion. How does a state that is using Islam as a political ideology get by forcing people to pray five times a day? In Saudi Arabia, you have a religious police.[16] You have to close your shop and go to prayer. That is not Qur'anic Islam. That's Islam being used as a political ideology.

In any case, in many parts of the Muslim world, you do have the state defining who's a Muslim and who's not a Muslim and what Islamic behavior is.

But what's great in the United States is that you can be Muslim and you can talk about it with other Muslims, and there is nobody that forces you into a mold.

You need dynamism in a religion, and I think this is what Islam in America is undergoing now. It's still a relatively new tradition in terms of the immigrant population. And people are negotiating their way through all of this, learning to recognize pluralism within Islam and recognizing that there are many ways of being Muslim without being judgmental about it.

[16] *Mutawin,* Saudi Arabia's religious police squad (known as the Committee for the Promotion of Virtue and the Prevention of Vice). They patrol the streets in jeeps, enforcing religious law.

My own personal *jihad* is on two issues: one is this double standard of how Islam is portrayed in the West; and two, I think it's a struggle to make Muslims understand that there are many ways of being Muslim. The *shahada* is like the thread holding prayer beads together. They're all there, and they're all strung together by that thread. And the beads need not all be of the same color.

A couple of years ago, we had the imam of the Islamic Center of New England, who's Sunni, who's Lebanese, as a student here. He got admitted into the Harvard Divinity School in the master's of theological sciences program. He enrolled in my course, Introduction to Islam. He has a degree from Al Azhar. When I first saw him I said, does this make any sense? Yes, it makes sense.

At Al Azhar, he was given a certain interpretation of Islam, very *shari'ah*-oriented, a very classical Sunni viewpoint. My course was basically looking at different ways of being Muslim. We talked about the Qur'an. We talked about the life of the Prophet. We looked at how Muslims interpret things. And we looked at how historians of religion who are not believing Muslims looked at the Qur'an and looked at the figure of the Prophet. But then we examined other ways of being Muslim, like the Sufi tradition, the Shi'a tradition, and then we looked at issues of Islam localized in indigenous forms of Islam, especially in the non-Arab world, and conflicts between those and scriptural forms of Islam.

In a sense you could say it's a Western academic approach to talk about Islam in localized contexts. We looked at Islamic modernist movements—the Wahhabis in Saudi Arabia, the West African reform movement, which he didn't know anything about, Turkey and its experiment with Islam. And then we looked at Islam and race—in the United States and Europe.

So I thought it was legitimate for the imam of the Quincy mosque to take a course like this, because he's learning things. I had lots of misgivings. Would he be able to have an open mind? But he did beautifully in the course. He wrote some very good papers.

Many Muslims look at this diversity and are threatened by it, because they think in all this diversity, with all these people claiming to be Muslim, that in fact you are going to lose out on some kind of essential Muslim identity. In fact, it is the strength of the tradition that you have all of this diversity. The moment you have a tradition that is monolithic or very uniform—that's the end. There's no life to it.

There are any number of *hadith* about the right of the individual to interpret the faith, the importance of using reason. I think one of the strengths of the early Islamic community, in the time of the Prophet, was the tremendous diversity of opinions and views; and the debates.

There is a *hadith* that every person should in fact have the right to interpret. Somebody questioned the Prophet: what if you interpret something and you interpret it the right way? He said you will get double the blessings, but if you interpret it and your interpretation is wrong, you still get blessings, because at least you tried.

At the end of the course, I asked the imam what he got from the course. He said one of the most useful things was that he learned how to talk about Islam to a Western audience. All too often you have imams who come from the Middle East who are interviewed by the media every time something happens in an Islamic context, and a lot of these people don't speak the idiom of Americans. They're always giving out the wrong image, or the wrong message. And of course the media loves it, because it confirms all of the stereotypes.

I've seen him in interviews being quoted. He does a good job.

To be able to communicate with a diverse congregation—with some people who are very educated—you have to be able to talk on their terms, and if you do not have that education, you're going to turn everybody off.

This whole office of the imam in the United States is itself being redefined in American terms, very much along the lines of ministers and pastors. He told me, "Oh, the things I'm supposed to do here are in no way comparable to what you have to do in the Middle East. It's like being a minister."

My most embarrassing moment was related to being a professor of Islam at this university. I was recently on a three-week trip taking a group of Harvard and Yale alumni on a study tour of South Asia and the Middle East. We were on this cruise ship. The cruise was called "The Great Trade Routes of the Indian Ocean and the Arabian Sea." We stopped at many different countries, went to many different ports, and on the days at sea, my job was to give lectures on the history, the culture, the language, the literature of the areas we were visiting. I'd had a good two weeks with these alumni—all of them having a good time, really curious to see the world. We'd had these lectures about Islam, trying to break the stereotypes.

We were going along the streets of Jedda in this bus, and we passed this magnificent white mosque. There was a big courtyard in front of it, and as we were passing, the tour guide said, "And in the courtyard of this mosque, every Friday, they have an execution." So the tourists asked, "What kind of execution?" He said, people's heads are chopped off with a sword. It's a public execution." He said that the only month that this is not done is in the month of Ramadan. And we had come in the month of Ramadan.

Someone sitting beside me on the bus said, "Too bad we didn't come here on bloody Friday."

Here's a country like Saudi Arabia. It tries so much to improve the image of Islam. They have that Arabia exhibit. They came up with a wonderful booklet on Islam. But sad to say, they're the worst enemies of Islam, at least in the public image. I saw my whole trip, everything that I'd done, go down the drain. You can tell people whatever you want to tell them, but what's going to stick in that head is that white mosque and that courtyard.

When we were passing by, all the cameras clicked. And you can imagine them showing their pictures to their friends back home.

The human mind is such that what it remembers is images. What they'll remember of the Middle East is the mosque and executions. Also the image of societies being very repressive. The role of women. These people were astonished. They asked me why women can't go to the mosque. There is absolutely nothing in the Qur'an that stops women from going to the mosque, and nothing in the *hadith*. In fact, we know that during the time of the Prophet women did go to the mosque. And I kept telling them, "In America, women do go to the mosque."

Hopefully they'll remember some of the things from the lectures. We tried to make a big distinction between Islam the faith and Islam the political ideology.

One woman told me, "The Qur'an may say one thing. But Muslims are practicing in this way, and *that* is Islam, the practice."

What else can you say?

Is it not a Sign to them that the Learned of the
Children of Israel knew it [as true]?

Qur'an 26:197

Rendezvous

Rabia van Hattum

Thirty-nine. She lives across the road from the mesa-top mosque in Abi-
quiu, New Mexico. Abiquiu (a Native American word meaning "sweet
water"), in the upper Rio Grande Valley, is the setting of Dar al-Islam, a
community of some twenty Muslim families and the first Islamic village in
the United States. Some in the community wear Islamic robes, others West-
ern attire.

Their hand-shaped, mud-brick mosque and the attached school, or
madrassah, together said to be the largest adobe structure in North Amer-
ica, sit atop a mesa fifty miles from Santa Fe and in view of the late artist
Georgia O'Keeffe's New Mexico estate.

The mosque, built in one year at a cost of $2 million contributed largely
by Saudis, was designed by the late Hassan Fathy, a renowned Egyptian
architect who learned how to construct mud-brick domes and vaults from
Nubians and intended to use the technique to house the world's poor.
Inside, beneath the dome, it is cool and dank, even during midday in the
desert.

To this new sort of holy land, on 8,500 acres of New Mexican desert,
have come Muslims from Los Angeles and Brooklyn, from Egypt and Eu-
rope. They claim not to be utopians, "just people."

Rabia was born in San Francisco into a family of conservative Jews; she
attended Hebrew school.

The interview took place in back of the house as a Paula Abdul record
blared from the living room and the children buzzed around and minor

43

*emergencies occurred (her carpenter husband, Benyamin, sawed away; her
son sprayed insect repellent into his own eyes).*

When I was a child my parents took me to Israel several times. The first
time they took me, I was eleven years old. I remember being in Jerusalem
and hearing the *adhan*[17] for the first time, and that was like the first seed
being planted. I went out on the balcony and it was warm and it was dawn
and I could hear the muezzin[18] from East Jerusalem. It was the most beautiful thing I had ever heard. That was in 1962.

The most extraordinary thing happened. When I was thirteen my mother
was going to some very high-class women's clothing store and she slipped
and broke her hip and she sued them and won. So she said let's take
another trip. So we did.

I went to Jerusalem in 1968 after I graduated from high school. I kind of
wandered around intimidated. I had a kibbutz[19] stay then. I liked the rural
aspect of the life but I found the community incredibly bourgeois and the
people extremely narrow-minded and bigoted. They just hated Arabs.

In Jerusalem the people are paranoid. The city is fraught with tension.
There's so much antagonism going on that everyone is suspect.

It was 1973 and we were driving through the eastern section and I
looked at the women in their long velvet dresses with the embroidered
bodices, carrying everything on their heads, and I saw Arabic calligraphy
and the beautiful architecture. I just said, completely spontaneously, to my
mother, "I feel such affinity with these people."

My mother nearly crashed the car.

She said, "How can you say that? They're Arabs!"

And I went, "It just came out."

The Israelis had become so Westernized and so modernized. Concrete
apartment houses. Supertechnology. I hated it.

The Yom Kippur War broke out in 1973.[20] The Syrians invaded from the
Golan and the Egyptians came over the Sinai. I was in Jerusalem and the
whole city was blacked out and curfewed and all the men disappeared.
They were all called up. It was a terribly frightening experience. There I
was with all my relatives and they were getting into the war effort. I real-

---

[17] Call to prayer.
[18] Caller to prayer.
[19] An Israeli collective settlement or farm.
[20] Egypt and Syria attacked Israel on October 6, 1973—Yom Kippur, the most solemn day of
the Jewish calendar.

Benyamin and Rabia van Hattum.

ized that I couldn't relate to it at all. I just said, "I don't understand why everybody's fighting. I can't get behind it nationally, and I can't relate to what's going on politically."

So I got on a plane and left.

She studied Sufism at a retreat in the Swiss Alps, where she met her husband-to-be. She stayed for several weeks and found people who were planning to go to East Jerusalem to study with a sheik on the Mount of Olives. She then returned to Israel.

I went to Jerusalem. This was a great moment for me because I thought, well, these are the people I was waiting for. These are the people that are going to understand what I'm looking for.

So they spent the night at my apartment and the next day they said, "Well, we're going to go see the sheik now." And I went, "Oh. The sheik."

They took me up to the Mount of Olives. To go into the eastern section was very intimidating for me. But we did, and I felt extremely suspicious of everything. It's a completely segregated and divided city. I suppose it's like Detroit.

We met this sheik, and I remember feeling very distrustful. He offered us tea and everybody was sitting there just glowing. They thought it was the greatest meeting they had ever had in their lives.

He kept looking at me and saying, "How are you?" I remember not being able to relax.

He got an apartment for them. That was a terrible blow for me because I just wasn't ready to move in. Islam and the Arabic culture was something that I was conditioned to feel very afraid of and very intimidated by. There was something there, but I didn't understand it.

They all took this house and the sheik went on *hajj* and for the next month I visited them regularly and found out what they were studying. I came over all the time because I just loved the people.

They were studying Islam. It was the truth wrapped in an Islamic package. But I think what was really important to me at that time in my life was that I actually found a group of people that understood what I was understanding. That kind of companionship and that kind of affinity I so desperately needed.

And then the sheik came back and I saw him differently. He said to me, "Move in."

I said, "Well, my mother—?"

And he said, "Forget your mother. Move in."

So I did.

My family was totally freaked out. They hired private investigators. They called the police to trail me. They thought the entire thing was political and national and subversive. But that's what I did. I moved in and I started to study Islam.

When I started practicing Islam, Jerusalem opened up completely. I understood it. Everything that I'd been wanting to experience, everything that I knew that was there and could never taste. It was just there.

And three months later, Benyamin and I got married. Our marriage and our Islam were fairly simultaneous. We studied Islam for six months, and we practiced for five months.

The sheik who married us said, "Allah is my beloved and I must see my beloved's face in everything. In every state, in every situation." He said, "This is Allah's face." He was talking about everything I could see. Even him. He said, "Allah is merciful but you must understand His mercy; it's not like what you think."

My future husband was waiting outside. The sheik kept asking if there was no difference between us. He just kept asking one question after the other and the answer was always, there's no difference between us. And it was like, well yes, of course we should be married.

This went on for hours. And then he said to me, "Okay, you're married."

This wasn't at all what I was anticipating. I said, "What do you mean I'm married?"

He said, "Go back and get two witnesses and get a paper saying that in the religion of the God you've married him at this hour and he's your husband and in the religion of the God, you're his wife at this hour. And then you go sleep with your husband."

So I left.

I came out at about midnight and Benyamin was there waiting for me. For four hours he'd been sitting in the road. He was ghostly white. And he goes, "Well what happened?"

"We're married."

He said, "What?"

And we walked back to the apartment and I explained to him what had happened. We woke up everybody in the apartment, and we wrote up a little paper. They signed it and that was it.

Allah changeth not the condition of a folk until they [first]
change that which is in their hearts.

Qur'an 13:11

Brand-New Old Revolution

Jamil Abdullah Al-Amin

(formerly H. Rap Brown)

Today, his name is Jamil Abdullah Al-Amin, and he is imam of the Community Mosque of Atlanta. As head of the former Dar-ul-Islam movement, once based in Brooklyn, he is one of the nation's most influential Muslim leaders. His followers are said to number around 10,000 Muslims in more than thirty cities across America, including Chicago, New York, and Detroit.

He's the proprietor of an Atlanta corner variety store that sits across from a basketball court. He sells candy to neighborhood children, who enter in a flurry but settle down to show him great respect. (Virtually the whole neighborhood calls him "the imam.") He counts their pennies with his long fingers.

The same fingers fervently punctuated his points during fiery speeches when he was known as H. Rap Brown, a Black Power advocate in the 1960s. Born in Baton Rouge, Louisiana, on October 4, 1943, he attended Southern University, joined the Student Nonviolent Coordinating Committee (SNCC) in 1963, and was named SNCC chairman in 1967. He calls his book Die Nigger Die[21] *a "political autobiography." It's a fast-paced story about growing up black in the segregated South, challenging authority in both the black and white communities and living as a fugitive.*

In one 1967 rally speech, he warned, "If America don't come around,

[21] New York: Dial Press, 1969.

we're going [to] burn it down." In another, he said, "Violence is very American, as American as the Fourth of July."

He says he earlier earned the name Rap because he could do just that, rap. ("I'm sweet peeter jeeter the womb beater / The baby maker the cradle shaker / The deerslayer the buckbinder the women finder . . .")

He was the subject of much concern by the FBI under J. Edgar Hoover, who put Brown under surveillance and sought ways to show that Brown posed a subversive threat to the law-abiding, tax-paying white citizenry of the "true" America.

A manhunt for him ended in a New York shoot-out in which he was wounded. He converted to Islam in jail. Up till then he made his reputation rebelling against authority. Now he acknowledges the divine authority of Allah and in impromptu sermons preaches revolutionary ideals that stem from the Qur'an.

While H. Rap Brown would have enjoined listeners to bear and tear down, Jamil Abdullah Al-Amin says discipline yourselves through prayer, fasting, charity, and steadfastness, so that you will be organized and prepared when Allah tears the system down. He adds: There's "intoxication" in speaking too much.

As to the name Rap, it was based upon what I tried to illustrate in *Die Nigger Die*—the ability to talk. "Sweet Peeter Jeeter the Womb Beater"? I don't recite that poem. That was a chronicle that was taken from the past, in terms of the language and how it was used when I was growing up. As a matter of fact, they named rap music after me. That was because it was consistent with what I was trying to bring out during that time. I'm not saying I was the first person to rap. But the word and its introduction to the popular language was as a result of the reference to the style that was attributed to me during that time.

I don't think I ever spoke over an hour in any speech that I gave, [in the 1960s] and now. I was sincere about what I talked about, and I think what the Prophet (peace and blessings be upon him) warned against was excess in speech. In other words, the rule being moderation. Because there's an intoxicant in speech. If you can't deliver your messages in less than two hours, then what is the message that you're giving?

I became Muslim in 1971. I was in prison in New York. The Dar-ul-Islam movement had a prison program and brothers would come in to conduct *juma* and for *dawah* purposes.

It is said in Islam, it is Allah who makes Muslims. And so everything that Allah does is a progression, an evolution. There's no one incident that I can recall or relate to that made me become inclined toward Islam or to accept Islam. In my travels I had been exposed to Muslims but I had never made any conscious effort to study or to look into Islam. So again it is Allah who makes Muslims.

The life of this world is a prison for the believers and a paradise for the unbelievers. Schools in some instances are similar to the prisons, so [I] had been "institutionalized" long before I was incarcerated.

Everywhere that you go is school. Some people go to Harvard and Yale and Dartmouth and Boston College. Other people go to Attica and Auburn and Sing Sing. But the learning process continues.

I was released in November of '76 and proceeded to *hajj*. I did five years [of prison time] in one stretch. Overall it's more if you count the times that I was arrested and the time I did. I think everybody who was in the [civil rights] movement during that particular time to some degree was upset and perturbed and angry. Islam enables you and it teaches you not to be controlled or to do things out of anger. The Prophet pointed out that the strong man is not he who is a good wrestler, but he who can control his

Jamil Abdullah Al-Amin.

anger. That doesn't mean that you don't get upset about things, but if you can't control it, then you will be victimized by it.

Allah has created man for struggle. This is what pervades the very essence of what man is; his nature deals with struggle, advancement; even from conception, when the sperms compete to fertilize the egg, to the fertilization of the egg, to the growth in the womb, there's a kind of struggle that becomes a part of, the imprint upon, the character of man. All men struggle.

But then there's a higher level of struggle in which Allah says *jihad* for the pleasure of Allah, which deals with conscious struggle. The Islamic movement itself is built up on that level of consciousness concerning struggle, so again the difference in my struggling in terms of the movement during [the 1960s] was that it was a struggle that was not based upon sound guidelines and principles. I think this was the case with many of the people [in] the movement during that time. We were using basically the ethics and morals of the people that we were fighting against. So if we were successful in replacing them, we would only run it the way they were running it.

Allah says in the Qur'an that they swore their strongest oath to Allah that they would follow the guidance better than any other people. Even in the movement in the sixties, if I knew a thing to be right, then it would be binding upon me to implement it or try to practice it. And so it was when it came to Islam.

Thus have We made of you an Ummah just balanced,
that ye might be witnesses over the nations, and
the Messenger a witness over yourselves.

Qur'an 2:143

Accidental Muslim

Sohail Humayun Hashmi

A Sunni Muslim, Sohail is a thirty-one-year-old doctoral student in the government department at Harvard University. He is studying international relations and Islam.

Sohail says there are about 200 declared Muslims in the Harvard student community, which numbers about 8,000. The Harvard Islamic Society was founded in the 1950s by graduate students but is now led by undergraduates. When Sohail headed the society, he conducted its activities out of his bedroom. The Muslim community is growing, Sohail says, and its membership reflects more active types. Harvard has seen its fair share of "cultural Muslims," he adds, Muslims by birth "who consciously avoid being associated with Muslim groups on campus."

I used to go to a school far away from my home in India. It was an Anglican school. I would get up at five in the morning, and my mother would get me ready to go to school. And this elderly gentleman would pick me up, and we would trudge off to school. First I would take a train and get off and take a bus. By the time I got to school I was exhausted. But I was going to that school because it was considered one of the best in Hyderabad, an English medium school.

While I was in school I would be busy playing during lunch break. This elderly gentleman, who was very poor, would come with hardly anything to eat and I would realize that he wasn't eating. Gradually I started telling him to eat my lunch. This became a regular pattern. My grandmother would fix my lunch and he would eat it. I would return home extremely hungry. My grandmother would say, "Why are you so hungry? Don't you eat your lunch?" At first I never confessed. Then one day she said, "Something's going on. Your lunch bag comes back empty but you're always hungry." I finally admitted that this old gentleman was eating my lunch. She scolded him and said, "How can you be taking food from a little boy like that? If you had told me I would have fixed lunch for you myself. You should not be hungry either. But it's not right to take food from a little boy and make him hungry all day." He was thoroughly embarrassed but my grandmother always afterwards gave him lunch along with me.

I remember that experience because it showed firmness as well as compassion and generosity which I associate with both my grandparents and my parents.

My mother returned to school after I was born, to finish her degrees, and my father was already in the United States. So I was raised by my extended family. My grandmother managed our household in India, which I think is typical in a lot of Muslim societies. I was never raised to think that women are subservient or subordinate to men in any way. Our religion doesn't teach that, and moreover I see that in my own life. It's the women in our family who run the family, and the men who are always following them.

My grandfather would never assume that he had any control over the money he earned. That money went directly to my grandmother, who would disburse the funds as she saw fit. The money he earned was not his own. This is the culture he was raised in; this was his ethical perspective. This was their division of labor.

My grandmother raised me with a very strong sense of my Muslim identity. All my uncles and aunts are imbued with this same kind of approach.

My grandmother lives Islam, she doesn't preach it. She never engaged in the trappings of the religion, such as making a show of her prayers or making a show of the fact that her children had learned Arabic enough to read the Qur'an. She had a different kind of approach which is that you have to be a good person, and that is something that is the essence of faith. It's not showing your religion outwardly; it's practicing it from within.

My family is from Uttar Pradesh in northern India. They migrated from Iran and settled in northern India for about three centuries near the city of Lucknow, which was imbued with a sense of culture, especially Urdu poetry and literature. My family still retains some of that old historical attachment to a dying civilization. When I go back and see my family in India, it seems like I am looking at a culture that has really passed away.

I lived in Statesboro, where my father teaches at Georgia Southern University. When we came to the United States, I was very fortunate in that we went to a small city, which is relatively conservative, very religious—Christian, Southern Baptist in particular. The environment that I grew up in was very much similar to the environment in which I was raised in India in terms of the cultural ethos. Of course, there were all kinds of problems in Statesboro, but on the aspect of religion and how my family was treated, there was never any kind of hostility or tension or bigotry or prejudice that I ever experienced. In fact, our friends there were always interested in finding out more about Islam.

Throughout the '70s and early '80s, we were definitely the representatives of Islam in that part of the country. My younger sister was married in 1990, and after her marriage, one of my father's closest friends said, "You know, this is a historic wedding."

My father said, "What do you mean?"

"Well, as far as I can tell, this is the first Muslim wedding in southern Georgia held in a Presbyterian church, conducted by a black imam."

The ironies were just so amazing. Not only was it a Muslim wedding being held in a church, but it was being held by a black imam who a few decades ago wouldn't have been allowed to set foot in that church. And now he's conducting the service there—for Indians!

To some extent that's what shaped my approach to religion, because I have talked to many friends who grew up in larger cities like New York or Washington, and they've been turned off by religion altogether. They were sent at a young age to Sunday schools where they were indoctrinated with the tenets of Islam and were taught by people who had no appreciation for growing up in the United States as teenagers. And they rebelled. Some of them actually think that Islam doesn't have any applicability to them in their environment, which I think is a great tragedy.

My experience was very different because Islam was taught to me in the home, and it was not taught so much as a form of dogma or ritual. Islam for me means basically the way my parents live, and they've always been the model for me of what a Muslim marriage and what a Muslim family should be like.

I never felt that I was being assimilated, and my parents never had that intention. I think they wanted me to appreciate the culture in which I was living and also be firm in my own beliefs and convictions.

When I was about eleven years old, I was cleaning the garage on a really hot, sultry summer day. As is usual in that part of Georgia, we had visitors from a church group. It was a man and a woman who were passing out leaflets for a revival meeting. The man asked, "What church do you go to?"

I said, "I don't go to church. My family is Muslim. Because we have no mosque here, we pray at home; this is basically our mosque."

He said, "Let me give you this flier anyway. It certainly won't hurt you to mix a little Southern Baptist in you."

[*Laughs.*]

At that point I realized how different I was.

In the sixth grade I was introduced to the fact that a boy and a girl were going out together. I thought that was very interesting. All of a sudden I found myself being asked to go to the local roller-skating rink. I was part of a group that had distinct couples. I was not matched up with anyone. But as time went on, I became more and more the odd person out. And I began to wonder, why should I be the odd person out? Maybe I should invite a girl.

I was at a crossroads. I could have gone either way. I could have asked my parents—look, I want to go on a date—and I don't know how they would have responded. But we went to India in 1975, and that made a big difference. I saw my cousins. I saw the way they behaved, and I realized I was not part of American culture. I wanted to emulate my cousins. In fact, I was very happy at that time contemplating the prospect of an arranged marriage. I just thought it was the greatest thing in the world—this is the way it's done, in a very secure fashion. You don't have any of the worries associated with "finding the right person."

At that point I parted course. I had close friends who were girls, and I knew they were dating and engaged in all that was expected of an American teenager, but I never was a participant in it.

When I reached the end of high school, there were some pressures along the dating line. I was extremely active in the arrangements for the high school prom. I decorated the gym. Then my friends said, Sohail, why aren't you coming to the prom? It's not as if you're morally opposed to it, otherwise you wouldn't be participating in the preparations. Even teachers were asking me, Why don't you date? I said this is something I don't do, and I told them that, more than likely, I will have an arranged marriage.

That immediately went all over the high school.

All of a sudden I was being introduced in the civics and history classes as the Muslim student from India who would probably have an arranged marriage. They thought that was just incomprehensible. And the girls especially were very curious about that. Nothing else about India concerned them.

I was amused by it. There were stereotypes developing, but they were not hostile in any way, and I tried my best to put it in context. I explained, "You know, I'm going to have some say-so as to whom I marry, but it's not going to be that I date in order to find that spouse." And I said, "If you're not interested in marrying someone, then dating is wrong."

It's morally wrong to have a casual relationship with someone and then part course after becoming intimate. I saw that as part of the general cul-

Sohail Humayun Hashmi.

ture that was contributing toward the breakdown of family. The parents of close friends of mine were getting divorces and that really bothered me.

I'm not saying that Indian culture is any better, because many couples who should get divorces just remain together for the sake of appearances or because it's the accepted thing to do. That's the other extreme. I think Islam is somewhere in the middle: if you get married, you settle down, and you try to make that marriage work at all costs. It's not a sacrament, it's a contract that is attested to in front of God. And only if it doesn't work out under extreme circumstances should you seek a divorce. That's an escape mechanism in case of severe problems in the marriage, but it's not an immediate recourse if something happens to go wrong along the way.

The Iranian revolution has had a tremendous effect on me personally, because at that point Islam exploded onto the Georgian consciousness with the taking of the hostages. For the first time, people were saying, oh, you're a Muslim, aren't you? What do you think about the hostage crisis, and Khomeini? So I began to explain Islam in a very political way. I had done it before from a historical, cultural, and religious point of view. Now it was politics. It was something that directly affected the lives of Americans.

I was a junior when the revolution occurred in January of 1979. Then the hostages were taken in November of '79, and all of a sudden everyone was really concerned. Are the Muslims about to rise up en masse against the United States everywhere? In other words, are they all like the Iranians, who obviously are fanatics? How come this guy whom we've known for more than a decade seems so palatable to us and yet he professes to be a Muslim? Is Sohail just the exception to the rule?

There was genuine concern and interest to try to figure out what Islam meant. I'm not sure what people were saying behind my back, but when I came to Harvard, I found a different situation than I expected. Supposedly, this is a very open and very objective kind of intellectual community. But again I found a lot of strange stereotypes propagated by people you'd expect to be able to dispel them.

It's not hostile, but it's much more aggressive and more prevalent than the situation in Georgia where Islam was a novelty and people were just discovering it. In Cambridge, people think they know what Islam is. And often I get the feeling when I try to counter these impressions, they see me as the exception or think that I'm deliberately trying to hide the realities. That I'm just a liberal on the fringes of the Islamic spectrum.

When Israel invaded Lebanon in '82, that was something that caused a great deal of concern here among my friends. And for me personally. It was during Ramadan, and watching day after day Beirut being pounded by heavy artillery was tormenting. And all the time you were hearing about "Shiite fundamentalists" or "Shiite terrorists," the people who blew up the American embassy.

Shi'ism is a branch of Islam, a school of interpretation. It's very much a religious phenomenon; it's not necessarily a political phenomenon. Yet the two are linked—Shiites and political terrorists—in American consciousness. They're code words. And when you see the word "fundamentalist," it's equated with "terrorist," or it's equated with someone who's fanatically hostile to U.S. culture and Western interests in general.

I blame the Muslims more or less, because the Muslims in this country have not established enough of a presence. They don't speak as a single voice yet, and they're bent on causing as little trouble as possible.

The Muslims are obsessed with issues that directly relate to their home countries. The Indian Muslims are often obsessed with what's happening in Kashmir or in India now. The Pakistanis are obsessed with U.S. policy toward Pakistan. The Arabs are fixated on the Palestinian issue. They're so fixated that they're hesitant to let any other issues cloud that agenda. And the Bosnians have very little presence in the United States. There hasn't developed a sense of an American Muslim community with interests abroad. That spills over not only to political activism but into social events —to mosque building, for example.

One of my closest friends who's a leader in Southern California categorized the mosques. There are what he calls the "homesick mosques," because they're formed by expatriates who just want a place to come together and speak their native language, make sure their children are in a safe environment and an endogamous group. The other mosques are somewhat complacent and willing to avoid politics altogether in order to maintain unity, so they don't ever form an agenda. They decide to bury the hatchet when it comes to their differences, and the result is that they're just a place where people come to pray. Maintaining the least common denominator of friction leaves them completely helpless.

A change is occurring in my generation. We're less likely to identify with the homesick-mosque culture and more likely to assert a very active political role for the Islamic center, and to do it as an American Muslim community—not as Egyptian, Pakistani, or Malaysian expatriates, but as Americans.

The Muslim *jihad* in America is to establish a sense of identity, because at this point there is no Muslim community. At every sermon, there's talk about the need for the reemergence of the Muslim *ummah*. *Ummah* is given a moral value in the Qur'an, which opposes giving moral value to the nation or race or ethnicity. It basically says that in the sight of God a community will be judged on the basis of its ethical standards and practice.

American Muslims at this point are not willing to enact certain measures which might move them beyond this kind of fragmentation which is characteristic. I think it's a problem of long-standing cultural differences, which can only be superseded as time passes on.

But there is a better climate in this country to live a Muslim life than there is anywhere else in the Muslim world, on the basis of my experience. Your American identity is what you make it, and there's more freedom in this country than there is anywhere else that I've seen.

I felt different from my American classmates in many ways. My children, however, may feel that they're completely American and at the same time they'll be able to share my values and know that they can never be total participants in this American culture—that they have a duty to reform it according to their own values. This is a task that I think can be shared with all the faiths in this country. The Christian friends that I have see this as originally a Christian country, but having completely diverged from Christian morals and values. They see themselves engaged in a *jihad* as well.

The Christian community, the Jewish community, and all the other religious communities are faced with a struggle to give identity to their religious missions in this country.

The opportunity is greatest for American Muslims to really shape the course of Islam in the future because American Islam is a microcosm of Muslims from all over the world who have to find a way to live together. They have to come to a common understanding of what Islam means in this country, and moreover they're free from the kinds of cultural and political repression that are prevalent in the Muslim countries.

The Egyptians are faced with this real challenge. They are living in a culture which prizes material achievement, uses material symbols as signs of status—à la the West; and they're bombarded with the television programs which glorify material consumption. If you are extremely poor,[22] you will either go in the direction of becoming a crass materialist, no matter what it takes—you'll struggle and bribe and sell your soul to achieve this status; or you'll have a complete backlash and become like the militants who reject that culture altogether and call for violent means to overturn it.

Sayyid Qutb,[23] who was one of the most influential Islamic writers, one of the leaders of the Muslim Brotherhood in the 1960s, spent a year or two in New York, where he was horrified by what he saw. He went back and began this campaign by saying that the West was not engaged in military invasion of the Muslim countries; it was engaged in a moral and a cultural invasion; and it was going to destroy the Muslim world just as surely as any military force could have done.

Many of his admirers see the TV shows that are aired, the casinos, the nightclubs—all these things that are very much the symbols of the degeneracy of Muslim society and Muslim culture—and they decide that only violent means can be used to stop the infiltration of the West.

The notion of *jihad* is a religious notion, but it is completely intertwined with political aspirations. You cannot separate Islam or *jihad* from politics. Because *jihad* is basically a struggle to achieve in the outward world a just social order, an order in which people are not hungry, and not being persecuted or abused or massacred; which is politics—essentially the allocation of scarce resources for the achievement of an equitable social system. Sometimes the system is highly skewed toward the rich, the powerful. Sometimes it is not. And Islam is trying to fight that tendency prevalent in all human societies toward the skewing of power and wealth to the few.

Ever since the secularization of Western politics, there's been this notion that somehow religion mixed with politics is going to produce warfare, conflict, killing, massacres. It's obvious why this notion developed, because Europe was rent for a hundred years by fighting and warfare between Protestants and Catholics, and that whole idea of secularism was an outgrowth of that—to reject religion as a political activity and to personalize religion.

[22] In spring 1993, Cairo's unemployment rate was 20 percent.
[23] 1906–66. Author of *al-'Adala al-ijtima'iyya fi'l-islam* (*Social Justice in Islam*) and *Ma'alim fi'l-tariq* (*Signposts on the Path*). A leading theoretician of the Muslim Brotherhood, Qutb was imprisoned from 1954 to 1964, released, rearrested, and executed in 1966.

People wonder if Islam is undergoing a similar type of reformation and whether politics is on the way out. I say no, exactly the opposite. Politics is coming back into Islam.

After World War II, the anticolonialist movements were led by people who wanted to get the West out of their countries. But that was in order to become Western—so they could join the "club" on an equal basis. The leaders wanted basically to assume the position of the colonialists within their own countries. *They* wanted to live in the villas, have a comfortable life.

But what they did as a result of that was to absorb and imbibe Western values so much that they began to treat Islam as merely a matter of personal conviction or faith.

The most prominent example of this is Turkey. It started in the 1920s, before World War II. It went to the absurd extent of ordering people how to dress. They couldn't wear traditional dress, because it was seen as backward, as antinationalist. As a result of that, the state started to try to shape people's lives in an overt way. It started becoming authoritarian. This was the objective. The state was to educate the people.

There was a time within the Islamic movement earlier this century when attempts were made to reconcile the modern world with Islamic principles; however, these modernist movements never became firm. They were always in the higher strata of intellectuals who were writing theories. They were never translated into an actual political movement or political party.

The field was left open for the appropriation of Islam in the political sphere by the "fundamentalist" groups. They say, we tried the nationalist experiment, it's not working. The Muslim countries are skewed toward favoring the rich and the masses of people are suffering from tremendous poverty. So obviously there's a very strong ground for a political movement to challenge that. And Islam is now providing the answer.

Islam has a very strong social ethic, which goes back to the time of the Prophet himself. The Prophet didn't surround himself with the elite of Mecca. He surrounded himself with former slaves, with the lower class, who became the first Muslims. So Islam has always had this appeal to the disinherited. And now that's what's spawning this Islamic movement.

Not that the masses of Muslims share the agenda of the fundamentalists —because the fundamentalists want to replace that postcolonial elite with themselves and then start to enact state policies from the top down. So it's becoming a vicious circle. They are cloaked in the rhetoric of Islamic universalism. They say that we will enact the universal ethics of Islam, and we will do away with state borders and state frontiers, and if need be we will intercede on behalf of the Bosnians and Palestinians.

But when it comes to actual practice, they themselves become a nationalist ideology. They set about to make sure that they don't lose power, that they are able to transform the state according to their own vision of what the state should be, and in the end they become just as oppressive as the nationalists that they're trying to overthrow.

This has happened in Iran.

Modernists believe that the Islamic notion of moral sanction is not derived from the state, but is derived from the community—the *ummah*. In other words, you don't legislate moral sanctions; you apply social pressure, which is much more benign than having the state enact it. The state shouldn't have any license whatsoever to enforce a moral code on the individual believer.

In America, we're starting from point zero. We're building our own community. It can go in the direction of continuing what the status quo is—the homesick-mosque versus the complacent-mosque culture. Or it can become politically organized and then split by all the different factions that are operating in the Muslim world today. Or it could evolve its own indigenous approach to Islam, which is based on interpretations.

There's a very strong concept in early Islam of *ijtihad*. It is derived directly from the word *jihad*. It's a form of *jihad*. It means struggle to interpret the faith. And it was used in a very technical way by the Muslim jurists, when they were struggling with their reason, based on all the sources of the law—the Qur'an, the *Sunnah,* and the prior practices of the community—to try to come up with legal injunctions for new situations. They had to engage in *ijtihad,* that was their personal *jihad*. And I think that's precisely what's facing the American Muslim community today, the need for *ijtihad*.

My *jihad* basically is to live as a Muslim according to my convictions, and if someone along the way likes what they see, then I'd be more than happy to explain to them. But I don't go out of my way to portray myself as Muslim. In fact, I have a deep antipathy for people who wear religion on their sleeves, who make a point of causing commotion and disturbance to perform a prayer, which I think is contrary to the purpose of prayer itself.

I don't think I am required to explain Islam. I live Islam the way I have been raised by my parents and the way I have come to understand Islam for myself. I've thought about the issues, and I've come to the conviction that I believe in the Islamic message. I've internalized it.

I call myself an "accidental Muslim." I was born into a Muslim family. In India I would have assumed certain things to be true, simply because everyone else believed them around me. But being in America forces you to really assess what you believe in and to act according to your beliefs.

The "nonaccidental Muslims" are the Muslims in America who have struggled really hard, sometimes coming from deeply religious Christian and Jewish backgrounds, and then come to the conclusion that Islam is the way of life that they have always been seeking. I think they're the future of Islam, especially in this country.

Work is prayer.
Arabic proverb

The Calligrapher

Mohamed Zakariya

Mohamed Zakariya was born in Ventura, California, in 1942, and his family subsequently moved to Los Angeles. As a restless teenager he dropped out of high school because he wanted to get out into the "real" world. In the early 1960s, he worked in a machine shop and was able to scrape together enough money for the adventure of a lifetime—a trip to Morocco. Zakariya boarded a Yugoslavian freighter in New York for a hundred-dollar trip to Casablanca, and from there he traveled to Marrakesh. In Morocco he found text fashioned in intriguing swirls of ink and gilded gold—calligraphy. He also found himself mesmerized by the sound of Arabic and drawn to the stately mosques. Upon returning to the states at nineteen, he took his shahada *and has never looked back.*

Zakariya (whose work adorns this book) is credited as the person who started Islamic calligraphy in the United States. During his second trip to Morocco he met an Egyptian calligrapher, Abdussalam Ali-Nour, who became his first teacher. Years later, in a correspondence course, he studied with master calligrapher Hasan Celebi in Istanbul. Zakariya learned the thulth *and* naskh *scripts. He also studied the* nasta'liq *script with Ali Alparslan. He has taught and exhibited in the Arabian Gulf, and his work is bought by the wealthiest and by the not-so-affluent alike. He works in all the major scripts as a genuine* hattat—*Turkish for calligrapher—and is the first American to receive an* icazet, *or diploma, from the Research Center for Islamic History, Art, and Culture in Istanbul. Today he lives with his family in Arlington, Virginia, quietly perfecting his craft.*

At work: Zakariya first designs a piece, practicing calligraphing the text.

64

He then creates a stencil, or mold (kalib), outlining letters with pin-pricks.
He places the stencil on the paper he will use for his final calligraphing, and
lightly dusts it with chalk powder, transferring his design as a series of dots
onto the surface he will use.

He utters "Bismillah," and works out his final draft, his pen moving
slowly across the page. When done, he cleans the edges of his pen work
with a scraping knife, then burnishes the page with agate to bond the
calligraphy to the paper. Finally, he may add decorative borders or gold
illumination.

Calligraphy is a way of celebrating God. It's like a song, like a visual *duah.*
There's a book written 750 years ago in Morocco by a guy who was the
Qadi of Fez at the time. He goes into a whole series of professions and how
they become Islamic professions by the way you make intentions when you
do the work. For instance: "I intend this to be pure work for the sake of
Allah." By making intentions as such you can transform any kind of work
as long as it's *halal*-type work into worship. Calligraphy is certainly one of
those types of professions.

The major thing with the Qur'an is it's oral. People in Islamic countries
are great memorizers of the Qur'an. But the visual aspect has been there
right from the beginning, when Muhammad said, Give your eyes their
share of worship—let them look at the pages of the Qur'an.

You've got to study literature, have concepts of what poetry is about.

Mohamed Zakariya.

You can bring a passage in the Qur'an to light using calligraphy. People read the Qur'an in a mechanical way where they don't stop to think sometimes. So when you do a calligraphy piece and it's on someone's wall, they may say, Oh I never thought of that.

People love the visual aspects of calligraphy. In most mosques there's lots of calligraphy. In the nineteenth century a new thing happened in Turkey—people began having large-scale calligraphy pieces done that could be independently hung on walls instead of paintings. Beforehand in the Muslim world people didn't have a concept of hanging framed works of art on the wall. They had things carved into the walls. But they didn't go out and buy a piece of art, frame it, and put it on their wall. That gave the calligrapher a whole new market.

Great art is great art. Great European art is not to be denied its place. There's never been the equivalent of Beethoven in Islamic music. Yet in calligraphy there were world-class works done by masters. It's not familiar to Americans—it has the flare of the exotic about it, and with the problems with Islamic countries right now, and those banners that said "Death to America" or "The Great Satan" in script, Americans don't feel too comfortable with it.

Oriental calligraphy is a concept that's radically different from ours. In Oriental culture calligraphy is a tremendous art as well. But it's more ceremonial than Islamic calligraphy. There's a whole series of rituals the calligrapher goes through in order to produce the work.

For us, we have to have the right intentions and we don't write anything without being clean. What's required is the same state as if you were ready for prayer. Then a customer can bring you a selection of text—either an *ayat,* a *hadith,* or a poem. Or I have to find something that has particular meaning for myself.

I'm kind of a traditionalist. I follow the precedents that have already been set. Within that framework there are a lot of possibilities for experimentation and growth, but it's also not cutting yourself off completely from the past. We have to have the past to tell us what we're doing today.

Recipe for writing:
It's a nightmare to make ink. It takes three to six months.

You mix up a tub of linseed oil and kerosene, 60 percent kerosene. You fill old V8 cans full of oil and stick a big ropelike wick in it. You burn it and put flower pots over the cans. After six weeks you scrape off the soot —enough to make a four-year supply of ink.

You mix it with gum arabic and grind it using a mortar and pestle. You have to grind it for thirty hours. So I generally take a month, and every night I get in front of the television and grind the mixture like a maniac—one hour a day for thirty days. It's real thick, like tar or black honey. It gleams like black diamonds.

Then you put the whole mess in the blender with a little distilled water, and for a week you grind it an hour a day, five minutes at a time, because otherwise you can burn the blender out. Then start adding water until it's the right thickness. And then you're done.

You get this wonderful ink! For the love of money you can't go and buy an ink as beautiful as this. It's got nothing but water, soot, and gum arabic. You can polish it with a stone and it won't get messed up.

It's not waterproof. If you get water on it, it will smear. But the control of it—it flows out like black gold. It flows just right when it comes out of your pen.

After the ink, the next problem is pens.[24] I make pens, but you have to start with the raw materials. The best pens we get today come from Iran. They come through Turkey. They're exactly like the reed for an oboe. It's the same genus. It's hard river cane. You have to cut one tip of the pen. Then you have to refine the shape of the pen.

The paper is the hard part. You can take practically any kind of paper and do calligraphy on it. But you have to put a coating on the paper. You take a big bowl of egg whites and a block of alum and mix it, and the egg whites turn into something like cottage cheese—lumpy, disgusting material. You keep going and it liquefies again. After it sits for a while you can paint it onto the surface of the paper. You put three or four coats on it. This transforms the paper into a surface that is usable for calligraphy. You rub it with a little dry soap on a paper towel, and wipe it onto the paper. Then you take a piece of agate and burnish the paper until it gleams. This mashes down all the fibers until they're very smooth and flat. It makes the paper feel very soft.

Before you write, you take chalk dust and rub it on the paper so that the oils from your hands are taken away, and then you can write on it.

By all these processes, the paper is made very valuable. That's an Islamic concept—where you take a humble material and turn it into something valuable by addressing your attention to it.

---

[24] The calligraphy pen, or *kalem*, is preferably made of reed or cane aged for a minimum of four years.

If you want your calligraphy to look authentic, you've got to use real gold. I buy regular gold leaf in $400 boxes of five hundred sheets. You mix the gold leaf with gum arabic and pulverize it with your finger on a big sheet of glass, and then you scoop it up and go through a washing process. It takes two or three days to make a big supply of it. The highest carat I use is twenty-three carats.

The gold transforms the calligraphy into something that really leaps off the page. The calligraphy needs the gold. The two elements in our worldly existence that last forever are gold and carbon. The ink is pure black carbon, it's eternal, nothing can change it. It's the most elemental element. Gold is the same. It doesn't change.

All Qur'anic calligraphy should have some gold work on it—this emphasizes its holiness.

The first people to write with gold were the Chinese. In Islam the same thing began happening in the second or third century *hijra*. In the first century gold would be used in chapter headings.

In calligraphy there can't be a focal point. We think of everything in weight—there has to be balance. We see it as a whole piece. If you keep looking at one spot, you've probably made a mistake.

(31) [Turn, then, away from all that is false,] turning unto
Him [alone]; and remain conscious of Him, and be constant
in prayer, and be not among those who ascribe divinity
to aught beside Him,

(32) [or] among those who have broken the unity of their faith
and have become sects, each group delighting in but what they
themselves hold [by way of tenets].

Qur'an 30:31–32

A Separate Peace

Abd Al-Hayy Moore

Born: Oakland, California, 1940. His father was vice president of a truck-
ing company there. The household was nonreligious. In junior high school,
he wrote plays, and in 1967, during the psychedelic era, he founded the
Floating Lotus Magic Opera Company, which lasted three years and did
three operas in the San Francisco Bay area. He wrote scripts and directed.
By 1971, his published and unpublished manuscripts were bought by the
Bancroft Library of the University of California at Berkeley.

Later, he became a Muslim, joined a Sufi order based in England, and
lived for a year in a Nigerian Muslim mission. He sought refuge back in
California after a falling-out with Shiites in Texas. Today, he lives in Phila-
delphia with his wife and two children.

I was propelled toward the Ka'aba on a sea of churning black arms toward
the Black Stone.[25] I kissed it and then I was propelled back like in a giant

[25] The Black Stone, an egg-shaped stone 18 centimeters in diameter, rests in a silver wire mesh
set in the southeast corner of the Ka'aba. The stone's origins are unclear (according to tradition, the angel Gabriel brought it to Adam in Paradise). One story is known, however: When
the Ka'aba was restored in A.D. 605, the stone was removed and tribal leaders were prepared
to fight for the privilege of returning it to its place of honor. To avoid bloodshed, Muham-

cyclotron. At some point when I was near the Black Stone I found myself being lifted up by these strong guys. It was like a gift in a way because I was on a carpet of Africans taking me to the Black Stone. I kissed it and I was drawn back. I remember these black arms like pistons in a giant machine.

A lot of Nigerians go on *hajj* every year. You have to be pretty wealthy to get there, but when you go on *hajj* one of the largest populations of Muslims is the Nigerian.

They're real strong, living as they do. You see women along the roads with a huge bucket on their heads, with a huge tin with grain in it, and they've got two buckets filled with water and they're running down the road and they've got children running after them. As far as physical beauty and strength and awareness, they're brilliant. They're bright.

After Nigeria, I found myself in Atlanta. I was very warmly greeted. And people had all had various histories about how they became Muslims. Some of them had been with Elijah Muhammad's organization and defected or grew out of it. There were orthodox Muslims.

I spent some time just being a Muslim and getting along with the imam of this community. And there were a number of people who expressed a strong desire to have a sheik and some Sufi practices. We found ourselves an old house and these people defected from one community to come and join us. We were very near to Jamil Al-Amin's mosque. And we had Sufi practices. A number of other people came and joined us.

But there were strong animosities toward us—some that disapproved of Sufism, some that were angry that we had taken the cream, the better people.

There was a large community in San Antonio and at one point the signal was given for all the people in San Antonio to come to Atlanta, so a sudden influx of people [came] from San Antonio. Now, that group was also racially mixed and they arrived and suddenly we had this big established group.

The sheik said we should all move back to San Antonio and we did. And at this point, into the picture comes another sheik, who was an Iraqi. Shiite. Businessman. He was living in a big house just outside of San Antonio. He was interested in setting up a Qur'anic studies college.

---

mad, the thirty-five-year-old whom they called *Al-Ameen* ("the Trustworthy"), was chosen to replace the stone. He called for a rug, placed the holy relic on it, asked representatives of each tribe to clasp the ends of the rug and lift the stone to its chosen spot. He then placed the Black Stone with his own hands into the wall and sealed it in.

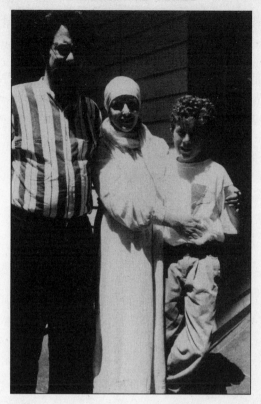

Abd Al-Hayy Moore with his wife, Malika, and son Farid.

We arrived as Sunnis and we were told that we could remain Sunnis. There were a lot of people leaving as we arrived. We stayed as Sunnis for maybe a month or so. After a month or two as a Shiite, I thought I was in Lilliput—everything was upside-down and backwards. They do lots of things differently, it seems. They combine prayers. They do prayers out loud that we never do out loud, and prayers silently that we do out loud. It was like being in Wonderland.

And their doctrine is extremely strong. And for me Shi'ism is the Catholicism of Islam. They have a priesthood. They have a mystery—the twelve imams, ending in the man who is hiding in the occult and who is going to come out one day. They have an iconography. And as a Muslim you think this is not allowed.

We were Shiites for about a year. In that time, I learned a lot about something I wouldn't have learned about. At some point we were in a communal meeting in Austin, Texas, and one of the members of the community was saying we have to teach our children that to be Shiite is like being black in South Africa. He wasn't black. [My wife] and I both looked at each other and I later said we did not become Muslims in order to live our lives as if we were black in South Africa, and hated and reviled by everyone and having to defend ourselves from sudden death.

At some point, we decided this was no longer viable and we fled. We got a rent-a-car and drove all the way to California. We put all the possessions we could in our car and what we didn't, we left behind. We took our children and just got out of there.

Chapter Two

Holy Empires

*O Prophet! Inspire the believers to conquer all fear of
death when fighting, [so that,] if there be twenty of you who
are patient in adversity, they might overcome two hundred;
and [that,] if there be one hundred of you, they overcome one
thousand of those who are bent on denying the truth,
because they are people who cannot grasp it.*

Qur'an 8:65

The Qur'an states: "And let there always be a community (of such people)
among you who should call people to goodness and enjoin equity and
forbid evil. It is these who shall attain their goal." And the Prophet reportedly said that nobody can be a true believer unless his neighbor feels safe
and secure from his side; and that no one should consider himself a true
believer if his neighbors go hungry while his own belly is full.

Islam, then, stresses the concept of community and of brotherhood and
sisterhood. Every major Muslim leader in America has striven to create a
Muslim minisociety in the United States. Ideally, it would guarantee freedom to practice Islam openly, provide freedom (and refuge) from discrimination, encourage the Islamic concept that mankind sprang from the same
mother and father, promote strong families in a land where too many have
been shattered, provide jobs for the disenfranchised and economic power
in ghettos forsaken by Christianity and Judaism. The Islamic community,
in short, would root out the evils associated with Christianity, Communism, or any other ideology.

America's Muslim leaders have proven resourceful. Calling himself "the

73

Messenger" and espousing nationalistic self-help principles borrowed from Marcus Garvey, as well as religious ideas from a forerunner, Noble Drew Ali, Elijah Muhammad succeeded handsomely, building a "lost-found" empire in Harlems and South Sides across America. He reigned as teacher, as harbinger of truth, as provider, as a divine-sent leader who offered the dispossessed a black-ruled community, a mighty black god, and a crystal-clear vision of the devil.

Elijah Muhammad—or, rather, Malcolm X, his national representative —got more press than any other Islamic leader in U.S. history. But Muhammad's ideas weren't always welcomed by orthodox Muslims, for whom Islam was—and is—a universal religion. Elijah Muhammad's own son and successor shunned the teachings and ended up dismantling the once-mighty nation bit by bit, temple by temple. In most instances, mosques arose in their place, and inside them black nationalism was forsaken in favor of piety and the universality of mankind, black or white or any other race.

Vestiges of Elijah's racial concepts linger, though, and while some former temples have been renamed mosques, others are still home to the tenets of his homegrown religion. There, the Fruit of Islam, a militia established in Elijah's day, stands guard in bow ties, and young fiery ministers pound the lectern and teach from Elijah's books in an angry sort of Sunday-school lesson.

Meanwhile, in mosques stripped of chairs, rows of Muslims squat on rugs, hear imams chide them for not living up to their Islamic heritage, and then prostrate to Allah.

A Nation Supreme

Are, then, they [who deny the life to come] not aware that Allah, who has created the heavens and the earth and never wearied by their creation, has [also] the power to bring the dead back to life? Yea, verily, He has the power to will anything!

Qur'an 46:33

The First Resurrection

Allah seemed to answer Elijah Muhammad's prayers: a mighty empire arose from the shambles. And Elijah, a fire-eater with a whispery soft voice, managed to lay a foundation for redemption. He redeemed drunks and addicts and invested them with pride; his Fruit formed a corps of dignified capitalists; and Muslim women, serene and chaste as angels, draped themselves in flowing gowns. The images spoke volumes in the sordid ghetto.

With charismatic men at his side—Muhammad Ali, his honorary son, and for a time Malcolm X, who, like a dynamic prosecutor, attempted to bring the United States to trial for crimes committed against black folk—Elijah's appeal was powerful. He found eager audiences. He told them Christianity was a religion of death—that its symbol, the crucifix, provided proof. Islam, he reasoned, was blacks' "natural religion."

But his ideas, particularly on racial segregation, bore little resemblance to the Islam of a billion adherents worldwide, which holds as ideal an all-embracing brotherhood of man. Orthodoxy, he said, had been contaminated with whiteness. It was spooky.

Many blacks could appreciate his empire-building skills but were dissuaded from joining his ranks because of his wild stories.

Born Robert Poole in rural Georgia, he met a silk peddler, Wallace Dodd Ford, in Detroit, who went by the name of W. D. Farad. Farad established an Islamic sect, and disappeared mysteriously. Leadership fell to Robert Poole, who, according to one researcher, accumulated more than a hun-

Elijah Muhammad.
PHOTO: ROBERT SENGSTACKE

dred aliases (including Elijah Poole, Elijah Karriem, Mohammed Allah, Elijah Black, Rassoul Mohammed, and Elijah Muck Muck)[1] before settling on Elijah Muhammad.

According to Elijah, blacks belonged to the tribe of Shabazz, which came from space 66 trillion years ago; whites were a race of Frankensteins foisted on the world by Mr. Yakub, a mad black scientist whose 600-year hybridization experiment produced devils lacking any ability to submit to God. Whites, Elijah said, had had 6,000 years to rule by "tricknology." Their time was up in 1914, but God had given them a 75-year grace period, the time necessary for blacks to arise from "mental death."

Elijah preached mythology, but rooted himself on solid ground. He abolished the hereafter, calling it a hoax devised by whites to put off payment to blacks until they were dead. What mattered, he said, was what you earned and acquired in life.

He practiced what he preached. Before he died, in 1975, he ruled over 76 temples nationwide and 50,000 to 100,000 people. His Nation included 15,000 acres of farmland, a newspaper with an estimated circulation of 500,000, several aircraft, a fish-importing business, restaurants, bakeries, and supermarkets. Elijah, born to a family of former slaves in Georgia, ended up amassing a fortune estimated at $25 million.

[1] Bruce Perry, *Malcolm: The Life of a Man Who Changed Black America* (Barrytown, New York: Station Hill Press, 1991), p. 143.

*God is black. All black men belong to Islam; they have been
chosen. And Islam shall rule the world. The dream, the sentiment
is old; only the color is new. And it is this dream, this sweet
possibility, that thousands of oppressed black men and women in
this country now carry away with them after the Muslim minister
has spoken, through the dark, noisome ghetto streets, into the hovels
where so many have perished. The white God has not delivered them;
perhaps the Black God will.*

James Baldwin, The Fire Next Time

Pioneers

Benjamin and Clara Muhammad

Elijah Muhammad's first converts in Washington, D.C., gave a history lesson.

She is eighty-five, he ninety. He is still a member of the Fruit of Islam, she a member of Muslim Girl Training. They live in a corner house on a sharp incline. The living room is dominated by a drawing of a young, bow-tied Elijah Muhammad.

In a self-published autobiography, Al-Wakeel Benjamin Ilyas Muhammad (formerly Benjamin X Mitchell) wrote that he is the oldest of twelve children born to farmers in Winchester, Arkansas, ninety miles from Little Rock, on September 7, 1901. Raised Baptist, he spent twenty-one years on a farm. One very hot day in 1922, he recalls, as he and his father were plowing and his feet began to hurt and swell, he sat down, rubbed his ankles, and asked his father, "Will we have to work like this all of our lives each year and not get anything for it?"

"No, sonny," his father answered. "We will get our pay up there."

"Up where, Daddy?"

"Up in heaven."

"I don't need anything after I'm dead," Benjamin said. "I need some-thing now."

Benjamin left the farm for Tuskegee in Alabama that year. He attended night school and during the day worked as a carpenter. He graduated and got work with the U.S. government hospital in Tuskegee.

In 1930, he married Clara Bryant of Bainbridge, Georgia, "eighty miles from the Messenger's home." The couple moved to Washington, D.C., where five years later they placed a room-for-rent sign in their window, at 1602 13th Street NW. On July 5, a small, delicate man inquired about the room. He called himself Mr. Evans. He moved in a short time later.

Mr. Mitchell worked at the U.S. Navy Yard from 4 P.M. till midnight. When he returned home, he would find Mr. Evans and Mrs. Mitchell up talking. Mr. Evans, who ate little and cut a mysterious figure, explained that he was doing missionary work among black people. He claimed to have met God, whom he said was black. Meetings were held in the Mitch-ells' living room and friends and neighbors heard Mr. Evans spread his message about Islam. Eventually, the meetings moved to storefront Baptist churches, and Mr. Evans won many converts, including the Mitchells.

But tensions grew as followers of Mr. Evans—who rented rooms in Vir-ginia, Maryland, and Washington, D.C., and whose name was Elijah Muhammad—refused to register for the army.

Clara: Elijah Muhammad was running from not only black people but white people. They were after him. So he left Detroit and went to Chicago. And when he got to Chicago, he had to leave and went to Milwaukee, Wisconsin. He said that's the last time that he saw Allah.[2] Then he came to Washington, D.C.

Benjamin: Washington, D.C., is the modern Jerusalem. Do you remem-ber reading about how they arrested Jesus in the streets of Jerusalem? Well, this is the place where they arrested the Messenger, you get me? History repeats itself.

We were right here at this house when the Messenger was here talking to one or two other brothers on the front porch. He said to me, "Brother, I'd like to speak to you privately." We went out there in the front yard, and the Honorable Elijah Muhammad said to me, "Brother, this evening at five o'clock I'm going to catch the fast train going out of Washington for Phila-_delphia. If anything happens to me, I want you to do something for me, and

---

[2] Master Farad Muhammad.

Benjamin and Clara Muhammad.

that is to take my car—here's the keys—and my two suitcases at Mrs. Williams' on the 1300 block of Gerard Street NW, and bring them to my wife."

I said, "What you mean, Holy Apostle, 'if something happens' to you?"

He said, "Well, I'll tell you. Things are very critical now in Washington, D.C., and in neighborhoods out here. Anything is subject to happen."

That kind of excited me, and I forgot where he said the car was. I said, "Where'd you say the car was?"

Elijah Muhammad was arrested after returning from Philadelphia. The next day, Benjamin drove to Chicago, delivered the bags, and returned to Washington.

"The FBI agents crucified Mr. Evans the Friday before Easter, May 8, 1942," Benjamin wrote in his autobiography. "The news quickly spread that the FBI had arrested this much-wanted man, teacher of Islam. They kept him in the D.C. jail for a few months." He was released, after followers raised $5,000 for bail. He warned Mr. Mitchell, "Brother, if you follow me, you will be locked up and you will lose your job." Benjamin X Mitchell ("X" signified he was formerly known as Mitchell) said, "They will have to lock me up."

Not long afterward, two neatly dressed white men paid Benjamin a visit while he was working in his garden at 1205 51st Avenue NE in Deanwood Park, Maryland, just outside of Washington.

"Are you Mr. Mitchell?" one asked.

"No, sir," he said.

"What is your name?"

"Really, I don't know."

"Well, who is Mr. Mitchell?"

"Mr. Mitchell is a white man. You know I am not white."

"What is your name?" he was asked again.

He said he had lost his name 379 years ago. "I am surprised at you asking me if I am Mr. Mitchell. You know that all of our people are named after your people."

The men showed him their FBI identification, then asked where he had registered.

"With my government," he replied.

"Your government? What is your government?"

"Islam."

"Were you not born here?"

"Yes, sir, I was. But that doesn't make me a citizen."

All persons born in this country are naturalized citizens, they said.

"No, sir, I disagree."

"Well, what are you?"

"Just a free slave," he said. "Because I was born here doesn't make me a citizen." Pointing to his new stove out on the porch, he said, "Because a cat gives birth to kittens in a cooking stove, that doesn't make them biscuits."

Frustrated, the agents left.

But Benjamin X was eventually arrested and sent to federal prison for Selective Service violations. He was joined by other followers of Elijah Muhammad as well as "the Messenger" himself. Benjamin was released four years later. Elijah eventually named him a field minister.

Clara: For eleven and a half years, we were in Richmond, Virginia.

Benjamin: We are pioneers. We had a lot of scared pioneers out there too. They were afraid to face Uncle Sam. Charlie. You know they didn't never intend for Islam to be taught in America. No, no, no. They were afraid. And we had a lot of scared ministers. They called themselves pioneers. I said, "You're scared pioneers."

*It is Allah Who has subjected the sea to you, that ships
may sail through it by His command, that ye may seek of
His Bounty, and that ye may be grateful.*

Qur'an 45:12

"Go Buy Fish!"

H. Nasif Mahmoud

*He is a partner in an international law firm based in Washington, D.C.,
and Pasadena, and a professor at Howard University's law school. He
remembers his start, in his mid-twenties, sitting in the Peruvian Fish Ministry negotiating multimillion-dollar contracts, and the memories send him
into song: "How you gonna keep 'em down on the farm after they've seen
Paree?"*

*In the 1970s, Nasif, fresh out of Harvard Law School, negotiated well in
Peru, despite roadblocks reputedly put up by U.S. government officials. His
legal expertise, as well as that of others like him, became indispensable to
Elijah Muhammad's plans for building a business empire.*

*But the old man taught Nasif some clever tricks of his own. Nasif, who
called himself an "academic athlete," used the lessons to launch a career in
international law that has taken him to Peru, Ecuador, Canada, Abu
Dhabi, Dubai, Kuwait, Morocco, Lebanon, Saudi Arabia, Germany, Switzerland, England, Belize, and El Salvador. But the road to globetrotting
was preceded by run-ins with a few fools.*

School was always easy for me because of the women in my family: my
Muslim grandmother, who was my father's mother, my Christian grandmother, who was my mother's mother, and my mother. They planted the
seeds in me to help me become a man.

My grandmother, bless her soul, was a Moorish Scientist. When I was a
kid, I would see her pray five times a day. She'd stop you in the middle of a

conversation, perform ablution, and go to a corner facing the east and pray. She had Islamic artifacts and memorabilia from the Moorish Science Temple all over her house.

She'd ask me, "Who are you?"

I'd say, "I'm Henry Camberlon Tyson Junior."

And she'd say, "No, that's not who you are. You are the Asiatic black man, that's who you really are. You come from a great tribe of people in Africa. You come from the black Moors. They were people of culture and refinement and riches and wealth, and the Europeans came to Africa and stole a lot of their wealth, and through taking blacks in Africa and bringing them here to America, that's how you came to be an American. So you're really a Moorish American."

Then she said, "The so-called white man is someone you should never call white, because whiteness denotes purity, purity denotes godliness, and these people certainly do not behave like gods. In fact, they are influenced by the devil, because racism is a devilish influence—that makes them the devil. As you grow this devil will try to stop you. He will call you out of your name. He will call you jigaboo. He'll call you coon, nigger. But don't listen to those names, because he's not talking about you—he doesn't know who you are."

Then she would say, "You're not supposed to let the devil beat you at anything—not reading, not writing, not arithmetic, not on the baseball diamond, not on the basketball court, not on the football field, not on the track field. When you come of age, you will change your name and you will do a great work before you die, and your people will be proud of you."

I felt I was supposed to speak well, write well, read well, communicate well, be an all-star athlete. To me that wasn't something that was supposed to be out of the ordinary. So throughout school, I was an academic athlete.

I'd walk along from school. Three guys would come behind me. And I always knew, of the three, one was going to be the leader. So the books were knocked out of my hand. I didn't know who knocked them out, but you don't turn and ask a question; you swing at somebody. So the closest one to me got hit. Now if he was the leader and he got hit, fine. If he wasn't and he got hit, and he said, "Hold it, you hit me and I didn't knock the books out of your hand," well, "That's for being with the one who did and not telling who did."

I had competing interest from my Christian grandmother. She would tell me white people aren't the devil. There are good white people, there are good Jews. She would give me *her* propaganda. And my mother wouldn't say an evil thing about anybody. She taught me to fight back, but she always taught me to be real humble first.

In handling this episode with people knocking the books out, my Muslim grandmother would applaud me and say, "That's right! You swing on the first one that you see." My Christian mother would probably say, "Well, you should have turned and asked who did it, and then you should have warned them not to do it again, and then you should have picked up your books and gone home, and if they tried it again, maybe you should have hit them."

I got an academic scholarship to Dartmouth. I was an economics major and I did well in the discipline. When I graduated I had two full scholarships, one to Harvard Business School and one to the Amos Tuck Business School at Dartmouth. I changed my mind and decided I did not want to go to business school. I had wanted to be a lawyer ever since the fourth grade. I worked a year, got married, and got accepted at Harvard Law School.

He lived in Providence, Rhode Island; his wife was a student at Brown University.

The year before I went, I did a lot of reading: philosophy, religion, history, government and politics. I then decided that not only did I want to be a lawyer but I was fascinated with international affairs and international relations.

I was also fascinated with this organization—the Nation of Islam. I said, I'm going to get on the inside. I called my grandmother and told her what I was going to do, and she said, "Elijah Muhammad's a false prophet with a good industrial program—just be careful." Back in '65, when Malcolm X was killed, she blamed him. She said he had him killed.

I wrote Elijah Muhammad and told him I was entering Harvard Law School in September; what should I study to be of most benefit to the Nation of Islam? If he wrote me back and said, Don't go to law school, sell my newspapers, I wouldn't have been in the organization, because I'd have thought he was a damn fool. But he wrote me back and said, "Brother, to be of most benefit to the Nation of Islam, you should study international law."

Before I heard that, I had read this study in 1970 that said that in the next twenty to thirty years the United States would be saturated with lawyers, but two fields would go wanting: international law and municipal law. And then Elijah Muhammad writes me and says this! I found that quite intriguing. So international law was it.

Elijah Muhammad had a game plan that no one knew about. And that was international trade. He had been planning this for years, but he had incompetent people around him; he had FBI moles and spies.

Many people talk about the experience of coming to Islam and having to give this up and give that up. I didn't eat pork, I didn't drink, I didn't smoke. I was married. I didn't run around with women. So there was no real change in my life. And I came to help. I wanted to help Elijah Muhammad build this great organization.

I didn't believe in the catechism. Not just because of my grandmother. I always felt "in" but "out." I saw the difference between the principle and the practice. In principle, we're all brothers, but in practice, you had these jealous paper captains and these lieutenants trying to get some kind of position in the temple to have some kind of social stature. I never wanted to be an officer or secretary in the temple.

One day these goons came down from Boston. The Providence temple was a satellite under the Boston temple. I was always very quiet. I wore glasses. I spoke correct English. So I'm sitting in the temple and somebody taps me on the shoulder and tells me the lieutenant wants to see me out in the car. I go out of the temple and get in the car, and he starts this psychological abuse.

He tells me I ain't nothing. That I'm not "with" Elijah Muhammad's program. I got to get "with" the program. It was just plain craziness.

One tact I could have taken was [*in crybaby voice*]: "I wrote Elijah Muhammad and he told me I could study international law." But my business with Elijah Muhammad ain't here with this ignorant lieutenant, captain, or whatever he was. So I said [*softly*], "Allah is God."

And he looked at me. "What do you mean, brother?"

I said, "Allah is God . . . [*leans forward and nearly shouts:*] "because if I had still been in the 'dead world,' I'd have beat your motherfucking ass by now!"

I told him he was silly for even bringing me out of the temple to try to psychologically abuse me this way, and he said, "I'm going to have to come down from Boston to teach you."

I said, "Bring a dozen of you motherfuckers when you come—because I ain't got that much time! I got civil procedure and property and contracts and international trade to study! So I'm going to whop all your mother-fucking asses in one swoop to get rid of you! Now, keep fucking with me, hear!"

I slam the door, and I go back into the temple, and I sit down. I'm just pissed. I feel it coming. So I'm thinking about how it's going to come.

Three weeks later, we get some red alert down in Providence. We get the call Saturday afternoon: Everybody *got* to come to Boston to meet at the temple at seven o'clock. I'm thinking that it's some problem in Boston with the police. We all jump in cars and we race up to Boston, and meet at the temple. We're told that everybody is lax. This was a special FOI[3] training class. We're going to do self-defense.

Now, I had seen all these programs where sons of bitches break boards and bricks. I have never been impressed with that shit. So you can break a board. It's a board. I slip your right hand lead, and then knock you out with a left or right, and you're gone.

They moved all the chairs out and put mats down. We're going to have one line, and then two lines opposing. People in the single line are going to be the defenders. Now the rules are: You can hit in the chest, in the stom-ach, on the thighs. No hits on the knee, in the face, in the groin. The guys in the single line are always waiting. Two guys attack them, and the guys in the single line always get the shit beat out of them.

I was in the double line. That captain came and took me out of that line and put me in the single line. And then he put a couple of goons in the double line. Put me three deep; put them three deep.

And I said, Lord have mercy! I done come up here this Saturday after-noon. The things I have to study have to wait so that they think I'm going to hold still and accept an ass-whopping in here! I started boiling. I never told them I was taught judo when I was seven. I was always a nice guy.

So they came. I picked a weak "sister." Instead of waiting, I rushed him and he did exactly what I thought he'd do: He went to kick. Now all I was going to do was block the kick and hit him in the chest or the stomach to debilitate him so I could work on the other guy. But I caught his heel in the crease of my arm and I slung him. And when I did, his heel went up and his ass went off the mat. He hit the linoleum floor with a thud, and he screamed like a stuffed pig.

[3] Fruit of Islam, the paramilitary wing of the Nation of Islam.

By this time, the strongest guy is in shock, because I guess he's been told I'm a pussy, take me out. So he who hesitates loses.

I rushed him. I'm angry now. I didn't really try to kick him in his face, in his groin. But damn if I'm trying and you move and I miss; that's your problem! I'm whipping your ass.

The whole temple is silent, except one guy. His name is Brother James X. He's yelling, "Go 'head, Brother Henry! Go '*head,* Brother Henry! I told them to leave you alone! I *told* them you was a fighter! I could *see* it in your eyes! I could see it in your *eyes!*"

I'm angry and I'm talking and I'm screaming. James grabs me from behind, and he pulls me off this guy. And everybody in the mosque is quiet—because they had come to see the brother who's going to Harvard Law School get his ass beat.

James pulled me to the side and said, "Brother Henry, calm down. I told them you were a fighter, even though you were quiet."

I said, "Brother James, you are my only brother in this temple."

He said, "Oh, brother, don't say that."

I said, "I know what brotherhood is. You are my only brother in this temple. Everybody else came here to see me get my ass kicked." Except, of course, my brothers from Providence.

And I said, "Brother James, I don't play. I'm going to Harvard Law School, because I chose to go to law school. And I'm not going to have them interfering with that because of some crazy small-minded bullshit they got on their brains."

He said, "Brother, brother, now don't turn your back on Islam."

I said, "It ain't about Islam; it's about these niggers."

He said, "Brother, I understand."

And that's when I made my secret vow, out of my protest: I would never buy or wear one of those FOI uniforms. And never did.

From that point on, nobody fucked with me. Why? Because they felt, Brother Henry from Providence, Rhode Island, will beat the shit out of you. Leave him alone!

So my third year in law school, my wife graduated from Brown and we moved to Cambridge. And even then, I rarely went to the Roxbury temple, if ever.

And when I came to Chicago, from the very beginning, I felt that pressure—with [selling] the papers. And I said I got to stop this right now.

I told an FOI captain, "Look, I know you don't know who I am, so I'm

Fruit of Islam member.
PHOTO: ROBERT SENGSTACKE

going to tell you. I practice law downtown, and I'm a son of a bitch that don't hold still and let nobody fuck over him. Now I'm here to learn Islam. I ain't here to kiss your ass or no other lieutenant, captain, or nobody else. Now, I'm telling you motherfuckers to leave me alone."

They left me alone.

I realized that my best suit would be to pursue my law practice at a major law firm and then develop the Nation as a client. Which I did.

Elijah Muhammad's wisdom is something that I saw from a distance. He always did things through intermediaries. You never sat and bullshitted with Elijah Muhammad. He was too busy.

When I got to Chicago, various businessmen in the temple took a liking to me, because they felt, well, he's a Harvard lawyer, he's international business, international law, and they began to pull me in. But I was able to do it on a professional basis, because I worked for this law firm. In order to get me, you got to retain the law firm.

Elijah Muhammad bought a bank on Stony Island Avenue. It wasn't something that was done just so it could be said that Muslims owned this bank. What basically happened was this:

After the first purchases of fish[4] from the Japanese, we found out that the fish really came from Peru. So we decided to go direct. Elijah Muhammad gave us instructions about not negotiating price: "Let them charge a fair price for themselves. Be as charming and gracious as you can. But get the deal."

See, he knew what we didn't know. He knew that the U.S. government was going to try to stop him. Which they did. Henry Kissinger[5] flew to Peru, telling the Peruvian government not to deal with us because the Nation of Islam was subversive. The Peruvians said, What are *you* doing for us? You can kiss our behinds—you *and* Nixon. The Peruvian attaché in Washington even sent us the documents that went back and forth between them.

Elijah Muhammad wanted the deal because he knew once he got the deal, the floodgates were going to open. So even though the price was a little high, that was fine. Because the next year when we went down to negotiate the price, they dropped it themselves because he had cornered the market.

Now, the reason Elijah Muhammad bought the bank wasn't for show; that was for international trade, because the other banks downtown were playing crazy: like, what is he doing wanting letters of credit to buy millions of fish from Peru? So Elijah Muhammad said, No, no, I can't be bothered with this; buy the damned bank.

Has there ever been a client like him? I say to myself, no. What other client has said, go down to whatever country and buy a half million dollars' worth of fish on the first load? And I was out of law school about two years. I was twenty-six, twenty-seven. The delegation had to rely on me in terms of legal judgments. This is where all that hard studying and all that proper attention to detail paid off, because if I hadn't studied and become a sharp lawyer, I could have made big mistakes for my client. Not having a senior attorney looking over my shoulder, having to make judgments and make calls. It was trial by fire.

On the one hand, he was a threat to the U.S. government. But on the other hand, he wasn't, because Elijah Muhammad never really exceeded

[4] The Nation of Islam operated a fish-importing business.
[5] U.S. Secretary of State, 1973–77.

his power. It's like he knew exactly how far to go. He would stretch out there farther than they wanted him to go. But he knew how to deal with people.

There was a secretary to Mayor Daley[6] in Chicago who told me that Mayor Daley once told her, "There's only one man on earth that I'm afraid of, and that's Elijah Muhammad." And I believe it, because Elijah Muhammad was not of this world.

He did things that were timed well, organized well, and they were successful because he had a way of diverting people's attention to other things.

The most beautiful maneuver he made was this thing about the South Shore Country Club. It was up for sale. White people galvanized trying to block the Muslims from buying the South Shore Country Club, because this was a symbol of white supremacy in Chicago. In the meantime, he bought the bank. He built the Pioneer Office Building. He purchased hundreds of thousands of dollars of real estate and apartment buildings—because they were all focused on keeping him from purchasing the country club. In his wisdom, he knew that that would be a rallying cry.

Oh, he was so wise! Lee Iacocca, Joseph Kennedy, none of these men could shake a stick at Elijah Muhammad, and he supposedly had just a third-grade education. And he was impeded by a system that was against him! Joe Kennedy had help. Lee Iacocca had help. Elijah Muhammad was fighting against a system full of Jim Crow discrimination, and he built an empire in the hells of North America that could be a symbol of what black Americans can do if they unite. What could he have done if he had had competent people and he didn't have people trying to hold him back!

In our heyday, easily we did $27–$30 million a year. We bought sardines from the Moroccans. We bought fish from other places. Various international trading projects were on the table. We had this fantastic project where we were going to become a joint venture with Islamic banks in the Middle East. Oh, the plans that were on the table! It makes you shake.

His son[7] had a different philosophy and things began to taper off because he didn't have the vision and the steam his father had.

Elijah Muhammad had come up with all of these ideas and directions from the very beginning. His vision was always that that was one of the ways to break this chain of slavery—to develop international trading business outside this country so that we are feeding, clothing, sheltering our-

---

[6] Mayor Richard Daley.
[7] Warith D. Mohammed, who inherited the mantle of leadership of the Nation of Islam.

selves. With the fish program, he was trying to feed people. Inflation under Nixon went rampant. At the time he did the fish deal, he was selling fish in African American communities for as low as 25, 30, 40, 50 cents a pound. This was when meat prices were $1.50.

And the distribution system. Everybody got upset because they couldn't get in on it. He controlled the shipping. The Nation of Islam chartered the ships. We controlled the stevedores. The FOI brothers would come from the temples to unload the fish. So when that started happening, the issue was: Wait a minute, they got all this multimillion-dollar stuff going on here! But if we attack him, then we're going to have hell to pay—these Muslims don't play. This is where I see that this paramilitary FOI group may have been needed.

The distribution system was closed, so all that money was made within the organization. That money was turned over and over and over and over.

Just think about it; it was the most beautiful thing. The emissaries go down and make the initial purchase from the Nation of Islam coffers that had been developed by people giving in charity. The fish is purchased in Peru. At any one time, there were twenty to thirty ships on the high seas going back and forth. The fish came into twelve to eighteen ports around the United States. It was handled by the temple, and all the temples would purchase the fish from the central temple in Chicago. But now that fish has to be sold. So the profit is going to be made by the local temple. This provided jobs for brothers who couldn't get work. They converted various trucks into cold-storage fish trucks.

This was happening all over the country. It was one of the most fantastic things I'd ever seen in my life, and this little black man with a third-grade education was showing the world. It was an economic system.

Elijah Muhammad raised Lazarus up. Lazy, stiff-necked, rebellious—he got up off his behind and did something.

So you see, I have a healthy respect for that man, because of his leadership, his genius, his wisdom, his love for African American people. I don't care that he had more than one wife. I wish every man that had more than one wife did in his lifetime what Elijah Muhammad did, if that's the measuring stick.

I feel that it has always been a benefit understanding Islam and Christianity and being moved by both religions. Just like there are things I didn't believe in when Elijah Muhammad taught his catechism, there are things that I never really accepted as a Christian. I never really accepted the Trinity—the Father, the Son, and the Holy Ghost. I always looked at God as being the Boss.

African Americans who came to Elijah Muhammad took their Islam *seriously,* and they were a great example, even though doctrinally there were differences. Elijah Muhammad had chairs in the temple, and some of his lectures went right through prayer time.

But in essence, had the orthodox Islamic community ever approached doing what Elijah Muhammad did for Islam in the West? No. The destruction of African Americans was complete, and from those ashes a phoenix had risen.

I think that those seeds that Elijah Muhammad planted have been scattered to the four corners of the earth. And from those seeds, great oak trees will grow. You have to realize, we were young bucks, and our lives aren't over. We're in our forties now. We're coming into our own.

Leave that which makes you doubt for that
which does not make you doubt.

Prophet Muhammad[8]

Prodigal Son

In April 1988, on the nightly news, Washington, D.C.-area television view-
ers watched bow-tied black men tackle a lone man, take his sawed-off
shotgun, and stomp him. The men apologized later for the rough tactics.
They were not vigilantes. They were the Fruit of the Islamic tree that grows
in America.

Improbable as it seemed, they had sided with people they considered
"devils"—whites—to establish law and order in the ghetto and kick drug
lords off their turf. They helped clean up Mayfair Mansions and Paradise
Manor, 9,000-resident complexes in the Northeast section, and became
local heroes: Dopebusters.

Shirley Douglas, who has lived there thirteen years, says so many push-
ers and users brazenly did business outside her door, "they looked like
locusts." The Fruit arrived, and dealers and buyers vanished. Now she
gives the Fruit ten dollars a week and wishes her son would convert.
"They're cute in their little bow ties," she says.

America learned of the Fruit in the late 1950s, when the news media
discovered the Nation of Islam and its leader, Elijah Muhammad, who
declared himself divine and whose homegrown religion, based on black
nationalism, was specially suited to deal with racism in the New World.
His clean-cut Fruit became familiar sights, hawking newspapers on street
corners across the country. They were fearless warriors in an age of black
protest, the 1960s, when tens of thousands joined the Nation.

[8] *Hadith* (Abu 'Isa Muhammad at-Tirmidhi [824–92] and al-Hasan ibn Sufyan an-Nasa'i
[d. 915]).

Elijah's disciples are still among the most visible American Muslims. But a theological rift divides them. Since Elijah's death in 1975, conflicts have taken place periodically among his spiritual heirs. The disputes have pitted those who have moved toward orthodoxy against a sect that believes the black man is the progenitor of all civilization and will inherit the earth.

These camps agree to at least one basic principle, the prophethood of Muhammad of Arabia. Otherwise, their ideas diverge—particularly about whites and about Elijah's role in establishing an Islamic toehold in America.

The camps are led by Elijah's dearest disciples: Warith D. Mohammed, Elijah's son, who threw out his father's teachings, and Louis Farrakhan, who favors them. Mohammed (who adopted the legal spelling of his father's surname) calls Elijah a "sincere but misguided" man. Farrakhan says Elijah was God's emissary. Mohammed's Islam teaches love for whites. Farrakhan preaches that they act evil. As both vie for leadership of America's Muslims, one thing they do in common is revere Elijah. Both call him "the Honorable," as though he were a mogul of American Islam.

Elijah Muhammad's empire, left to his son Warith, has since crumbled.

Warith, a short, bearded man, does not have the burning eyes of a zealot. He smiles tenderly and has the comportment of a man who would melt under the sun of hard physical labor. He likes boxing, yet is more music lover than flamethrower. And though born into the Nation's "royal family"—of Elijah's loins—he is unpretentious, dressing like a professor and emanating about as much charisma as an accountant. However dulled his killer instincts may be, though, with just a few strokes he managed to lay low the Nation, dethroning himself in the process.

After Elijah died, Warith, then known as Wallace D. Muhammad, was voted ruler of the Nation during Savior's Day, the birthday celebration of the founder, Farad. Almost immediately, Warith began dismantling the NOI [Nation of Islam], welcoming whites into an organization founded on separatism. Only a handful enrolled, but civil rights leaders embraced the idea. So did mainstream Muslims who felt he was bringing the Nation closer to their beliefs.

Warith depoliticized the Nation, rescinding its call for reparation for blacks, encouraging patriotism and voting, striking "devil" as a reference to whites in the NOI lexicon, phasing out Savior's Day, and enjoining Arabic prayers.

He relaxed the dress code, approved of women going out alone at night, capped ministers' salaries at $300 a week, broke up power bases by reassigning ministers, and summoned Louis Farrakhan, a contender for leadership, to Chicago for closer surveillance.

Still, he was not finished. Upon discovering that ten people were killed "for no other reason than that they didn't want the FOI completely dominating their lives," he decriminalized the Nation, disbanding its Fruit, whom he called enforcers—the Nation's "punch your teeth out" arm.

He seemed to specialize in name changing. He became Warith Deen Mohammed and encouraged followers to adopt Islamic names. He also had chairs ripped out of temples, renamed them mosques, and dedicated Harlem's to Malcolm X, restoring official honor to the minister who helped build the NOI before falling from grace with Elijah. Warith even renamed the Nation twice: in 1976, it became the World Community of Al-Islam in the West; in 1980, it was the American Muslim Mission.

His changes caused dissension, particularly among hard-nosed nationalists for whom rallying round the flag would have felt as perverse as buddying up to Jim Crow.

Mohammed also was no saving grace for his business empire, which was failing. To reduce debt, he scrapped unprofitable businesses. The bottom fell out after he ended "forced charity" (dues) and dropped sales quotas for the group's newspaper. The lifeblood of the Nation, its weekly income, simply dried up.

Mohammed sent deeds of mosques to imams around the country, an assistant said. And in 1985, he decentralized leadership.

The Nation's fate was sealed with the rap of a gavel in a Chicago probate court, where the Nation's bank account, properties, and businesses were disentangled from Elijah's estate and a $13 million judgment was handed down. The Nation claimed bankruptcy and sold its Chicago mosque to Farrakhan's organization to pay off debts to Progressive Land Developers, its principal creditor.

Most of Elijah's heirs—eight legitimate and thirteen illegitimate children —haven't seen a dime yet. After ten years, the courts were still unraveling the legal mess, although the Nation has already been deconstructed and Mohammed has lost his father's house, where he lived for a while.

Others reportedly profited, including law firms. Some observers refer to the lawyer retained by members of the Muhammad family as Elijah's "twenty-second heir." He owns 25 percent of Progressive's stock.

Mohammed, who says he never staked a claim as an heir, moved from Chicago to Rialto, California, then to Little Rock, Arkansas, to lead a more private life.

Still, he has more followers than any other American Muslim leader has ever had, estimated by some at a million. They call him "Muslim American Spokesman for Human Salvation." As his father had done, he stays in touch with them through articles in the community's newspaper, which survives, and in radio broadcasts. In turn, they mail him donations totaling $7,000–$10,000 a month for his propagation. With it, he travels abroad and visits the loose federation of 100 mosques around the country, all that remains of Elijah's glorious empire.

Mohammed's audiences are mainly Muslim, and he limits himself to conservative discourses on Islam. His followers no longer "fish" on the streets for converts; more likely they share daises with rabbis and reverends. Whereas Louis Farrakhan's followers importune blacks to join Farrakhan with impassioned appeals to snap out of "mass hypnosis," Mohammed's followers simply invite people to the mosque. Pressure is not a tactic used to win converts.

Mohammed sparked controversy among fellow believers long before ruling the Nation. Decades ago, he moved toward orthodoxy, performing his first *hajj* in 1967. He brought home lessons about "true Islam," but NOI courts, with Elijah's backing, ousted him from the Nation three times for heresy.

Not long after Warith was expelled, he repented on a Chicago stage, begging thousands of NOI members to take him back. They did, and ten years later they named the prodigal son "supreme minister."

Later, he said the Nation never had a place in American society—that it had "spaced out" millions. "I feel they were always losing contact with reality and the nature of the teachings," he says, sipping tea in a coffee shop on Chicago's South Side, "especially the theological teachings, or the mythical teachings. A lot of followers don't like that term, but yes, that kind of teachings attracted some people who had, I would say, unreal ideas about the world."

Some disagree. What is unreal, says Johnny Lee X, who quit Mohammed's NOI and joined Louis Farrakhan's to return to Elijah's old teachings, is the concept that God is a spirit.

"God is a human being just like us, you know?" he says. Allah is flesh and blood—W. D. Farad Muhammad, who is alive and well. Admiral of the Motherplane, the UFO on which Elijah Muhammad is now a passenger.

Warith Mohammed, who in 1992 became the first imam to offer morning prayers in the U.S. Senate,[9] challenges followers to adhere to Islamic doctrine, and says that Islam is simple: Merely uphold its five tenets—faith in Allah, prayer five times daily, almsgiving, self-purification through fasting, and *hajj* if affordable. Elijah's mythology, he says, has no place in this religion.

[9] February 6, 1992. On June 15, 1991, Siraj Wahhaj of Brooklyn, New York, offered the opening prayer for the U.S. House of Representatives.

Warith Deen Mohammed

October 29, 1990, at Chicago's Hyde Park Hilton.

I would have to say that I'm a religious preacher or teacher.

My father never made it conclusive that any person should be the leader behind him. But he did give support to certain people. He helped make them popular with his following, and the one that he gave the most support and the one that he made the strongest statements in support of was myself, going way back.

Perhaps I've redefined his role. I see him as a social reformer but that doesn't mean that he wasn't a religious man. He was a student of the Bible. His father, my grandfather, was minister of his church in the South. He had a strong religious background although he was a rebel even in the South. My grandfather said that he always would question him and differ with him, and he wasn't a churchgoing person, but for some reason he believed in God and he believed in the Bible. He had his own ideas.

Other Muslims say that the movement cannot be divorced from the Honorable Elijah Muhammad. Are you following in your father's shadow?

In a sense yes. It's a continued respect for the sincerity of the Honorable Elijah Muhammad. I definitely believe he was sincere. He was ignorant and misinformed, and when I say ignorant, I'm not saying it in the ugly sense. I'm saying that he didn't know world religions or anything. He came from the South with no high school education, and he had no way of knowing

99

Warith Deen Mohammed.
PHOTO: JACQUES M. CHENET

what the Islamic world believed in or what it didn't believe in. His mystic teacher, whose name was W. F. Muhammad or Farad, presented the religion to the Honorable Elijah Muhammad, and if someone would come and present the religion in the backwoods now, they wouldn't know the rights and wrongs of it. They would accept what they were given.

You grew up with a large painting of Farad on your wall?

When progress came for the Nation of Islam during the 1960s a big painting was made by Herbert Jr., my brother Jabir's son. He's called Isa now.

Isn't that similar to going to a church and seeing a figure on a cross?

Certainly, that's the way I thought about it. As I grew as a young man, and I got in my teens—at fifteen, sixteen—I started to wonder why this man looking so white was supposed to be black and a black god. I started to see similarity between the way Jesus is portrayed in Christianity and the way he was portrayed. Maybe the Qur'an had started to influence my thinking without me knowing.

Why did you decentralize the community?

To make it democratic in an Islamic sense; fix it so we could make progress without certain strong personalities being a hindrance. Not that they were promoting themselves that much, but I think the membership, like church membership, was inclined to carry all their burdens to the preacher or the minister—like he's Jesus Christ.

Did you offer Minister Louis Farrakhan any position he wanted if he wouldn't leave the Nation of Islam?

No, no, I didn't. I told him the West Side to me was a better situation for our mosque than the Southeast Side. I asked him to go over there and establish the mosque on the West Side. We had just secured the property on Division Street and also in the suburbs.

I came in after being away, after serving a prison term for refusing Selective Service order. And I came back out of touch with what had been happening for the national staff in terms of their problems and concerns and the Honorable Elijah Muhammad had certain people in place as his national staff. I thought it best to leave them there because they had first-hand knowledge of what was going on. I didn't want to change horses in midstream. I felt comfortable leaving them in place and waited for the opportunity to gradually bring the understanding of the Muslims to the way it should be. That's the international understanding of our religion. So I didn't remove anybody.

But you brought him to Chicago?

Yes, but at the request of the national staff, not my request. It wasn't my orders. It was a request that he be brought. And they told me it was for his own good, that he was threatened out there. That he would be killed if he stayed in New York. And he never complained to me that he didn't want to be in Chicago. He never to this day told me he wanted to go back to New York. That made me think there was some truth to the threats.

You were one of his harshest critics—for following the old teachings.

I never spent much time on Farrakhan at all. That was exaggerated. It was clear what I represented, and when he differed with that, I accepted it. He said, "I have to leave. I've tried to go along with this." He didn't use strong language, but I got the impression that he was saying that I discredit my father, or reduced him in the eyes of the people, and he couldn't go along with that.

Are you divinely authorized to lead this community?

No, we don't believe in any divinely ordained people in this religion. The Qur'an is divine. The word of God is divine. Prophet Muhammad didn't even accept being called divine. And he said no human beings are angels. We are human beings, not angels.

Farrakhan says your father is still alive.

I know in the past he has given the impression that the Honorable Elijah Muhammad is still living in some kind of form. But I say he is saying one thing to appease or to make people who believe in the old teachings of the Mothership and all that feel comfortable and feel that he is representing them too.

George Lincoln Rockwell called your father the "Adolf Hitler of the black man." What's your reaction?

Because of the strong race-consciousness and the idea of the black man being superior and god, and God being black, I can understand him saying that. But the moral character of the Honorable Elijah Muhammad didn't deserve that ugly expression from Rockwell. No, he was quite different. He told his followers not to do violence, even against the white man, though he preached the white man was a devil. He told them to give the white man a decent day's work, if they were employed—not to shortchange the white man. And he wasn't for destroying anybody. He believed that God was going to destroy. And I hear many Christian preachers preaching doom, you know. Their language sounds as strong as the Honorable Elijah Muhammad's.

What did excommunication do for your religiosity?

It helped prepare me for leadership, especially the way the Honorable Elijah Muhammad handled my case. They actually brought me to a court situation, a hearing, which was the normal procedure. When anyone had a problem with the Nation of Islam or the teachings, they were questioned before the believers and actually given a sentence. Sometimes if it was a person on the staff or some person of importance, the Honorable Elijah Muhammad would have a private hearing in a private court that pronounced sentence. That's the way my problem was handled. And several others that I recall were handled the same way.

One of the things you did as head of the Nation was end mandatory contributions from the local mosques to the central mosque. And also, adult males had to buy 300 papers a month. You cut this off too?

It's true. My policy was to discontinue all forced obedience.

When you did this, you cut off the lifeblood of the Nation—the money that came into Chicago.

When I was in Philadelphia,[10] I believed in the same policy, and I did the same thing. It was voluntary. No one could be put out of the mosque or the temple for not coming up with $8.50, if that's what it was for a week to give in charity. Or if they didn't sell 300 papers, no one would be put out for that. That was my policy. The national staff reported me to the Honorable Elijah Muhammad. The Honorable Elijah Muhammad never insisted that I change my policy. In Philadelphia, we had one of the biggest temples. In fact, our membership was second only to New York, when I was a minister there. When I got there, they had about 67 people attending. Over the less than three years that I was there, the attendance grew to 500. And we didn't have huge sums of money to bring to Chicago, but we had very sincere supporters of the Honorable Elijah Muhammad, and the proof of it is, Philadelphia still stands out as a leading community of Muslims with those same pioneers that were there when I was there. There are two or three mosques now in Philadelphia. So what I'm saying is my policy was known before, and the national secretary, John Ali, feared that if I would become the leader I would set that policy for the whole Nation of Islam. And I did. And the money stopped coming in in the big sums. But I didn't cut it off. The money continued to come in moderate amounts.

What was the membership of the Nation of Islam?

The [active] membership hardly ever went over maybe 10,000 people. That was for the whole Nation of Islam. Under the Honorable Elijah Muhammad, the membership was transient. People were coming in and going out regularly. The pressure was too much. That's why they had a program just to get men; what they called "fishing." The men would go out and fish all during the week, especially just before the speaker speaks on Sunday. And those new people would be converted. At the peak at that kind of activity on Sundays we would have like anywhere from 30 to 50

[10] In the 1960s.

new people at one spot, in Chicago, at the *masjid*. And out of that 30 to 50, most of the time, half or more of them would actually join. Now, if we were converting people to the membership that fast, if those people stayed, can you imagine how many people would be in?

I would say it hasn't changed that much. In fact, for most of the mosques we don't have the size membership that we used to have, because we don't have people going out fishing and bringing people in. The great difference between the situation now and the situation then is that then you were obligated to come and if you didn't come for a certain number of meetings you were actually put out.

Is that why you had fewer than 10,000 active members?

I believe that's one of the reasons why. Also the quota of papers. Also if you smoked, drank, committed adultery, or if they caught you out at a party or going to a movie. Many things accounted for the mosques not having a big membership. But the national staff and the Honorable Elijah Muhammad believed that that strict discipline really accounted for them keeping a strong membership. If they relaxed those disciplines, they felt that they wouldn't have much of anything.

Right now, everybody knows they don't have to attend a location to be a member in this religion. They don't even have to listen to me to be a member in it. They can come and hear me and be converted. They don't have to ever come back to me again and they're accepted as Muslim and I see them ten years later, they're still Muslim. The Muslim membership is international and you can't throw anybody out of it.

I hope what I leave behind is enough evidence of my sincerity as a Muslim for people to say, well, maybe he had ups and downs, maybe he didn't do a lot of things we thought he should do, but one thing we have no doubts about: he was a sincere believer in his religion. That'll make me comfortable in my grave if I knew that.

And lower thy wing to the Believers who follow thee.

Qur'an 26:215

Everybody's Grandfather

Ozier Muhammad

Born to Eleanor Pascal and Nathaniel Muhammad; grandson of the late Elijah Muhammad. Ozier, thirty-nine, lives near Columbia University in the Morningside Heights section of New York City. He is now a photojournalist for the New York Times, *and while at* New York Newsday, *he won a Pulitzer Prize in international reporting in 1985. His twentieth-floor apartment offers a spectacular view of Harlem.*

I remember Muhammad Ali shadowboxing with me right after he beat Sonny Liston. He came over to see my father. All the kids just gathered around him, like the Pied Piper, and he said, "Hey, you guys are like family. You're royal family. You're special." He'd grab me by the ear and he'd pull me to him and I'd hug him, then he'd box. He was very warm and affectionate. He knew that we just loved him to death and he reciprocated with kindness. That's the way I wanted my grandfather to be. More like Ali.

I remember that I felt kind of a special responsibility to be well behaved because I was the Messenger's grandson. I remember teachers telling me, "You know, you're the Messenger's grandson and we expect you to behave. We expect you to be an example." That was pretty stultifying in a way. When I reflect on it, I say, Gee, you shouldn't put that kind of pressure on little kids. I felt like they clipped my wings.

We went to school in very small classrooms—maybe one teacher to four or five kids. The first time I realized how significant the movement was in the political and religious sense was when I was old enough to read something that said, "Up, you mighty race. You can accomplish what you will."

105

This was just above the blackboard. And then seeing pictures of my grand-father all over the school. In each corner it had like the crescent and the star and all of these slogans about "There is no god but Allah."

They called us "royal family" and they called us "soldiers" and the ideal was to be a good soldier. It was daunting to me to be expected to be exemplary. And then my uncle Wallace, who's now Warith, had a long stint at the school in the 1950s. He was teaching Arabic and Islamic law. God, he was so rigid! I didn't like him. Being in his class, he would single me out and spank me. Sometimes he would make me stand out in the hallway. One occasion he racked me across my knuckles. I said, God, how come Uncle Wallace is treating me like this?

But I remember being enamored of him too because he could speak Arabic fluently and he really understood Islamic law and he had made *hajj*. The first five kids were born in a period of deprivation and in the absence of their father. Their father was a fugitive and he had a lot of enemies within the Nation and he had the U.S. government on him for sedition, for supposedly preaching the overthrow of the country. So the first five chil-dren were not nearly as well educated as Wallace or Akbar were. They were allowed to go to college and my father and uncles and aunts were not.

I was fascinated by the stories of W. D. Farad. He could make water disappear from a glass. He could walk through a door. And my grandfa-ther had this library and most of this wall was taken up by this huge portrait of W. D. Farad Muhammad. That was pretty overwhelming. A three-quarter profile of a man holding a Qur'an. This man didn't look like he was Afro-American; he looked like he was Pakistani and we're thinking that this man is God, like Jesus, the son of God. I remember when I used to go into my grandfather's study I would almost feel like I was in the pres-ence of a picture of God. I thought he was someone supernatural.

When I went to school I had to dress up and wear a suit, and the teach-ers were like our mothers away from home. They took us into their bosom. I remember learning songs. Some of them were to the melody of popular songs. Some of the melodies were almost a paradox to the message of the song. The melody was like so out of the realm of what the message of the lyrics was trying to convey to us. Like it may have been a cowboy song to convey something about the reverence of God.

My father forced us, of course, to go to all the Temple Number 2 meet-ings on Sundays. As a child it was more or less an ordeal for me: "Oh,

Jesus Christ, I gotta go to that nauseating sermon at the temple in Hyde Park!" It was torturous for me to sit there as a child. Minister James Shabazz would speak every Sunday. I remember getting sick and nauseous and vomiting, just having to sit still as a child for hours, traveling to Gary, Indiana, and going to Detroit all squashed up in these cars.

At the time I was ten or eleven was the first time I ever heard my grandfather speak. It was at a Savior's Day convention. I went to hear my grandfather speak in front of maybe 10,000 people. I had never realized the magnitude of the man's importance to African Americans. Even though I was his grandson I was searched. I really should not have been searched, and someone said, "Hey, that's royal family, let him through!" Hey, I didn't know. My father had gotten separated from me.

I went in that room and I saw all of these slogans that had been pasted around the school—they were in this huge arena. "One God, One Aim, One Destiny"—all these are borrowed from [Marcus] Garvey—and "There is no god but Allah, and Muhammad is His Messenger."

I saw all of these people all dressed the same, looking very prosperous. Thousands and thousands of people. Then it hit me: This is something special.

It made me feel like maybe I *am* royal family; maybe I do shoulder responsibility that's extraordinary for many of my peers. And then I began to become a little intimidated by my grandfather. I began to look at him not as my grandfather but as my leader.

I withdrew. I felt like now this man is my leader. I don't have this special access to him. He didn't help the situation either. My grandfather *acted* like he was reverential. He acted like he was *everybody's* grandfather.

I really couldn't make a breakthrough with him even though I was like his boy Friday. But a couple of times he let down his guard. At those times I felt like maybe he is more than just a king. Maybe he can actually talk to people and actually be a grandfather.

I remember how smooth his skin was. He had a very regal face with high cheekbones. It was always so clean, as if he was some sort of alabaster Greek mask.

I was with my grandfather when the flash came across the radio that Malcolm X had been assassinated. He was in [his office]. I was the only person there with him. As soon as he heard the flash he said, "Oh my God!" And then he leaned back and said, "Um um *um!*" He decided about a half hour later to cut it short. He said, "You know, I really want to go home now." So he gathered his things and I grabbed my coat. He was very, very somber.

It seemed to me that he was hurt by the news. I'm not trying to defend him, because I know that he precipitated a lot of bad feelings about Malcolm. He may have encouraged those three brothers to assassinate Malcolm, if they in fact are the ones.

We always prayed at the dinner table. We prayed in the Christian manner. We said the *Fatihah*. It would be in English. I didn't really get involved in the rituals until the time I was thirteen or fourteen. My father asked us if we would fast the month of Ramadan.[11]

My grandfather imposed this different calendar on us because he felt that in the first manifestation of the movement, there was no way in the world that the Nation of Islam would be palatable to black folks if it was as rigid as Islam can be. When you follow the lunar calendar, the days you fast can be very, very long. So my grandfather was smart in this way. He said December will be the month of Ramadan, which has the shortest days of the year. Dawn is perhaps at six-thirty and dusk is at four-thirty in the afternoon. So he got us used to fasting that way.

I got real close to my cousin Hassan Sharif. He took me under his wings. I don't know why; maybe because I was so disciplined. The difference in our ages is almost ten years.

Hassan was very close to my uncle Wallace.[12] At this time Wallace was excommunicated because he called his father an impostor. He said his father wasn't a prophet.

It wasn't as if Wallace had rolled out of bed and said, "Hey, wait a minute. This man can't possibly be a prophet. The prophethood ended with Muhammad, you know, or Jesus." He mulled it over for a while and then he approached his dad and said, "Well, Dad, I've studied Islamic history for years and I've studied the Qur'an and the *shari'ah* and all that, and, Dad, this thing about you being the apostle of God and the Qur'an just doesn't jibe. Because I'm studying Islamic law and you sent me to Egypt, and here it is saying the finality of the prophethood is with the Prophet Muhammad and that's the end. It stopped there."

I remember people saying, Woe is me. My aunt Ethel and my father were

---

[11] One of the five pillars of Islam. The others are faith, prayer, *zakat*, and *hajj*.
[12] Now Warith D. Mohammed.

Ozier Muhammad.
PHOTO: VIOREL FLORESCU

very concerned because they felt that Wallace was puzzled. Wallace was the Philadelphia minister and he was torn. There was too much ambiguity between what he was teaching and what he was learning from the Qur'an. He went to his father on several occasions and said, "Dad, explain this to me. How could you be the prophet?" He tried to work it out with his father. His father said, "Yes, son, I *am* the prophet."

My uncle Wallace returned to the Philadelphia temple and he started to preach the transliteration of the Qur'an—I mean, none of this hocus-pocus about Elijah Muhammad, and none of this hocus-pocus about W. D. Farad. He said they were just mortal men like anybody else. He said the reason why they brought it to you this way is because you would never have accepted it in this form. But this is not Islam. You have to understand that this is a black nationalist movement predicated on some kind of palatable form of Islam, something that you would find more acceptable.

My grandfather went off. He just blew a blood vessel. And he said that you have been relieved of your duties as the minister at the Philadelphia temple, and he brought somebody else in. And he was excommunicated. And my grandfather said, "If you don't recant I'm going to disinherit you too."

In other words, Wallace would not receive a stipend every week as the other children received. It was like seventy-five dollars every week in the late 1950s or early 1960s, and Wallace being a minister, his stipend was greater. He was relieved of that and he accepted it. He said, "Look, I can't continue to do what I feel is contrary to Islam."

Hassan actually worshipped his uncle Wallace, while he would make jokes about Grandfather. I laughed at them too. I had never heard anybody be so irreverent about Grandfather. Hassan made me feel like I didn't have to be such a good soldier. I could be myself; I didn't have to be so rigid, austere. He was a real person.

He used to talk about Wallace in such glowing terms that I replaced my grandfather as being my kind of hero with Wallace.

Hassan started taking me by Wallace's house, and Wallace was excommunicated at the time; we weren't supposed to associate with him. I was about fifteen. I had to be very discreet about it because Hassan was getting a stipend and he would have been excommunicated.

Wallace was very kind. He was nothing like that austere teacher that I remembered as a kid. He laughed a lot and he was very logical about his father. There wasn't any of that vitriolic kind of ranting and raving about Grandfather. He didn't counterattack. He shrugged it off and said, "Well, everybody has their cross to bear. I love my father and I miss my father and well, that's it."

He talked about his trips to the East and the last *hajj*. He would ask me how my parents were doing. I'd just sit down and listen to the conversations they were having.

On one occasion, Hassan asked me if I wanted to pray with him and Uncle Wallace. I said, "Yes, but you know I don't know how to pray like that." And he said, "We'll teach you how. First you have to wash up." So Hassan taught me how to wash up and then they taught me how to pray. Uncle Wallace would spread out these prayer rugs and he would be right in front and Hassan would be right behind him and I would be just a couple of inches behind Hassan. They would go through the whole prayer ritual and I would just follow. After I had become more familiar with the prayers, I could move right up next to Hassan; we were on the same line, and Wallace was the one to always lead the prayer.

So Hassan through Wallace introduced me to the orthodoxies of the religion. Man, it was like I was reborn. Finally I felt like well, gee, there is something greater than the Nation. All of a sudden my horizons expanded.

I felt like I was connected with the greater Islamic world. I began to fast, even fast weekend fasts, just short fasts.

I used to have nightmares as a kid. My grandfather used to say that there was no hereafter, and I had thought, Gee, I'm not going to ever see my parents again when they die. I didn't like that. All these good people who are dying because of being victims of crime or some injustice—their lives have been snuffed out and there's no justice after this life? But I think that my grandfather was saying, Don't overendow afterlife. Transform your life condition in this world, then there is a heaven to look forward to. But I didn't get that message when I was a kid.

But Wallace and Hassan opened up a whole new world to me and I really accepted it wholeheartedly. It like really lifted a weight off of my shoulders. I felt like I could be human and I could make transgressions and be forgiven. Wallace could explain why my behavior could be erratic and that there was nothing wrong with it.

There were some cousins who were very disciplined in following the teachings of the Honorable Elijah Muhammad, like my cousin Herbert. I used to think he was a lunatic, he was in such lockstep with the teachings.

I began to stop believing in Yakub[13] as soon as I started hanging out with Hassan. Hassan in a very subtle way started to deconstruct the Nation of Islam dogma. He would reveal things to me about the Cro-Magnon man being discovered and he'd inform me of the Leakey findings in the Serengeti Plain and Tanzania and Kenya, so he brought up all this stuff that predated my grandfather's teachings that white men were created 6,000 years ago.

I was encouraged to get an apprenticeship with some minister and study Islam in its first manifestation with the Nation of Islam. I didn't want to be like my father and my uncles and aunts. I wanted to go to college. I wanted my world to be much more extensive than my parents' had been. So I thrust myself into the greater world.

I did well in college, I think because of the discipline. Frivolity was foreign to me. But Hassan and Wallace helped me to get through. Thank God for Wallace and Hassan because white people weren't so intimidating to me when I went to Columbia College. They said that they weren't devils.

I began to make friends with whites. I was nineteen when I finally left home. My first year and a half was at colleges that had predominantly

[13] The black scientist who rebelled against Allah, according to the central myth of the Nation of Islam, creating the white race and peopling the world with "blue-eyed devils."

black student bodies. I was surrounded by black students, so I felt very comfortable. But all the instructors were white. At this time people were profoundly politicized and people who weren't Muslims were acting like Muslims. They were challenging professors on any kind of innuendo.

When I went to Columbia College I was finally in a school that was predominantly white. They had some interesting people on the faculty who were black; Gwendolyn Brooks was there and Hoyt Fuller, who was editor of *Negro Digest,* which later became *Black World*. It took me a while not only to get used to my fellow students but the white instructors. I mean, they had long hair. They were very left of center politically. Some were gay, but they were very likable.

I liked photography. My instructor was very interested in who I was. He thought I was one of his better students because I seemed to show a lot of promise. At that time I was working for *Muhammad Speaks*.[14] I used to bring a lot of pictures in of Muslim sisters in their dress.

My instructor asked me, "Are you Muslim?"

I said, "Yes."

Then he said, "Oh, Elijah Muhammad's your grandfather? Well, gee, that must be a pretty heavy burden for one's grandfather to be God."

I was taken aback. Hassan kind of laughed, but I became suspicious of him from then on. I felt that he was cutting the legs off from under my grandfather, taking a cheap shot at him.

I became very guarded after that. I would say I'm a Muslim, yes; that's why I had the name. But I wouldn't say I was Elijah Muhammad's grandson. Maybe his perception was I was acting like royal family.

I came into adulthood during the Vietnam War and the black consciousness movement and all the other offshoots of that. I began to do drugs. I began to smoke marijuana.

Now that I became an adult, other adults began to reveal their lives more to me. I found out that a lot of Muslims were also doing marijuana in the Nation. I felt conflicted because I felt how could I follow the Qur'an to the letter while I'm polluting my mind with marijuana?

I tried every once in a while to fast and just purge my system. This lasted a long time, until I was about thirty years old. I still considered myself an orthodox Muslim, a Sunni Muslim.

I was conflicted with my smoking marijuana, but I was also much more interested in pursuing my interest in black literature and history. I began to

[14] The newspaper published by the Nation.

read a lot and I began to move away from the Qur'an. At that point I was collecting a lot of Islamic literature and the proof of the finality of the prophethood of Muhammad. I began to expand my repertoire of prayers. And then I started to move away from this when I traveled to Africa and worked for *Ebony* magazine.

When I came to New York City in 1980 I became immersed in my job, with my reading. I became more involved with other drugs. If I was under the influence of marijuana or cocaine or anything like that, I just wouldn't pray because I would never approach God in that way. I would never approach God impaired.

One day, it must have been '82 or '83, I couldn't buy any marijuana in the streets. They said, "We don't have any marijuana but we have crack," and I said, "Well, what is that?" They said, "It's coke." I said, "Well, you know, I've done coke, but I don't buy coke off the streets from nobody."

It was a clean break. I just stopped doing marijuana and then I started to really get back into the orthodoxy of Islam. I started praying five times a day.

I haven't lost faith. I think Islam is a wonderful religion, but I don't look at Islam as being perfection. I don't think there is any perfection. My wife is a Buddhist. I find certain things very appealing about Buddhism.

Buddhism, Islam, and Judaism are all trying to achieve the same thing and that is to center people, give people a sense of presence, a sense of mission, a sense of purpose in their lives, making them feel whole, connected.

I do think that my grandfather was somebody extremely important in world history. I think that he did something that was very profoundly needed by African American people. I think that he was an extension of Garvey but he was greater than Garvey because he was actually able to make things happen. He actually built a nation. He was a profound nationalist. He built an economic base. He gave people a sense of purpose. He gave people a sense of unity. He reformed people. He actually saved people's lives. He made men responsible to themselves and to their families.

I'd say after college up until the time I was about thirty-four, I was very angry at my grandfather. I've never thought that my grandfather didn't achieve great things. But I felt that his family had to pay a dear price in order for him to achieve these things. I thought, Gee, it would have been nice to have gone fishing with my grandfather, to have been hugged by my grandfather, to have seen my grandfather cry. I don't remember my grandfather ever hugging me. I'm not certain that my grandfather actually knew how.

*Verily the most honored of you in the sight of Allah is
[he who is] the most righteous of you.*

Qur'an 49:13

Converting the Converted

A Mosque in Newark

*Masjid Mohammed in Newark, New Jersey, has seen great change since
Warith D. Mohammed became a Muslim leader. In the past, some mem-
bers of its predecessor, the Nation of Islam's Temple Number 25, prayed
five times a day and raised hell in between. Some believed the minister,
James Shabazz, stood in the way of a "new world of Islam" in which
Elijah Muhammad, leader of the Nation of Islam, would be revered as
Allah. Shabazz was shot dead in 1973.*

*A war broke out. A month later, two headless bodies were found in a
Newark park. The heads were found in a lot four miles away, near the
home of the late Shabazz. Members of the New World of Islam splinter
group were convicted of killing Shabazz and police said they uncovered a
plot to take over the temple.*

Ali K. Muslim: When I heard Minister James teach, one of the points he
made was that whites were blond-haired, blue-eyed devils. I said, "Yes,
that's right! I agree!" I think that was probably one of the main things that
inspired me to come in. But I didn't really know and understand.

After I came to understand the teachings of the Qur'an and the *Sunnah*
of the Prophet I began to grow out of the racist mind. Because I *had* a
racist mind.

*One-man wars were waged. One afternoon in the early 1970s, when Ali
K. Muslim, then Charles 41X (there were 40 Charleses registered in the
Newark mosque before he joined), was guarding the temple, a man carry-*

115

ing a sack asked to meet a temple official. The man, thoroughly confused about Elijah Muhammad's teachings, believed that if he killed four white "devils" he would win a star-and-crescent lapel pin and a trip to the Holy Land. He had come to redeem his prizes. In the sack, Ali K. Muslim says, were four severed heads.

He never got to the door. We wanted no association. The police were contacted and he was arrested. These are the kinds of things that happened and we're not proud of the experiences, but we have had some unique ones in Newark and in the development of the Islamic community.

Today, about 6,500 Muslims are affiliated with the Newark mosque, Americans, Africans, West Indians, and others. During congregational prayers, some wear jeans, others traditional garb. Women and girls cover their heads and pray peaceably behind men and boys.

Imam Ali K. Muslim was born Charles Sharpe, a Southerner. Under Warith D. Mohammed's leadership, Imam Muslim, a husky, bearded man, has changed his beliefs so dramatically that he voted for Ronald Reagan twice, as well as for George Bush.

One Sunday, the imam told the congregation, "God didn't choose Arab over non-Arab, white man over black or black over white. What distinguishes a person in the eyes of Allah are his deeds, his righteousness."

No chorus of "That's right!" arose from worshippers as in the past, when sermons there elicited fist-in-the-air responses. The imam's middle name, Khutbah, means "sermon" in Arabic yet his speech lacked the soul-stinging fury of ministers who had preceded him. Still, he was strong on conviction, even though many of the 200 congregants squatting on the rug dozed.

Imam Muslim laughs with detached humor about his evolutionary steps from "the straitjacket days" to mainstream Islam. He remembers one meeting in which a Nation of Islam official said, "Okay, we got to raise $13,000. I'm going to lock the door." That was unnecessary, Muslim says.

With the Fruit of Islam standing around, it was as good as locked. To get out the door you'd have to go through a 250-pound Fruit.

No one dared to try.

The lieutenant said, "Do you believe in this teaching?"
I said, "Yes, sir, Brother Lieutenant!"

"Well, then, why don't you bear witness with your wallet."

"Yes, sir, Brother Lieutenant!"

Imam Muslim gave money smilingly. But he now says:

People sacrificed too much. They would hand over food stamps and welfare checks.

Warith Deen Mohammed said this is not our religion—to force people to give charity.

Imam Muslim now calls W. D. Farad, Elijah Muhammad's teacher, a "witch doctor" and has replaced martial arts training as a Fruit with five daily prayers. In September 1990, the New Jersey State Council of Black Social Workers named him citizen of the year for his social activism. His mosque spends $1,200 in charity each month, and buys food for 100 homeless people a day. It also runs a school and Islamic congregational services for 700 inmates at five New Jersey prisons.

*Verily Allah has prescribed proficiency in all things. Thus,
if you kill, kill well; and if you slaughter, slaughter well. Let
each one of you sharpen his blade and let him spare
suffering to the animals he slaughters.*

Prophet Muhammad, *Hadith* (Muslim[15])

From Dust to Industry

Akbar Salaam

Every empire needs its merchants. Religious communities are no different.

Salaam is the great-grandson of "King" Saul, who made sausages; cousin of butchers in Brooklyn whom he has never met. Butchering, Salaam says, "is genetic. It's in the blood."

Many of Warith D. Mohammed's followers are in business. He challenged them to adhere to Islamic doctrine. It would bring them "from dust to industry," he said. The community now publishes a nationwide directory of more than 1,500 Muslim-owned firms.

Akbar T. Salaam, forty-five, paid $800 for a steer at an auction and went into the meat-processing business. Today, his company, New Unity Beef Sausage, is the largest Muslim-owned and -operated firm of its kind in New York and New Jersey. It slaughters, processes, and sells halal *(lawful) meats, an equivalent to kosher products.*

When Salaam started slaughtering, area Muslims were eating unlawful meat unless they slaughtered animals themselves. Now, each week, New Unity slaughters 10 to 15 steers, 25 to 30 lambs, and 15 to 20 goats according to Muslim ritual.

New Unity's clients are 60 percent American-born Muslims and 40 percent immigrants. The company, which started as a retail operation, now

[15] Abul Husayn Muslim ibn al-Hajjaj (d. 875).

118

grosses almost $1 million annually, a 66 percent increase since 1975, when Mohammed became spiritual leader.

Salaam does not denigrate the old teachings. "We're standing on the Honorable Elijah Muhammad's shoulders right now," says Salaam. "Imam W. D. Mohammed gave us the blueprint for the new system."

Salaam has accepted another Mohammed challenge: to raise animals so as to be sure they are bred healthily. And he is helping others draft plans for the largest halal *plant in the United States. It is expected to generate over $1.4 billion in sales within its first two years.*

If you slaughter one animal you have a hide, you have by-products. One hide tanned and stretched can produce four leather coats, 135 pairs of shoes, belts, hats. And if it's a steer, maybe you get a two-way split out of that. So there's many other functions that the cow serves other than just eating.

Take medical research. You may have one foot of spinal cord. It sells for twenty dollars. Eyes sell for twenty dollars apiece. It's a known fact now that the blood of the unborn calf is perfect for human transfusion—AIDS-free. And the glucose in the eyes of the unborn calf is being used now in treating glaucoma. The bone of the cow: Now because Africa is banning the slaughter of the elephants, there's a shortage of ivory. The Japanese have come up with a process to put the bone in a special acid and it's bleached white. This is being used in the jewelry industry now to replace ivory.

I went to the auction and I was told to select some animals. What we found was different communities bidding, trying to get the best to take it back to their community, and we found that there was no one there representing the African American community. After everyone made their selections, the product that was left of course found its way back to the black community.

I bought a Black Angus steer. We paid approximately $800, and we had the animal transferred to a German facility, and we were actually talked through the whole procedure, because slaughtering an animal is a dangerous task, because you could end up being kicked; they could swing and hit you with their head, their body. They can get loose and trample you. I've been chased several times over the last fifteen, twenty years. I've been thrown up in the air, gored in the shoulder.

First, we read the Qur'an and the *Sunnah* to find out how the Prophet wanted us to slaughter this animal. And there's a certain procedure that you must follow, and that is, first of all, your knife must be very very *very* sharp. The Prophet said whatever a Muslim does, he should do it with excellence, even in the sharpening of your knife. So the knives that I took out there really weren't sharp enough. There was a grinding stone there, so I just put a better edge on the knife. Then the Prophet has told us, when you slaughter you say, *"Bismillah"*—In the name of Allah.

Then you make your cut.

Then you say, *"Allahu akbar"*—Allah is the greatest.

The imam[16] said when you slaughter you should give respect for the creator of that animal. You should have a certain mental state when you approach, one of humility, and have an understanding that this animal that you're about to slaughter is for the service of humanity and particularly for the service of your community.

When you go to a slaughterhouse you see certain cruelties. You see the animals being stunned, kicked, hit in the head with pipes. So the humane standards that are established aren't followed. The USDA feels the stunning process is more effective, so they stun the animal and slit its throat.

But stunning gets the adrenaline going and also produces fear. It goes all through the meat. So therefore our process is this:

We approach the animal. We make sure the animal is relaxed. We face the animal toward the east, and with a fast stroke you say *Allahu akbar,* and what happens is, you don't sever the neck. You make sure you cut the main arteries but you leave the neck intact so that the involuntary muscles can take control and force the blood out. The animal gasps and dies from a loss of blood, not from being stunned: no fear.

We are still a thriving business trying to establish ourselves. Success is not here yet but the cornerstone is definitely in place.

Salaam's clients aren't only Muslims. There's a huge market to tap in Newark and beyond. Warith Mohammed offers further encouragement for Islamic businesses like New Unity, drumming up support among prospective clients. "If Americans like kosher wienies and corned beef," he says, "I'm sure they'll like halal products too."

---

[16] Warith D. Mohammed.

*Those who listen [in truth], be sure, will accept: As to
the dead, Allah will raise them up: then will they
be returned unto Him.*

Qur'an 6:36

A Clear Sign

Johnny Lee X

Former bodyguard of Malcolm X. He came to Islam, abandoned the Nation, then returned. He was sharp, clean-pressed, wore a plaid suit, bow tie, long black leather coat—the picture of health at sixty-seven years old in the Seaman's Net restaurant on Harlem's central artery, 125th Street.

I was looking for God, I guess. I went to a Holy Roller church. It was so funny, I just started laughing. They were laying a sheet down on the floor and they were rolling around. They were kicking and hollering, and they had an old stovepipe, and they knocked the stovepipe and it flew and I said, "Nah, man, this can't be right."

This fat lady was screaming and jumping and she fell into this fellow and he pulled a knife out. I said, "I *know* this ain't right."

I started laughing. So somebody said, "Open the door." They held me by the collar and helped me to the door.

I said, "Oh, well."

So one day I was walking in New York and I saw this sign that said: MUHAMMAD IS COMING.

I said, "That's a strange name. Who is *that?*" Well, why not check that out?

I went down there. I saw all these young men. All of them had on neckties and they were so disciplined. I said, "Maybe this is what I been looking for."

121

When I saw the Honorable Elijah Muhammad and I heard them talking, I knew then that's what I was looking for.

I said, "I ain't never heard nobody talk the kind of talk they talk."

And that man was *talkin'* about white folks!

I said, "I knew something was wrong with them."

Then he asked who believed in what he was teaching—would they stand up? I didn't stand up right then; I just listened and I went home and I studied.

So the next time I went to hear them teach at Rockland Palace down here on 155th Street, I stood up and accepted Islam. That was 1959.

I had to write a letter.[17] My first letter didn't pass. I wrote six or seven letters. But it made me more determined to get that letter off.

A sister told me, "When we get through with you, you're going to be able to talk to everyone from the man in the ditch to the President." In other words, they were making me very wise.

I began to pray. Then I could feel my life changing. Some people talk religion, but I'm living it. Yeah. I quit smoking, I quit eating pork, and I started praying five times a day.

A letter granting him his "X" came on October 24, 1959.

After I got my "X" I went back to my hometown and got into a debate with my uncle. When the rooster crowed the next morning, we were still debating about who is the devil and why we were brought here and who we are. They had never heard no talk like that.

My uncle said, "We can't do a *thing* with him."

I came to 116th Street and that's the first time I saw Malcolm. I saw him with his briefcase walking down and I said, "Who is that guy?"

Somebody said, "That's Malcolm X. You ain't never heard him?"

I said, "No."

He said, "Man, that dude is *bad*."

That's when he got up on the rostrum and began to teach.

I said, "*Wooooooo*, this guy can talk."

I went around with Malcolm a lot. He never embraced you like Far-

[17] Converts in the Nation of Islam were required to drop their surname and take on "X." It symbolized the repudiation of the slave name and the rebirth of the black man. This was done only after seeking permission in writing from the Honorable Elijah Muhammad. Letters had to be written perfectly legibly.

rakhan[18] did. He was a very stern person. You couldn't loosen up around him like I do with Farrakhan. With Malcolm, a sister could be saying something to me, and I'd be scared to even look at her in the First Resurrection.[19]

I stayed close by him, made sure no strange person come up on him. We were having a speech down on 125th Street where the State Building's at now, and a fellow had something stuck up in his pocket. We thought that was a gun. We were getting ready to kick this brother off the planet.

We were supposed to have a meeting downtown. But when John F. Kennedy got killed, the Honorable Elijah Muhammad called off the meeting. Malcolm told him he done spent all this money and we can't get it back. Just let me go ahead and have the meeting. The Messenger said, If you do, don't mention the President. Don't say nothing about the President.

The meeting went beautiful. I was standing right in front of Malcolm. Just before the meeting was over, one person asked about the President being killed. Malcolm said, "It's like the chicken comin' home to roost. It never made me sad; it always made me glad." And that was the end of the meeting.

That night it came on the radio that the Minister suspended Malcolm for making that statement. He was suspended for ninety days. So instead of Malcolm doing his ninety days and being cool and staying out of the limelight, the next thing we know he was down in Florida and all over the TV. So he was suspended indefinitely and then he started his own thing.

I came to the mosque after he was suspended, and this person was going this way and that one was going the other way.

I said, "What's going on?"

They said, "We're going with Malcolm. What are you going to do?"

I said, "There's too much dust. I'm not moving till the dust settles."

I knew that the Honorable Elijah Muhammad was the author of this teaching. I can't leave and go with this man, although I love him.

When Malcolm was shot they had sent me out on an errand. Just as I pulled up to the temple on 116th Street, Edward 15X came running out and said, "Let's go up to the Audubon.[20] Malcolm just got killed!"

I said, "What!"

---

[18] Louis Farrakhan, head of the reconstituted Nation of Islam.
[19] Members of the present-day Nation of Islam refer to the Nation in Elijah Muhammad's day as the First Resurrection.
[20] The Audubon Ballroom.

We jumped in the car. We saw a lot of people still hanging around. We drove around the block and then we came back to 116th Street.

I was really shocked. I couldn't hardly believe that would happen. I still grieve over that when I think about it, you know. We all loved him. When Malcolm talked I could memorize it word for word. I still got notes that Malcolm used to teach on.

When Malcolm first got killed they said six carloads of Muslims were headed for Chicago. Going to get Elijah Muhammad. The papers were jumping. That's all you heard on the news.

I really wanted to go to Malcolm's funeral. But I didn't want to get into bad standing with the Nation.

I see a lot of brothers who were in the Nation. They deviated so much. After 1975 I deviated a little bit. I began to smoke a little bit. I never did eat no pork no more. But every now and then I would take maybe a social drink. But then when I heard the minister[21] was going to teach, I said, "Where?" I dropped all that stuff.

Malcolm always taught that Wallace[22] was going to do a great job, because he was named after Master Farad.[23] But when Elijah Muhammad passed away I thought Farrakhan was going to take over.

There might have been bloodshed. A lot of brothers would have got killed because some would have been on Farrakhan's side and some on Wallace's side.

I got confused, the way Wallace was teaching. He took all of the uniforms away from us and he broke up the FOI and he started having white folks coming into the Nation.

I said, "Man, what is he *doing?*"

Wallace's teaching seemed like it did the same thing to me the Christian church did. I used to go to sleep. I stood up there and I listened to the preacher and just when I think the preacher is getting ready to tell who God is, he breaks out and starts to singing. I said, "What is he talking about!"

Actually there was nothing really to do. There was nothing to look forward to. When I heard the teaching again, that's where I wanted to be. I was so happy, man. When I heard Farrakhan teaching again, it drew tears to my eyes.

[21] Louis Farrakhan.
[22] Warith D. Mohammed.
[23] Founder of the Nation of Islam. Members of the Nation believe he is Allah incarnate.

See, I done lived both sides of the coin. Now I got a chance to live on the good side.

I was shooting, cutting. When I was in "the grave" I carried me a gun just about all the time. I started carrying a gun again after I got out of the Nation. I just thought that was the "in" thing, to carry a gun—and a black-handled razor. I feel if my gun misfired I got a razor to back me up. When I was a young kid in Virginia, I used to go to some of the roughest places. I call them the Bucket of Blood. I thought that was it, you know— eating that bad food and getting hot, wanting to fight. But now, I don't harm nobody. I don't think I really had the heart to really hurt somebody. I didn't have that killing instinct.

Now, I don't have no kind of weapon. Only thing I believe in that will protect me will be Allah. If I'm supposed to go I feel it will be the time for me to go.

Farrakhan reminds me of Malcolm a lot. We call ourselves the *new* Nation of Islam. The First Resurrection is with the Honorable Elijah Muhammad; the Second is with Farrakhan. It's a change of command, that's all it is.

Since I came back to the Nation, I became a lieutenant. They said I had a lot to tell.

Second Coming

The ignorant man is a soldier without weapons.

Arabic proverb

Survival Course

A young man lovingly unwrapped his Qur'an, which he carried in a towel. He kissed it and laid it on his lap. Class began with the study group leader asking, "What stimulates you spiritually?"

"Soldiering," answered one man, "because it makes me more accepting of the message than before." An elderly woman replied, "When I see a young Fruit; when I see the power in his eyes."

About seventy-five members of Louis Farrakhan's Nation of Islam gathered in the gymnasium of the University of Islam in Chicago. The study group session felt like a class of Dale Carnegie course students for whom blackness equated with things positive.

For religious inspiration among members, the Nation of Islam has created a series of study guides. Taken verbatim from Farrakhan's speeches, they amount to a compilation that could well be entitled *The Sayings of Minister Farrakhan*. The guides are used in question-and-answer study sessions.

In one, questions were asked on conquering "low desires," spiritual healing, and overcoming personal problems. Each of four groups mulled over the questions separately, then together listened to Farrakhan's representative, Ava Muhammad, read the "correct" answers.

"These questions are for leadership—for people who are on the move," said Ava, dressed in a flowing yellow gown. "These are not questions for couch potatoes."

One question was: "The first step in the resurrection process is the awakening of the person—what is the next necessary step?"

Answer: "The nurturing of that person into the strength that would enable that person to live an Islamic or righteous life."

The "correct answers" she read appeared to animate those in attendance.

"Oh, man!" exclaimed Walter 3X, a seventeen-year-old high school student with flattop haircut and chrome-pointed shoes.

"Go ahead, sister!" another man said. "This is more powerful than any weapon the white man has!"

At the end of the meeting, members of the paramilitary Fruit of Islam sharply saluted a star-and-crescent flag and marched out. Others followed, beaming, as though they had just heard Allah's words.

And never have We sent forth any apostle otherwise than
[with a message] in his own people's tongue, so that he might
make [the truth] clear unto them; but Allah lets go astray
him that wills [to go astray], and guides him that wills
[to be guided]—for He alone is almighty, truly wise.

Qur'an 14:4

Extended Royal Family

Some years after Elijah Muhammad's death, Louis Farrakhan chided those who went astray. "You have gone back to drinking alcohol, smoking reefers, eating pork, and boogieing," he told a Harlem audience in 1980. "All the progress we made has been lost."

Disgruntled, Farrakhan himself had left Warith D. Mohammed's organization two years earlier to found his own, a "new" Nation of Islam based on Elijah's doctrines.

With his new Nation, Farrakhan catapulted himself to prominence among those who felt betrayed by Warith Mohammed. Farrakhan reinstated the ascetic lifestyle and dress code: bow ties and dapper suits, gowns and head coverings. He re-created the Fruit and brought back Muslim Girl Training, a homemakers' group. And as in Elijah's NOI, recruits joined after being awarded an "X." Used as a prefix to a surname or as a surname, it indicated a person was known formerly by a "slave name." Recruits could apply for an "X" by writing to Farad and Elijah, whom they believed were alive; mail went to Farrakhan's Chicago office.

Louis Farrakhan was born Louis Eugene Walcott in 1933 to a West Indian domestic-worker mother in the Bronx.

Farrakhan, who stuttered as a child, was raised Episcopalian. The family moved to Boston, where he attended public schools. He went on to college in North Carolina, where he ran track. But music was his first love. In the

Louis Farrakhan and a security squad at Madison Square Garden in New York City in 1985.
PHOTO: JACQUES M. CHENET

1950s, he became a nightclub singer billed as the Charmer. He sang ca-lypso songs and was a virtuoso violinist. In those days, he confesses, "I smoked a reefer or two."

He first heard about Islam when a friend invited him to a Chicago con-vention. Later, he visited the Nation's Harlem temple, heard Malcolm X, and joined.

Elijah prohibited his followers from being entertainers, so Farrakhan abandoned his career, reportedly rejecting a movie contract later signed by Harry Belafonte. But he put his talent to use writing, singing, and accom-panying on violin the NOI's unofficial anthem, "A White Man's Heaven Is a Black Man's Hell."

Leadership has changed Farrakhan's life. During Elijah's heyday, when he was an NOI minister in Boston, his family ate baked beans every night, he says. Today, the Farrakhans (there are nine children) live royally in what his followers call "the Palace"—the limestone-and-marble mansion in Chi-cago's integrated Hyde Park section that was once owned by Elijah. It is a fortress with high brick walls and an electric fence.

In 1973, Farrakhan escorted Elijah Muhammad into the mansion. As Farrakhan remembers, while people marveled at the stately home, Elijah told him, "Brother, Muhammad will not be in this house with his foot propped up enjoying this mighty fine home. Muhammad will be in this home planning on how to get seventeen million of our people into homes just like this."

Farrakhan says he bought the estate for $500,000, paying off delinquent taxes. He compares it to the White House. "It belongs to the community," he says, "and whoever sits in the seat of the Honorable Elijah Muhammad at this point would run the Nation of Islam from this residence."

There, Farrakhan holds court, plucking his 200-year-old Guadagnini violin when time allows.[24] "Whenever I can find a moment, my violin is to me like a golf club is to a golfer, or like some pastime is to a business executive," he says. He plays music composed by whites, justifying it this way: "You think that I as a musician should not respect the beauty of Mozart! . . . No. We have to respect greatness wherever it is, from whatever race of people manifest it. Now, that would make me a racist if I said no, I will not play Mozart's music."

Farrakhan also presides over Elijah's old flagship temple, which he bought for $2.3 million from Mohammed's bankrupt organization. Renamed Mosque Maryam, the elegant, high-vaulted former Greek Orthodox church is the crown jewel of the modern-day NOI. An illuminated star and crescent revolving atop its dome shines at night like a beacon over the South Side neighborhood.

Dues support his organization, estimated in 1993 to have more than 20,000 members nationwide.

Farrakhan says members give only what they can afford. However, dues are expected, though proportionately less goes to Farrakhan's organization than went to Elijah's. In years past, members gave as much as a third of their earnings to Elijah's "do-for-self" program.

Yet for all his work in raising a Nation, Farrakhan has not been able to fill Elijah's business shoes. Elijah was venerated for creating a conglomerate of restaurants and supermarkets near his temples. By comparison, Farrakhan is no entrepreneur.

[24] In 1993, celebrating his sixtieth birthday, he played before an audience of 3,000 at Christ Universal Temple on Chicago's South Side. The concert featured the music of German-Jewish composer Felix Mendelssohn. He called the concert a peace offering to other religions, saying, "I desire for us to use the universal language of music to help us rise above the fray that has been created by the usage of words." Earlier in the year, he performed in a Winston-Salem, North Carolina, concert. The New York Times, on April 19, reviewed the concert. It reported: "Can Louis Farrakhan play the violin? God bless us, he can. He makes a lot of mistakes, not surprising for a man who had virtually abandoned the instrument for 40 years and has only owned one since 1974. Yet Mr. Farrakhan's sound is that of the authentic player. It is wide, deep and full of the energy that makes the violin gleam." In 1955, when he was a professional entertainer, he was asked by Elijah Muhammad to choose between music and Islam. Farrakhan put the instrument away until Elijah Muhammad asked him to pick it up again in 1974.

In 1985, he lent his name to a line of health and beauty-aid products made by POWER (People Organized and Working for Economic Rebirth). The venture might have broadened his appeal to middle-class blacks but it proved a disaster. Fallout from his own rhetoric was the reason.

Five black-owned companies promised to make POWER products. But by the end of 1985 they pulled out. Reportedly they feared Farrakhan's inflammatory statements would alienate Jewish distributors.

Farrakhan persuaded Muammar Khaddafi to fund the venture with a $5 million, interest-free loan. POWER products were sold at Farrakhan's mosques and door to door. But in crime-ridden areas potential customers kept their doors shut to canvassers, and salespeople were reluctant to go knocking. "We are struggling," Farrakhan confesses.

Farrakhan is easily the most controversial Muslim leader in America. The media, he says, has manufactured a monster image of him. He is partly correct. Reporters turn his sensationalistic statements against him, and his own recklessness with words leaves him open to criticism. During Jesse Jackson's 1984 presidential campaign, Farrakhan, a supporter, threatened a reporter for disclosing that Jackson had called New York "Hymietown." Farrakhan also called Judaism "a gutter religion" and described Hitler as "a great man, but wicked." (He tried to counterbalance the Hitler statement with "How dare you say I love a man who hated blacks!" But irreparable damage had already been done.)

His statements have caused him to be barred from Britain and Bermuda and driven from a Nigerian stage at gunpoint. But his audaciousness has struck a responsive chord among blacks in America. Many thousands attended his national "Stop the Killing" tour, where they dumped many thousands of dollars into donation buckets, then heard him run down his theory on how the U.S. government had declared "covert war" on blacks.

The crowds—26,000 in Detroit, 19,000 in Atlanta, 10,000 in Chicago—were eclectic. Nearly as many people wore kinte clothes as bow ties. Some women wore miniskirts.

In Milwaukee, Wisconsin, in 1990, bow-tied men and white-gowned women frisked a crowd of 6,000 one by one. Even matchbooks were confiscated. "We want to protect Minister Farrakhan," a young minister explained onstage. "And also we want to make it safe for you in here."

After donations were collected, Farrakhan, emerging from a knot of bodyguards, breezed onstage, wearing a bow tie, a blue suit, spoon-sized gold cuff links bearing an image of Elijah Muhammad encircled in diamonds, a matching ring, and a diamond-encrusted watch. He worked the crowd like a master, and it hooted back at him like a jubilant late-night television-studio audience.

In a two-and-a-half-hour impromptu speech, he lambasted the "enemy," saying AIDS had been "manufactured" and then spread purposefully among blacks, whites had introduced crack to kill blacks, and black neighborhoods were "war zones." "It's safer to rear your children in the jungles of Vietnam—in an actual war zone!—than to rear your children in the inner cities," he said.

(His "enemy" conceded the point. In November 1990, the U.S. government released a report stating it was more likely for black males between fifteen and twenty-four to be murdered in some areas than it was for an American soldier to be killed in Vietnam.)

Who will lead a counterattack in this "war"? "Prophets can't handle this," Farrakhan submitted. "You take Noah and give Noah one look at Milwaukee, and Noah will get in his ark and paddle away."

In the last days of the world, he prophesied, God will work miracles "through a man."

Presumably, Farrakhan.

He stirs as much controversy among Muslims as he does among non-Muslims. One reason is that he considers himself god-sent.

In a vision in 1985, he says, he was beamed aboard a UFO, which docked in the Motherplane, a planetlike object a half mile in diameter. Inside, he says, he heard Elijah Muhammad speak:

"President Reagan has met with the Joint Chiefs of Staff to plan a war. I want you to hold a press conference in Washington, D.C., and announce their plan and say to the world that you got the information from me on the wheel."

Farrakhan says he came to realize that Elijah's message meant American military forces would attack Libya, so he forewarned Libyan officials.

Many mainstream Muslims write off his mystical experience as hallucinatory. Still, they invite him to speak at their conferences. In September 1990, before 750 imams, including Meccan officials, Farrakhan professed belief in Allah and the prophethood of Muhammad of Arabia. W. D. Farad Muhammad, Elijah Muhammad's teacher, he added, came to aid American blacks. The remark offended imams who consider Farad a heretic.

"I don't want to look like an illegitimate child of Islam," Farrakhan said. "I don't want my brothers to look down on me and call me an infidel, hypocrite, or call me words I don't think correctly describe me and my work in America."

He asked the imams to be patient; Islam is evolving peacefully among his and Warith D. Mohammed's followers. "Even though we have differences," he continued, "we have never so much as given each other's followers a bloody nose. You can't say that for Iran and Iraq."

Onstage, he hugged Mohammed, ending, publicly at least, a theological dispute. Mohammed then said all Muslims should accept Farrakhan as a fellow believer. Many did.

Farrakhan, however, clings to the old teachings. In his mosques, banners declare: "THERE IS NO GOD BUT ALLAH. MUHAMMAD IS HIS MESSENGER"— referring, implicitly, to Elijah. Mainstream Muslims consider the implication sacrilege. Muhammad of Arabia, they insist, is the "seal of the prophets," the last in a line that includes Adam, Noah, Abraham, Moses, Jesus.

Further evidence of his unorthodox views appears in his group's newspaper, *The Final Call*. It carries pictures of Elijah in a bejeweled fez along with an article of faith: "We believe that Allah (God) appeared in the Person of Master W. Farad Muhammad, July 1930; the long-awaited 'Messiah' of the Christians and the 'Mahdi' of the Muslims."

What's more, Farrakhan posed this challenge in his newspaper:

I, Louis Farrakhan, am saying to the world that the Honorable Elijah Muhammad is not physically dead. I am further stating that he was made to appear as such as written in the Bible and in the Holy Koran, in order that the Scriptures might be fulfilled.

We stand ready, at any time, to pay for the exhuming of that "body" of the Honorable Elijah Muhammad and we stand ready to pay for the two dentists who worked on his teeth to compare their dental records with the dental records obtained from examination of the "body."

In an interview, Farrakhan said, "I've taken a position that would automatically render me insane, or render me a charlatan at best and insane at worst. Yet I'm the most successful of all of his students. If I'm not in error then the world is in for a terrible surprise."

Some Muslims believe Farrakhan shifts gears with each audience, saying one thing to appease those who hang on to Elijah Muhammad's teachings and quite another to please orthodox Muslims.

He bristles at doubters. In a Washington, D.C., hotel room, he said, "I was created a Muslim—not by any *fatwa*[25] coming out of Mecca or any edict coming from Prophet Muhammad."

Farrakhan's followers are busy. His Dopebusters made national headlines, improving his group's public image. So Farrakhan tested his Nation's popularity in D.C. polls in 1990. His handpicked candidates ran on a platform of incorruptibility and Elijah Muhammad's self-help principles. They did not call for reestablishing the District as a black territory and ignored an opponent's "overlooked" income tax payments. In fact, they campaigned so cleanly, per Farrakhan's orders, the news media virtually ignored them.

So did voters.

Dr. Abdul Alim Muhammad, a surgeon and Farrakhan's national spokesman, ran for Congress in Maryland's 5th District, which was 60 percent black, winning less than a quarter of the vote in the primaries. Still, he declared victory, charging vote tampering.

The Muslim candidate for congressional delegate, an attorney, got 5 percent of the vote. He, too, claimed victory. Dr. Muhammad told supporters, "We are planting the idea of our ultimate victory in the minds and the hearts of all the people, black and white."

Farrakhan does not think it is inconsistent to call for a separate nation for blacks and yet participate in the American political process. "How will that come about except through politics?" he says. His goal is "to put the Muslim program before Congress that the Congress itself may reason as to whether or not separation is a viable alternative to genocide."

Farrakhan lashes out when that works best for him and extols when it serves his purpose. After Elijah expelled Warith (then Wallace) from the old Nation for heresy, Farrakhan announced that Warith had chosen "the road of hypocrites." Later, when Warith became head of the Nation, naming Farrakhan his spokesman, Farrakhan publicly endorsed him, saying he had Allah's blessing: "No other man holds the key to divinity. There is no one wise enough to approach the shoelace of Wallace D. Muhammad."

In 1964, Farrakhan led the attack against Malcolm X when Malcolm accused Elijah Muhammad of fakery and adultery. In a series of articles in the Nation's newspaper, Farrakhan, once Malcolm's protégé, wrote: "Only those who wish to be led to hell or to their doom will follow Malcolm. Such a man is worthy of death and would have met his death if it had not

[25] Religious decision.

been for Muhammad's confidence." He also called Malcolm a "silly general without an army." Within months, Malcolm was assassinated. He died with twenty-one gunshot wounds.

Farrakhan, who ascended to Malcolm's position as Elijah Muhammad's national spokesman, absolves himself of guilt in connection with Malcolm's assassination. He admits contributing to the murderous atmosphere, but, he says, Malcolm himself created it.

Farrakhan also stands by his articles. "Nothing that I wrote or said yesterday do I disagree with today—not one thing that I said!" he says. "I wouldn't have done a thing different. Anybody that rose up against the Honorable Elijah Muhammad in that way, I would rise up against them."

Farrakhan, who has cast himself as an antihero, surrounds himself with bodyguards. He may not inspire the blind devotion that Elijah once did. Nevertheless, if he is harmed, his Fruit, who can be as ferocious as Elijah's were, would retaliate. They believe submission to Allah's will goes hand in hand with obeying Farrakhan's. To lead, Farrakhan depends on their lock-step resignation, much as Elijah did. In his autobiography,[26] Malcolm X described his former devotion to Elijah: "I was like a zombie then—like all Muslims—I was hypnotized, pointed in a certain direction and told to march. Well, I guess a man's entitled to make a fool of himself if he's ready to pay the cost. It cost me 12 years."

As Elijah Muhammad had, Farrakhan bars whites from his mosque. Therein may lay his Nation's major attraction: It is a refuge for angry blacks in a land that is perhaps becoming more, not less, race-conscious.

But to many Muslims, including Warith Mohammed's followers, Farrakhan's rhetoric is a relic of the 1960s, and his version of Islam, based on Elijah Muhammad's myths, lacks spiritual breadth. He is a one-man show, and the fate of his Nation depends heavily on his charisma.

More loosely organized, Mohammed's followers look to historical Islam for answers to the day's pressing questions. To them, Islam was perfected during the Arabian prophet's time. Updating it would prove futile, since Allah had foreseen the future and made Islam infallible—a religion for all time.

In black America, further growth of Islam depends, in part, on whether Muslim leaders can build coalitions. To do so, Elijah Muhammad's place in

[26] *The Autobiography of Malcolm X,* as told to Alex Haley, first published in 1964.

history must be worked out. At this point, Warith Mohammed considers him merely a "social reformer" who was duped by "a satirist," W. D. Farad Muhammad.

In Farrakhan's world, and in his Nation, Elijah Muhammad still reigns —and Farrakhan himself is Elijah's rightfully guided spiritual heir.

Louis Farrakhan

I would not describe us as a nationalist movement although we desire to have an independent nation of our people.[27] Having an independent nation is not a new idea, but it is an idea the acceptance of which is growing at a very fast pace in America, both among whites and among blacks. We who are serious about our people have to think in terms of a real solution to our problems; and a solution cannot be a solution only for the middle class of black people, but it must be a solution that will ultimately prepare a future for the least of our people, and we don't see that in integration. We see that in the form of an independent nation with the backing of the government of the United States in that effort.

What leadership model would you choose if you had independence?

I don't see any leadership model except those that preceded us from the prophets of God. When Israel, according to Scripture, was in bondage in Egypt, God wanted the children of Israel for His purpose, for His own glory. So He raised Moses to separate the children of Israel from the Egyptians and to lead them out of Egypt into a land of their own, where they set up a theocracy based upon the rules and laws of God. The latest example of such leadership was Prophet Muhammad of Arabia, peace be upon him,

[27] At a prayer breakfast meeting in Libreville, Gabon, at the second African/African American Summit in 1993, Farrakhan said black Americans should be able to form a country of their own on the African continent. He planned, he said, to ask African leaders to "carve out a territory for all people in the diaspora." He added that black Americans should be granted dual citizenship by all African countries, "because we don't know where we came from."

Louis Farrakhan.
PHOTO: JACQUES M. CHENET

who found the Arabs divided as tribes with no nation, no national focus, no institutions of learning, and Prophet Muhammad, with the Qur'an, welded these human beings together and formed them into a nation—not a nation such as America or France or Britain, but a nation that expanded beyond the boundaries of Arabia. And that nation included human beings of every color and of every racial strain who accepted Islam. They became members of the Nation of Islam.

Is the Honorable Elijah Muhammad a prophet, and who was the last prophet?

The Honorable Elijah Muhammad never said to us that he was a prophet. Prophets prophesize. The Prophet Muhammad, peace be upon him, is the end of those prophets. He brought the final book or revelation, which is of course the Qur'an. We do not believe that there is any prophet after Prophet Muhammad. But we see that the Qur'an teaches us that every nation has received a messenger. Every nation has received a warner.

Since the time of Prophet Muhammad, we have in America a new reality that came up. Here's a country that was populated by Native Americans.

We don't have any record of a prophet of Allah coming to the Native Americans. The Caucasians from Europe came here. They had the prophets but the scriptures of the prophets had long been corrupted. So what you have in America are Caucasian people who set up a nation and a government on the basis of a corrupted version of the Torah of Moses and the *Injil*[28] of Jesus. So here now, you have a new nation that has no real contact with the true message of Moses, the true message of Jesus, even the true message of Muhammad. So now, who will bring the message to the West and establish it among the Native Americans, among the Chicanos, among the blacks, and among the whites? That person can never do that without divine backing, and we believe that as God in the past always raised His servants up from among the ranks of the oppressed—we believe that God has raised Elijah Muhammad up from among us, not as a prophet, but to bring us the message of Islam according to the condition in which he found us.

A few years back, you said about Warith Deen Mohammed, "No other man holds the key to divinity. There is no one wise enough to approach the shoelace of Wallace D. Muhammad." Are you, Minister Farrakhan, divinely chosen to lead?

I believe that I am divinely chosen. I don't see any way that I could be successful without God's choice and backing of me, especially to try to establish Islam in America. I think that any of us that stand up today on behalf of Islam, on behalf of truth, and on behalf of Allah—if we're not divinely chosen to do the job, we won't be successful, and I believe that I'm divinely chosen and divinely backed by Allah to be successful in raising black people up.

So you should have succeeded the Honorable Elijah Muhammad?

I have.

What does the name Farrakhan mean and how did you get it?

The name Farrakhan was given to me by the Honorable Elijah Muhammad. When I asked him what it meant he said it had very many good meanings. It was one of the modern names of God. He said, "I have the meaning upstairs, and one day I will give you its meaning." I never did get

28 Bible.

the knowledge of its meaning. So I can tell you in truth, I really don't know.

Do you foresee ever reuniting with Warith D. Mohammed's community?

There are efforts that have started in the past, and like a tender plant they have to be nurtured. We believe that, as Muslims, we all will be united. We hope that it will come soon. But Allah is the best knower and the best judge. We believe that the process has started, and we intend to feed that process, hoping that it will grow ever stronger every day.

You embraced Imam W.D. at an Islamic convention in Chicago. What did that symbolize?

Well, it was a very important day; it was a very meaningful day, because as Muslims we are facing great crises in the world and in the United States and we do not wish to see our differences manipulated by those who are not lovers of Islam at all, causing us to shed the blood of a brother believer. So in that sense, it was historic, it was glorious, it was wonderful, but it is only a beginning step.

I have known Imam Warith Deen since we were very young men, and I have loved him as a brother, and if you study my history, when I could not agree with him any longer, I separated myself from him. Not to take up stones to throw them at him but because I honestly could not abide his criticism of his father, who had laid the basis for our development Islamically in America. And I told the imam as much. And if I cannot agree with you, then I cannot walk with you. That's just basic, but that does not mean that I would join any effort to do harm to him or to the movement that he represents. None of these [people] who follow me will show any hatred toward *any* Muslim. When a Muslim says he believes in Allah, he believes in the Qur'an, he believes in Prophet Muhammad and is trying to follow the *Sunnah* of the Prophet, we have nothing but respect for such Muslims.

But the problem is when Muslims see us. We say we believe in Prophet Muhammad. We believe in the Qur'an. We believe in Allah. But we also believe in the Honorable Elijah Muhammad, his mission and his work among us.

And now all of a sudden we have to come and prove to somebody that we are Muslim!

I want to say this to you and through you to all those who would read what you write: I wouldn't care and don't care if none of you believe that I am a Muslim. You are not my judge. As I said to those 750 imams: Take off the robes of Allah. They don't fit you well. You don't know *who* a Muslim is. You really don't know anything about *anybody's* Islam except your own. So why don't you leave that to Allah! He says in the Qur'an, He knows best who errs from His path and He knows best who walk aright. Why not leave that to God! So I'm a self-respecting man and I don't feel that I should bend and scrape to try and prove to you or the imam or the rulers of Mecca that I am a Muslim. *You* don't make me a Muslim. And saying the thing that pleases you or Mecca doesn't make me a Muslim. I was created a Muslim by Allah. Isn't that sufficient?

Why do you think black people around the country are drawn to you? Do you think it's for religious reasons?

People are drawn to persons and personalities for various and sundry reasons. Go back and look at those who first followed the Prophet. Everybody had a different reason for joining the Prophet, but that's not the important thing—what their motive was. But after they got with the Prophet, he gradually changed their motivation and brought them fully into the Islamic way of life. To see thousands of people all across this nation bearing witness to the one God, to Muhammad the Prophet, to the Qur'an, is a start. That's all it represents. It's a start in the right direction. But now, we must get Qur'ans into their hands. We must get the knowledge to them of how to be a Muslim, and as time goes on, we will see tens of hundreds of thousands of Muslims in America growing as the Muslims did in Arabia. It took the Prophet twenty-three years to get them from where he found them to where he left them. And their state of *jahiliyyah*[29] in my judgment was not as terrible as ours. So it's going to take time to make us the kind and quality of Muslims that the world needs. But we are on our way. We are in that process. Allah will do for us what He did for the Arabs, what He did for the Jews, what He did for all those nations and peoples that received a messenger. He will give value to our lives.

One Muslim man in New York told me that the men are in the mosques and the women are in church. Do you think that may be true?

The teaching is not being handled properly. One of the marks of the Prophet is that the Prophet was always able to draw women and young

[29] State of ignorance, such as in the pre-Islamic era.

people. You go back and you look at the history of the Prophet. He didn't have all men around him. He had believing men and strong believing women. So what are we doing in deviation from the *Sunnah* of the Prophet that the mosque is full of men and the women are not desired there? It's not the separation of the sexes, but it is the attitude of many men in Islam that is a negative attitude, sometimes even hostile toward women in the mosque. And to me this attitude is backward and improper . . . women don't have equal access to the mosque but have equal access to *al-Haram*[30] in Mecca. Sometimes during *hajj* or *umrah*,[31] you will see a woman bowing down right beside a man and no one tells her, "Get up, get out of here." Well, if we don't do that in *al-Haram,* why should we do that in any other mosque?

In your own mosques, you have the men on one side and the women on another.

Of course. We're not saying that the sexes should not be separated. But we are saying that the sexes should have equal access to the wisdom of God. And in our Islamic world, you find many of the children of those who have been Muslims for many, many centuries going away from Islam today. Why? It is because there's a dissatisfaction in the women of how women are perceived, how women are treated, and it's causing a growing rebellion among the females. It's not that they want to be with men. They don't mind the separate status, but it is this separate and disrespected state. When I was in Mecca performing *hajj,* we were staying in Mina, and when it was time for lunch, the men took their lunch in an air-conditioned room while the women were on the roof in an unclean situation. And they were so upset over it that they rebelled against it and complained bitterly about the way they were being treated. So if you're going to put men in air-conditioned surroundings to eat, separating the males from the females, why put the women on a hot roof in the midday sun? We as Muslims need to really look again at our practice and analyze it principally against the practice of the Prophet and why the women in the time of Prophet Muhammad loved him intensely and honored him and followed him.

The position of the Nation of Islam is to get a separate nation and yet you have political candidates running for office in Washington, D.C. Isn't

[30] *al-Masjid al-Haram,* the Grand Mosque.
[31] A lesser, off-season pilgrimage.

that inconsistent? You're participating in this system and yet you want out of it. You want your own.

Well, every decision that is made, whether it's a decision for reparation, a decision for separation, a decision for integration, those are political decisions. If we can affect the process and our goal is ultimately to see our people have reparations and a separate nation status, how will that come about except through politics? When you look at nearly 26 million black people in the inner cities of America, where there are diminishing jobs and a diminishing tax base, the scholars and scientists refer to us as a permanent underclass. We cannot accept that. If the U.S. government does not have the will to tax itself to provide better opportunities for our people, how will they get that will unless we are on the inside as well as on the outside? And so we have decided that it is time now for us to become a part of a process that we feel is not just for our people, to get from it every atom's weight of justice that we can for our people.

I was disturbed to go back through Muhammad Speaks *and read some of the things you had written back before Malcolm X's assassination. Do you think that in some way you contributed to the environment in which Malcolm was killed?*

Let me speak very, very candidly. Nothing that I wrote or said yesterday do I disagree with today—not one thing that I said! Not one thing! Malcolm himself created the atmosphere when he deviated from the teaching of his teacher, or left his teacher. It was not his teacher that attacked Malcolm; it was Malcolm who attacked his teacher's domestic life. Now, when Malcolm did that, I who loved both Malcolm and the Honorable Elijah Muhammad felt the need to defend my leader and teacher against what I called then and now the vicious slander of Malcolm against his teacher. When it came to our knowledge that Elijah Muhammad didn't have secretaries—he had wives! If Elijah Muhammad had wives, what's the problem? Does it create a problem for you or for Malcolm or for anybody else? How many of the kings and rulers over there have wives, huh? And some of them in Africa don't just have one or two or three or four. They have many. Some of the Islamic kings have many wives and concubines. Does that create a problem for you in that context? No. Malcolm and I discussed this in the context of the Qur'an and Malcolm understood that. Well, then you should ask yourself the question that if the Qur'an says that a Muslim can have up to four wives, but [Prophet] Muhammad was given the privilege of having nine, but he had eleven and also concubines, hmm— now if he's the Prophet, and you don't have nothing to say about him, what are you going to say about a man that raised you up from prison and taught you and put you before the world, cleaned you up, and all of a sudden in this man's fifties he begins taking on wives? Not little teenage secretaries as Malcolm put it. Wives that he supported. Children that came from those wives. He bought them homes. He took care of them. A very wise teacher, in my judgment.

If Elijah Muhammad believed himself to be the messenger of Allah and acted on that belief, who can judge him? Certainly not you. Certainly not Malcolm. Malcolm was out of place. And when he spoke those words, I defended the right of Elijah Muhammad. And in that defense and in condemning Malcolm, that fostered the atmosphere. But Malcolm himself helped to create it, and we lent to that atmosphere in our polemic with Malcolm over Elijah Muhammad's right or wrong depending upon perception, and I would do the same today. I wouldn't do one thing different. Anybody that rose up against the Honorable Elijah Muhammad in that way, I would rise up against them.

You met the Ku Klux Klan in California in 1985?

No.

Did you meet them at all?

No. Mr. Metzger[32] was in attendance at a public rally, and when the basket was passed for charity, Mr. Metzger gave, I think, a hundred dollars, and the press seized the fact that a white man, who loves white people and does not like black people, respects a black man who wants to see his people in a nation of their own. I have no reason to meet with the Klan or the Nazis or any people of that kind. But I will say this: that among them I'm probably the most respected black man in America. Among them. And the reason for that is they don't want to see black men with white women. They don't want to see integration and mongrelization of the races. They want to see black folk separate. In that sense we have some common ground. But that's all there is to that.

[32] White supremacist Tom Metzger, leader of the White Aryan Resistance.

A Hunter College professor said, "What is going on in the black commu-
nity that you can trace to the Muslims? They haven't built one building.
They haven't housed anybody. Farrakhan is hype."

I wouldn't even dignify that. I'm sure that *he* hasn't built one building
either. What is the duty of a messenger? Is it to build buildings, or is it to
deliver a message? I never came to our people in Harlem and said, "I am a
building builder. I am a real estate developer." I am a student of the Honorable Elijah Muhammad with a message in my mouth to the black man.
Now, though we have not built buildings in Harlem, we did own the corner of 116th Street. We did set up four Universities of Islam—in each of the
boroughs. We had 22 businesses in New York. We employed over 500
people in New York. We didn't build a lot of businesses, but we reclaimed
lives. Malcolm didn't build any buildings either. Was he just hype, man?
Frederick Douglass didn't build any buildings. The NAACP don't own
none, except their own headquarters. Is that hype? C'mon, man. Judge me
with fair yardstick. My mission is the resurrection of our people, and I'm
on that job. Jam up.

Was there one shining moment in your conversion to Islam?

No. From as far back as I can remember myself, I've always had a yearning to see black people free. I grew up in the church. I sang in the choir. I
carried the cross. I loved the church. But the church did not speak to the
liberation of black people and so I was constantly searching.

When I was eleven years old, I visited my uncle in New York and he had
a picture of a black man on his wall, and that was very strange, for people
from the Caribbean who are from the British West Indies usually had King
George or somebody like that on the mantelpiece. But my uncle had the
face of a black man on his wall. I asked him who was this man, and he said
this man had come to unite black people. Well, I knew that that must have
been the man that I was looking for. I was very short. I asked my uncle if I
could stand on a chair and I looked up into this man's face to drink in his
features, and I asked, "Where is this man that I may go and meet him?"
And my uncle said, "He's dead." Right then the tears rolled down my
cheeks because I had come so close to a man who had come to unite black
people, but he was gone. And that was Marcus Garvey.

And so my search went on and on until I went to college in the South
and saw and felt the victimization of black people and knew that something was wrong with Christianity, the way that it was practiced, because I

couldn't go to a white church, except to sit in the balcony, and I knew that that was not the teachings of Jesus, and I saw the abuse of our young girls by so-called pastors, and I just decided I had to search for something better, and so when I found Elijah Muhammad, my soul, I would say, and my heart and mind, were opened but I was not yet thoroughly convinced. And when I heard Malcolm X, I became thoroughly convinced that Elijah Muhammad was the man I had been looking for all my life.

To this day you are compared with Malcolm X. Do you think it's a fair comparison, and what do you say about that?

Malcolm X is Malcolm X, and Louis Farrakhan is Louis Farrakhan. But Malcolm X had a profound effect on my life. He became the father that I never had. The big brother that I never had. The teacher in the place of the Honorable Elijah Muhammad. And I literally adored him. And so in my infancy, in whatever field we choose we choose someone that we admire and we attempt to be like that person. Malcolm was the person closest to me in the Nation of Islam. He was the person I admired. He was the person I attempted to be like. But as I evolved, I saw that Malcolm had a political astuteness that seemed to overshadow his spiritual development. Malcolm proved to be at the root spiritual, but he was more the political figure than the spiritual leader. Warithudeen,[33] known as Wallace Muhammad at that time, was much more the spiritual man.

I remember one day, we were in the mosque together, and Malcolm said to the Muslims, "Well, Farrakhan is spiritual; he'll handle that." He chose the political arena more than the spiritual. When he even went overseas and (I put this in quotes) became "converted" (and the reason I put that in quotes is because he was sent to the Holy Land in 1959 and he went to Jedda), he did not go to Mecca, because he wanted Elijah Muhammad, as the leader, to have that first experience as a member of the Nation of Islam. He knew then that there were white Muslims, there were brown, black, red, and yellow Muslims. That was no strange thing to Malcolm. This was '59. Then Malcolm went back in '64, four years later, and had this "conversion." But be that as it may, when Malcolm came back to the United States, if you recall, Malcolm [said] his political philosophy was black nationalism, his religion was Islam. And he allowed those who were more in harmony or more knowledgeable of the spiritual aspect of the teachings to teach that.

[33] Warith Deen Mohammed.

Woe to every [kind of] scandalmonger and backbiter . . .

Qur'an 104:1

Black Devils

Murad Muhammad

Born: October 14, 1950. Profession: Boxing promoter. Some of the boxers he has promoted include Larry Holmes, Donovan "Razor" Ruddock, James "Bonecrusher" Smith, Juan LaPorte, Wilfredo Gomez, E. Pedrosa, Mathew Saad Muhammad, Eddie Mustafa Muhammad, Dwight Quai Muhammad, Marvis Frazier, Rodney Frazier, Burt Cooper, Timmy Witherspoon, Elijah Tillery, and Alfonso Ratliffe.

We killed Malcolm out of ignorance. But what Malcolm was teaching at that time wasn't for us. You could not fault Elijah [Muhammad]. Elijah was the Man and either you joined him or you left him the hell alone. And if you messed with him, I don't care whether you be black or Caucasian, you had to deal with us! And that's how Malcolm lost his life.[34]

I feel that during that time, my mother would have been killed for Elijah. All you had to do was plant the seed. Just so happened it was them. It could have been me, because that's how we felt about our leader and teacher. You could not talk about our leader and teacher, and when Elijah Muhammad Junior left New York telling us that we got a man that we put

---

[34] Three followers of Elijah Muhammad were convicted and sentenced for the assassination: Mujahid Abdul Halim (formerly Talmadge Hayer), Muhammad Abd al-Aziz (Norman 3X Butler), and Khalil Islam (Thomas 15X Johnson). In 1977, Abdul Halim, who was also known as Thomas Hagan, filed a handwritten affidavit in Supreme Court in Manhattan saying Abd al-Aziz and Islam "had nothing to do with this crime whatsoever." He said he was aided in the assassination by four men he named only as Lee, Ben, Willie X, and Willbour. Abdul Halim confessed to using a .45 caliber weapon to shoot Malcolm X. Abd al-Aziz and Islam were paroled after serving 20 years and 22 years respectively; Abdul Halim was scheduled for a parole review in December 1994.

in *our* house,[35] talking about *our* leader and teacher, and we were a bunch of chumps, a bunch of punks, well as far as we were concerned that was dictated to us, "Get rid of him!" You follow what I'm saying? And that's how we felt—to the point that the Chief Imam[36] said we were like *black devils*. And that's what we were. We were like black devils.

One man confessed. The other two were innocent. I couldn't put my life on it, but again, by you being in the midst of the majority of those who knew what was going on, we were told at that time that they had found men that were innocent. But we were all Muslim. If they'd have caught me, I'd-a took it—even though I didn't do it. You gotta understand.

People don't understand—the Honorable Elijah Muhammad had an unbelievable power in America—more than any other black man, ever. Because if someone would have assassinated him like they did Malcolm or like they did King, we'd-a tore this country up. Because he taught us, as babies, if a plane come over and drop a bomb, don't chase the pilot, get the one next door that looks just like him. So the FBI and the CIA knew that. *They* protected Elijah. People don't know that—that his real security men were the CIA and the FBI, because they could not afford Elijah to be assassinated by some ignorant Caucasian who thought that he should die. So *they* protected him.

His power was so strong, when he said *"Ten-hut!"* 30 million minorities jumped to attention. And he didn't have to be here per se to tell us what to do; all he had to do was send a message. I don't know no other black man who ever lived, even today, has the power Elijah had.

So he was a threat to America. But today, now that he's gone, he was an asset. Because he raised the pimps, the hustlers, the drug dealers. Wasn't no such thing as drugs in our community. Wasn't no such thing as a pimp coming in our community. Wasn't no such thing as a woman prostituting in our community. He cleaned all them up, because his message was not to the college man, not to the brother who was educated who had a family. He wanted the rejected one, the one that was in jail, no one cared nothing about. The one standing on the corner and don't think that he could make it in life. That's who Elijah said bring to me.

His intention was honorable, to direct us to the *Sunnah*. In order to do that, you can't bring a filthy person to the religion. So he cleaned us up. He took the drugs out of our system. He taught us what to put in our bodies.

---

[35] Malcolm X and his family lived in a house in Elmhurst owned by the Nation of Islam.
[36] Warith D. Mohammed.

Murad Muhammad.

We stayed away from drugs. But he said, I didn't come here to teach you religion. I came to clean you up. And one will come after me to teach you your true religion.

We didn't understand it at the time, but now we do.

[Minister Louis] Farrakhan said something—I don't care if he says nothing else. He said we're just babies, and me and Chief Imam Warith D., we differ but not one of our followers ever drew blood from one another, and yet you all had religion all your life and you're killing one another. So I say *Allahu akbar!* because that is a plus for us. The first thing we were taught was love self, even though we might differ.

For he who hateth thee—
He will be cut off [from Future Hope].

Qur'an 108:3

Cold War

Sulaiman Abdul-Haqq

Abdul-Haqq was born and raised in Indianapolis. He escaped the draft by dressing "like Kunte Kinte" with beads and a fez and a robe, and saying, "Yeah! Teach me how to kill!" Army recruiters told him, "We don't want you in our army," he says.

For a while he lived in Brooklyn and in Harlem. Acted in street plays on black revolution there. After he converted to Islam, he returned to Indianapolis and founded a mosque attended by Sunni Muslims.

He moved to Abiquiu, New Mexico, in 1986 after reading an article about Georgia O'Keeffe, the late artist who had lived near the community's mosque. The article mentioned the Muslims in the area. He arrived to check it out and never left.

This interview took place at a picnic in Abiquiu. While guests ate barbecued chicken off paper plates Islamic-style—without utensils—he spoke about an undeclared war back in his hometown.

We found an old house, ran the rats out, sealed up all the rat holes, and painted it and made it a *masjid.*[37] Al-Fajr Masjid.

It was burned. It was arson. It was this cold war thing going on at the time between us and Elijah's people.[38] They would say, "Elijah's a prophet," and we would say, "Man, ain't no *way* he's a prophet. The Prophet was Muhammad [of Arabia] and that's *it.*"

When I became Muslim the first thing people would ask, "Are you a

[37] Mosque.
[38] Elijah Muhammad's followers.

Black Muslim[39]?" No. First of all, I am black. I am Muslim. But I'm not no *Black* Muslim.

The Nation [of Islam] had a place right down on Central, almost a rock's throw from where our place was. I had a good relationship with some in the Nation because in Indianapolis I was raised with a bunch of them, so there were times we'd have them over for dinner.

But they were so [dogmatized] with Elijah being the prophet at that time, with Savior's Days. They felt that we were attacking them. And we *were* because they, as far as we were concerned, were attacking Islam with this black junk, this hate-whitey stuff that doesn't have anything to do with Islam. So we were against them in that sense but we never openly attacked them physically. Whenever we would try to explain what Islam is and what it isn't, then they automatically got on the offensive, and we couldn't change what we're going to say. We had to stand on our ground.

I was living in the *masjid* at the time and I was living upstairs. It was right next to an alley. There was a back porch there and one night we had taken out the garbage out in the alley, so there was nothing back in the porch area, which was lit. Around three o'clock I heard a thumping sound and I thought there was something in the *masjid* that fell. A little time went by and I saw this little flicker on the side of the fence. I looked out and the whole back porch was on fire.

There was never no gasoline, nothing flammable out there. I looked around the playground and I recognized a van. I saw that it was people from the Nation. It wasn't like they were hanging out.

The fire department said it was definitely arson because the fire started right in a little corner where they found a gas can, and we didn't have any gas cans. A third of the *masjid* burned.

Everybody was ready to go out and do them in. I said, "We can't because we don't have enough proof."

We never did.

I came here and it felt like a little Muslim country. It felt very warm and very good. At that time, we had the Islamic school. I decided to just up and go. Being I'm a builder and carpenter, I felt I could make enough money to make a living. Fortunately the living expenses are not that much. You can make it very easy here.

[39] Member of the Nation of Islam.

Sulaiman Abdul-Haqq and his daughters.

You're dressed and you go down the street, and people shout, "Hey, Jesus! Hey, Moses!"

But you can't get uptight about it because they're calling you a good name, you know. [*Laughs.*]

I say, "Yeah! Yeah!" The funny thing is, they don't understand that they are giving me a compliment.

Chapter Three

Agony

On no soul doth Allah place a burden greater than
it can bear. It gets every good that it earns. And it suffers
every ill that it earns.

Qur'an 2:286

Conversion to Islam is an event that is triggered sometimes by struggling with one's past, transgressions, or fate and deciding a dramatic transformation is necessary. Converts develop a new worldview after trashing initial assumptions about faith which underpinned their old outlooks. The experience, often emotional as well as spiritual, enables them to begin their lives anew by allowing them to seek spiritual growth or regrowth based on a new religious foundation. With Allah's healing mercy, they learn to forgive themselves, reorder their lives, mature, and move from hopelessness to hope.

Some Muslims, afflicted with diseases through no fault of their own, are struggling for acceptance among fellow Muslims. Their sad stories reflect a community that hasn't yet come to terms with AIDS and the stigma it brings. The bolder victims refuse to be shunted aside or ignored.

Meanwhile, each year, thousands of conversions take place in prisons across America, where communities of Muslims have evolved over the years and where Malcolm X himself converted in the early 1950s. There are more than 140,000 Muslim inmates in federal and state correctional facilities.[1] New York State alone has 32 Muslims, including 2 women,

[1] Source: American Muslim Council, 1993.

among its corps of 170 chaplains, ministering to the needs of a state prison population that is about 21 percent Muslim.

When they arrive in prison, some potential converts seek out Muslims for the protection they offer from agitators among inmates. Muslim inmates are known for their closeness and supportiveness. In many cases, Muslims are assigned to cells that are separate from the general population.

With time, and earnest studying, a potential convert may come around to understand the meaning of Muslims' messages behind bars—a radical idea for many prisoners: that people are held accountable by Allah for their own actions and must not blame scapegoats for their troubles. Islam can afford the pious convert a semblance of freedom, even behind bars and razor wire. But the road to fervor and piety, especially following a life of crime, comes not without some agonizing.

If Allah touch thee with affliction, none can remove it
but He; if He touch thee with happiness,
He hath power over all things.

Qur'an 6:17

Under the Prayer Rug

Tarajee Abdur-Rahim

At forty-two, she publishes Jihad Wa Tauheed,[2] *a bimonthly newsletter about AIDS that contains clinical trial reviews, articles about common traits among PWAs (People With AIDS), social service listings, Q&As, advertisements and editorials, along with Qur'anic verses. She also offers to PWAs a discussion group, outreach, apartment cleaning, laundry, shopping, errands, escorting, personal visitation. She is a fireball and a fortress of strength for her five daughters. But she is struggling to feel protected and valued by the Muslim community.*

I took a *shahada* sixteen years ago. My husband had been Muslim for two years before I took the *shahada*. I thought Islam was cute. For him.

I liked to wear his *thobe*[3] and *kufi*. It looked nice on me. But I just was not interested. I called myself almost proudly an atheist.

I picked up the Qur'an one day and started reading it. It absolutely blew me away. I knew that this was the truth. It made so much sense, I couldn't take *shahada* fast enough. So that meant burning all my micro-miniskirts and my hot pants. And I didn't mind. It didn't faze me in the least. I never wanted to be anything else since.

My oldest daughter must have been about six, and the next was about

[2] The June–July 1993 issue was dedicated to Abdul Malik Abdur-Rahim, Aisha Salaam, Taiba Lythcott, Yusef Muhammad M. Rahman, Shareef Muhammad, Sheikh Jamal, Karima Abdul Wahhab, Sabir Tawwab, Abdul Gardinier, Shahida Uqdah, Katrina Haslip, and Dawud Rivera.
[3] One-piece, long-sleeved robe.

two. They're twenty-three and eighteen now. Nadine and Hillary. Now they are Latifa and Malika—same children. I've had three more since, all girls.

When I did get married my oldest child was about four or five. We decided we wanted to do it right. We'd already left Harlem to get to Brooklyn. Malik was my friend, my lover, my buddy.

Malik had a drug problem. I used to tease him, tell him he wasn't a good junkie. He was trying so hard, and he just wasn't good at this. He might be clean five or six years, and then go on a binge for a year.

He was quite capable of supporting his own habit. Never took anything from the house. Watching the metamorphosis that he would undergo while he was on drugs—that was the hard part. I'd never seen him use. He never did it in front of me or the girls, but I always knew when he'd be using again.

There was no reason to leave this man. He just had a problem that he didn't know how to deal with. And that was the bottom line.

When they started talking about AIDS, I listened and I thought to myself, I don't have anything to worry about: I'm Muslim. I pray five times a day. Malik is Muslim. I told myself, he's doing drugs, not me.

But then I kept hearing about AIDS, and I said, let's go get tested. At first, he didn't want to go, but I needed to know, because by this time I'm hearing that your direct association places you in a high-risk category. He finally agreed and we did go. We were both diagnosed eleven years ago as being HIV-positive.

I was absolutely stunned. I just couldn't believe that I had this virus. But I didn't cry very long. Islam teaches you how to handle anything that occurs in your life. And the way to handle anything is simple: You have faith in Allah. It's that cut and dried. I thought about it and I said to myself, well, at least we have each other. Maybe now he'll leave the drugs alone. And so as quickly as I was afraid, I wasn't afraid anymore.

I said, let's just deal with it. Malik got angry. He got bitter.

There was no support system within the Muslim community that he could turn to. There weren't many support systems available to heterosexuals. This was a gay disease. It was a Haitian disease, it was a white, gay disease, which we now know is absolute foolishness. But at that time, this is what everyone believed. Well, we weren't white, gay, or Haitian. And I

Tarajee Abdur-Rahim.

knew that this was a bigger thing than what people were realizing. I was very angry at Malik because I wanted him to protect me, not from the virus, but from the elements surrounding the virus. I wanted to sit behind Malik and not worry. I didn't want to worry about the gas bill. I didn't want to worry about what other Muslims thought. And I wanted Malik to make life safe for me. I got angry with Malik behind that, but never about the disease.

I had to venture out. I wanted to see what they were doing in the way of AIDS to use to my advantage. I knew other people had this besides me. Better yet, I knew other Muslims had this besides me. I knew I couldn't be the only one with this virus.

Malik didn't want to attend support groups. He didn't want to know anything. He was just angry: Why would Allah do something like this to him? Why would Allah put him in a position where the strong possibility existed where he would die from something that there was no cure for, and leave his children and his wife behind? I'm not a man, and I don't always understand how a man thinks, but I think I understood that.

We fought constantly after that—verbally. I fought his bitterness and his anger, and he fought the way I handled it. I think that as a man maybe it bothered him that his wife was being stronger than him. I wasn't trying to flex muscles. I wanted to protect him too. But I felt like crying sometimes. I wanted to cry but I couldn't. I was too busy being strong to deal with the situation.

Somehow or other as a woman, I found myself slowly leaving my feminine center and approaching things from a masculine center, because I felt that no one was protecting me. So *I* had to protect me. And so I put on my suit of armor, and I had a shield in one hand and a spear in the other. I started going from one support group to another, just to see.

I met everything from little green Martians. But I had fun. [*Laughs.*]

The Gay Men's Health Crisis Center in [Greenwich] Village treated me like a queen.

I knew that it was exclusively gay before I went, so I wasn't thrown aback by that. *They* were thrown aback by *my* presence. Forget the fact that I'm female. But I'm a black female, and I'm a Muslim female. I fell into categories all by myself.

When I walked in the door of GMHC and many other AIDS organizations that were exclusively run by gays, the first thing that they did was always the same: They would just sit there looking at me. On some faces I saw [*affected effeminate voice*]: *Oh, she's* clearly *in the wrong place.*

And on some faces, I could see: *I wonder what she's doing here.* And there were some faces that said: *Oooooo, I* like *that outfit she has.*

It was so amusing to me. They treated me very nice. Of course, they didn't waste any time asking me why I was there. I started talking immediately. I'd go right into introducing myself: "My name is Tarajee. I'm also HIV-positive. I know I'm in the right place."

They had as much fun with me as I had with them. They wanted to know why my hair was covered up and how long it was. They were asking me female questions. That's why it was amusing to me. I could relate. I felt comfortable with them. I was with "the girls." I didn't feel cast aside.

They left the door wide open. I could come and go as I liked. The majority of them found me fascinating. We didn't relate so much on an HIV level as we did on a humanistic level. I went in there not sure what I was looking for, but I came out with a lot. I learned a lot of things about them—their fears, their ways of dealing. More than that, I learned that they bleed when they're cut just like I do. They feel like I feel. They hurt like I hurt. They're no different.

I didn't immediately go into the Muslim community disclosing my HIV status. I would toss a question at a group or an individual, just bring up the subject of AIDS just to watch the reaction. And most Muslims believed that whoever had AIDS had committed a sin and Allah was punishing them.

I saw a lot of fear and anger and denial at the highest level. I suggested to an imam that we needed support groups within the Muslim community to deal with Muslims who had the virus. And he said to me, "Sister, you don't need support groups, you got us."

And I said, "That's not being realistic. Suppose I get tired of being single. What measures have you taken to ensure that I find a husband? I can't fornicate. I can't commit adultery. So what measures have you taken to ensure that I stay within the limitations of my *deen?*"

He said, "Well, we'll cross that bridge when we get to it."

This is typical of the kinds of reactions. He was upset with me because I talked about it too much. I had become too brazen.

He was the first imam that I told it to.

I started raising questions: Why isn't the Muslim community dealing with this? Why is everybody so cloak-and-dagger with this issue? What's going on here?

I met a Muslim brother in Manhattan who said to me, "They need to put all Muslims with this AIDS virus in leper colonies. They need to just lock them all away and throw the key away."

So I said to him, "Well, brother, I don't want to be in a leper colony."

He looked at me and said, "I ain't talking about you, I'm talking about all them other people with that virus."

I said, "Brother, I am one of those people with 'that virus.'"

What could he do? He already put his foot all the way down his throat. I just helped him shove it down a little further, that's all. [*Laughs.*] And I enjoyed myself immensely. I made prayer: *Allah, please forgive me for enjoying myself.*

I asked Allah not to let me be afraid, and that's exactly what I got. You get what you strive for. Allah says man can only get what he strives for. I don't strive for material things. I ask Allah for guidance. I ask Him to protect. I ask Him to show me how to get through this murky water. And He shows me how. And I get other blessings with it to boot.

Malik died three years ago from AIDS. He started back on the drugs again, and he did something that I never saw in twenty-four years of knowing Malik: He turned into a junkie. He finally succeeded, yes he did. When he got finished, Malik wiped out two savings accounts, a checking account; all our insurance policies lapsed. Everything was gone when Malik died. I had to get social services to bury him.

The day he died I was home. I woke up feeling funny, and I knew Malik had died. I knew. And they called me from the hospital and told me. I wasn't surprised. I was glad Malik died. I was glad it was over for him, because he went through sheer hell, and I was always saying to him, get up off your ass and fight this! Don't let this thing take you out of here like that! This is not the way to go. You don't *have* to be miserable. Misery, to me, is optional.

I couldn't make him see what I saw. He was so bitter and so angry he was blinded by it. So I got to a point where I couldn't say much else to Malik on that issue. He just didn't hear what I said. He tore his body down with the drug. I believe that he died from bitterness and anger. It ate him alive.

He had full-blown AIDS about two years before he died. I saw it—before he was diagnosed. We had gone to the Eid prayer, and we were in Prospect Park and I was standing out in the distance talking to a sister, and I just looked up and saw Malik, and I thought to myself, oh my God, he has full-blown AIDS. He wasn't emaciated at that point, but I just knew. I never told him what I saw. The fear bothered me more than anything, because as Muslims we are taught to fear nothing but Allah. I *believed* this.

Malik was afraid of being ostracized. He was afraid of being treated in a condescending manner. He was afraid to let others know that he'd messed up, that he'd made a mistake.

Sometimes Muslims want everyone to believe that they've never done anything wrong, or they're not capable of doing anything wrong. But we're humans. We all mess up from time to time. Allah says this in the Qur'an. This is the way He made us.

This is how many Muslims deal with it. They're more afraid of what other people are going to think than they are of having the virus. And I don't understand it. Because I still maintain we are Muslims. If you say, *La illaha ill Allah,* you've entered into a covenant with Allah. You have agreed with Allah that He is going to lead you, guide you, take you where you're going. I'm even clearer on that now, since I've had this virus.

I was afraid to put out this newsletter at first. It's almost two years old. I wanted imams' names so I could send it to them. I bought a Muslim directory with addresses for all kinds of businesses and organizations. I ended up in a one-year period with a circulation of over 900.

The real purpose of the newsletter is to put out information that most people don't have access to. Most people are not going to go to an AIDS organization to seek out this literature. Especially Muslims.

I'm giving the information straight up. What I've done, however, is include suras from the Qur'an so people will be able to read something that goes to the heart. They're little reminders.

I got quite a few angry responses through the mail and on the telephone: Why would a Muslima[4] put out this stuff about AIDS?

Put out what "stuff"? I'm giving you information. You don't think you need it? How many sisters are in situations like mine with a brother who had a drug problem? A lot of people change husbands and wives like people change socks. The brothers can have more than one wife.

There was a Muslim brother from Sri Lanka who lives in Manhattan who wrote me a lovely letter explaining how he used to do bad things when he came to the United States, and now he's back in his *kufi* and his *thobe,* and he is going to find him a nice Muslima and live happily ever after. He told me if I redeemed myself and stopped doing whatever it was I was doing, then Allah wouldn't punish me with AIDS.

I was incensed. How dare you assume that I had to be doing something wrong, which shows me the level of your ignorance!

So I wrote him and told him, "I'm glad you put your *thobe* and your *kufi* back on. However, *you* screwed everything with a pulse, not me. I was with one man for half my life. Got five kids by the *same* one man. Never did drugs. Ever! I was baking bread and making cookies when you were out there doing all this stuff.

"And now that you've got your *thobe* and your *kufi* back on, when a Muslima sees you, she's not going to question your past. She's going to look at you and say, '*Al-hamdulillah!*' You tell me if that's right or wrong. You're so arrogant that you believe that you don't even have to go get tested. To me, you are dangerous! I'm scared of you. Because all these people who don't have the virus will look at you and others like you and

[4] Female Muslim.

be lulled into a false sense of security based on what you project. Because you ain't going to say nothing.

"Don't worry. I ain't going to tell, because I don't know who you are. And you ain't going to let me know who you are either. You know what I'm saying is the truth."

So I've learned to deal with people on that level.

I know of least 150 Muslims with AIDS, male and female. Mostly males. I can't draw the females for nothing. I'm working on them. I'm corresponding with brothers all over the place. And they're scared. They don't even want to meet each other, because they don't want the other one to know they have the virus—even though that other one has it too.

I have a list—I call it my pen-pal list of Muslims who are all HIV-positive. What I do is circulate the list to Muslims who have the virus, so they don't feel that they have no options. Everyone who's on the list has agreed to be on it. And if you don't want your name on the list, then you can't have a copy of the list either. I just give name, rank, and serial number. To keep them communicating.

There's an imam I know—his wife has AIDS. The person who told me also has AIDS, but the imam didn't know that. I wanted the imam to let his wife know that there were others like her, who spoke the same language that she spoke. Who were all Muslim. I'm not interested in how she got it or why she got it. I'm just concerned about the fact that I think it's a horrible way to die. Not from AIDS—from loneliness, from anger and bitterness.

Allah says, do not despair, do not lose heart. That means you don't go bananas over a situation that you have no control over. You can't do anything about it, so you turn it inside out and you look for the good in it.

The only thing the imam was concerned about was how I found out. He said, "I want to know who told you."

I said, "I don't want to get into that."

He didn't care: "You ain't going to have this conversation with me without telling me who told you."

So I said, "Why are you making that the issue? Your wife has AIDS! I have the virus too. Let me be her friend, because if *you* don't have this virus, Imam, there's no way you could understand what she's going through, I don't care what you read in a book."

I never got past that point.

When I realized that who told me became the issue for him, I realized that AIDS was not the issue. So I just excused myself.

But I want them to understand, yes, I have this virus, but you are not going to push me out of this community. So I walk around and I make sure they see me: Yeah, I'm still here. Allah hasn't called me back yet.

I went to Masjid Al-Farooq on Atlantic Avenue [in Brooklyn]. Some service providers from AIDS organizations all over Brooklyn, Manhattan, and Queens were invited. We had posters up everywhere.

So we go for the meeting, and no Muslims turn up. There were about twenty-five non-Muslims there, which I thought was fantastic. They had to sit on the floor. This is hard for them.

The imam eventually wandered in. And the sister who put the program together, she said, "Um, Imam, would you like to say a few words?"

He said, "Yes. Muslims have the cure for AIDS: no boyfriend, no girlfriend, no AIDS! End of story."

We couldn't believe that he said this.

So I said to him, "Imam, may I say a few words?"

He said, "Yes."

"I'm the sister who sends you the newsletter. Forget the boyfriend-girlfriend thing. I don't have a boyfriend. I never did. I had a husband. And I have the virus too. Why am I treated as though I should just be quiet about this whole issue?"

He was so stunned that someone with HIV was sitting that close to him that he just looked at me. He never answered the question. He got up and said, *"Assalaamu alaikum wa rahmatullah wa barakatuh."*[5] And he left. And left us all sitting there with our mouths hanging open. I looked at all these non-Muslims sitting there. I thought to myself: There's no way I could invite them to Islam. They wouldn't listen to squat I had to say.

Now, maybe I'm misinterpreting something somewhere along the line. But if support is necessary, then you give it up. Nobody should have to ask for that. That is the Islam that I know. That's what Allah is teaching us. He's teaching us the fine art of being human.

· · ·

[5] "Peace be unto you, and the mercy and blessings of Allah."

I'm not looking for anything out of this newsletter. Who wants to be known as the famous AIDS person? But if I have to do that in order to get the other Muslims to come out, I'm sad for them.

What other choices did I have? I watched what happened to Malik when he didn't deal with it. I watch it happen to people all the time. I watch them die from a lot of other things that I don't feel are AIDS-related.

I know there are other Muslims out there. I know that if I wasn't there with my hand out, they wouldn't have that. They get in touch with me and they keep their correspondence going. People have a million ways of crying out. I've broken some of the *Sunnah* laws. For instance, contact between a man and a woman. I've gone to Muslim brothers' apartments and I say, "Okay, your surrogate wife is here." And I go to the store for them, and I keep them company. I've gone to the funeral parlors with them to help them pay for the plots. I shop and I cook for them.

This whole thing has been an adventure. I have met some of the most beautiful people on this planet. I used to think that everybody was a demon thinly disguised as a human being and I was the square peg that didn't fit the round hole, but wasn't trying to fit the round hole either. I never understood what man was capable of.

I've sat with groups of people. I don't see them as: he's all right . . . she's a lesbian. AIDS has divided us into two groups: those without AIDS and those with AIDS. It's us. And it's them.

I'm holding onto Allah's coattails, and I'm not letting go. I don't know where He's taking me, but I know it's right, wherever I go. And you can feel this in here. [*Taps her chest with a fist.*] You know it's right.

I never wanted to be an AIDS advocate but if this is what I have to do, I'll do it.

Everything is geared and designed to teach you. It's what makes your character. It's what redefines you. You're constantly in the state of redefinition. It's what makes you who you are. That's what adversity is for—it's to strengthen our character. Without it you would not be a strong individual.

Before I started the newsletter, one issue for me was: how am I supposed to meet somebody? I really don't like my choices let alone I got to find somebody with this virus too.

I was reading *The Village Voice* and looking through the personals section. Never looked at it in my life. I spotted a few ads from men. They were all gay, but they still had the virus, and they were looking for other people that had the virus. I said, oh, this is a great idea! So I placed an ad. I put something in there like:

MUSLIM WOMAN, HIV-POSITIVE, YOUNG 40S, ROCK-STEADY, STRAIGHT-SHOOT-ING. AIN'T LOOKING FOR NO FOOLISHNESS, LOOKING FOR MUSLIM BROTHER THE SAME. WHERE ARE YOU? LET'S GO.

I got a lot of responses. I got some non-Muslims tossed in there too. All of whom I know to this day. And I'm very close to them, but none of them would I want to spend the rest of my life with.

I got one call from a Muslim brother who knew I was doing things [about] AIDS, but didn't know I had the virus. He was absolutely incensed. The ad was pointed out to him by another Muslim who had read it. They were up in Al-Farooq for a little powwow over this ad. They didn't know it was me.

He said, "Guess what? This sister put an ad in the Sodom and Gomorrah paper. She's got AIDS and she's advertising for a husband!"

And I said, "Well, why were you all reading the personals section if you all thought it was such a yucky paper?"

"No, no, no. This dude just brought it to us and said, 'I didn't know Muslims get this virus too.' "

So I said, "Well, are any of the brothers HIV-positive?"

"No, no, ain't nobody got that virus."

I said, " 'Cause if they are, tell them to call that extension number in the paper."

He says, "What do you mean, 'call the extension number'?"

I said, "That's my ad."

I haven't heard from him since. Never. I made myself an enemy.

The Muslim greeting, male or female, is to hug. Before the virus it was something I used to do automatically. After I contracted the virus and I started to disclose, I stopped doing that.

I stopped for two reasons. Number one: I don't know how afraid people really are. Why subject myself to that kind of pain watching them with-draw? I've seen that happen. Those I know I can do it with, I'm all over them, because they know they can't catch it from me that way. But some people don't know that. I don't want to frighten them, and I don't want to hurt their feelings.

I watched that happen to a Muslim brother. He passed two years ago.

He contracted AIDS through blood transfusion. He was a hemophiliac. And he was young. He had never been out there in the world.

I remember being at his house when his aunt and her two children came to visit him. He sat on the edge of the bed, and he said to the two little girls, "Come give me a hug." The little girls froze, and right then I understood what was going on.

I thought that maybe he would leave it alone, but he didn't. And he said, "Come; come give me a hug."

Then the oldest little girl, who had to be about eight, said, "My mommy said I can't hug you because you got AIDS."

I was absolutely floored. Not for myself—I understand these things—but for the effect that it had on him. There were several people in the room. I asked them to leave.

He cried and just went to pieces. And I said, "Now listen. You know, even though they love you, everybody is not going to be able to handle this. Some people are very afraid and you have to understand that. They'll be concerned, yes, but they'll still be afraid to touch you. That's just the way it is. Now, you're just going to wipe your face, and you don't put yourself in that position anymore. Ever."

He was twenty-two when he died. He was in the hospital, and I go visit him. I got some oil. I say, "Okay, your surrogate wife is here." I done seen his butt and everything. I'm helping him to the bathroom when he needs it. And I'm giving him a rubdown and making jokes. And a couple of Muslim brothers walk in, and they look at me and: "*Astaghfirlah*, sister! That's not your husband, you can't touch him!"

It was just a bunch of foolishness, and they went on so bad with it that I took the bottle of oil and I said, "Well, then, you all do it."

Nobody touched him.

I said to them, "Could I speak to you all for a minute in the lounge, please?"

I told them, "How dare you be so thoughtless. Allah knows my intentions. If breaking my *wudu* is all that I did back there, then I'll make another one. If you're not going to offer to help, if you're not going to stick your feet in the murky water, then get out of my way. I got my boots on."

Alcoholism, homelessness, wife abuse, child abuse, homosexuality—it's all the same. These are issues that have to be dealt with. If you sweep them all up under the rug every time you're confronted with them, you're not dealing with anything. And this is the natural tendency.

When Malik was on drugs and I wanted support from the Muslim community, and I'd gone to them with this. I was saying in effect: Help me. Show me what to do. Tell me how to deal with this. I don't want him to be like this. I didn't ask for a divorce. You're a man, he's a man, talk man talk to him. Talk to him the language that you speak better than I can. Maybe he will hear something in what you're saying that I don't know how to convey to him. Malik would not go to the counsel with me, so I was trying to bring the counsel to my house. I want help, and I want it Islamically.

I was told some cute little stuff like: "Who? Abdul Malik on drugs? That brother works every day." In other words: I don't see him doing anything.

AIDS is out there. I want the Muslims who don't have the virus to make AIDS service accessible, and I would like to see the brothers running it Islamically, not based on how they feel.

Brothers get in touch with me, get scared and hang up and not call back ever again. I've had them call, and maybe speak to them for a year, and they won't tell me who they are. And they know I have the virus too.

There's another brother that I've been corresponding with for about three years now. He lives in California. He's married to someone who doesn't have the virus. He found out he had it, and fortunately she doesn't have it. She knows, and they've been married sixteen years. She doesn't deal with him sexually. My heart goes out to this brother. There's no hugs, there's no kisses, there's no intimate interaction between them. They just deal with the kids. She cooks dinner. That's it. He's miserable to the point where he's talking about how easy it is to commit adultery.

Meanwhile, he's getting ready to have a nervous breakdown, because he has no one to hold his hand. And that's what he's dying from. He's not dying from the virus. I understand her fear. Let him go. Or let him get another wife—someone who's going to take care of his needs. That can't be ignored. That doesn't go away because you have this virus. Touching and holding hands is something profound now. It's not the same anymore. It means something different now.

I remember sitting on a train and this old woman sat next to me, and she went to sleep, and she was leaning on me, and I was just thinking about the beauty of it. The warmth from her. The feeling of her leaning on me, and even when my little girl gets in the bed, I'm so aware of her presence in a way I was never aware before.

So I know what he's talking about.

But I also know what she's talking about.

I had remarried for a hot minute. For about four months to a brother I've known for fifteen years. He knew I had the virus; for four years he asked me to marry him, and I said no because he didn't have the virus.

I finally said yes, but I was uncomfortable the whole time in the marriage. Of course, we used protection. But all I could think about was suppose this thing breaks. My mind was full of supposes. I wanted to kiss. And I wouldn't kiss him. Because I was always worrying about it. I got *nothing* out of that intimately because I couldn't relax, no matter what he said. I don't want the responsibility of hurting somebody that way. So I believe that people with the virus should be with people who have the virus. I just couldn't deal with it anymore. Someone with the virus needs me much more than someone who doesn't have it.

The struggle is not about dealing with the AIDS virus. It's about recognizing the fact that Allah's in charge. It's that simple. People complicate things. People want what they want when they want it. And it's not like that.

I know Who to go to. I took a *shahada*. I entered into a covenant with Allah. I feel like I found that pot of gold at the end of the rainbow. It's almost like I can sense things. AIDS has made me understand who Allah is.

How do I see AIDS at this point? I see it as Allah having presented us with an outrageous opportunity to get our spiritual acts together. But I can't get up there with my spear and my shield and come from an Amazon center and say, "Now look! You all got to get up and do this!" I have to say in a gentler tone, "Protect us. Be there to support us when we run into these brick walls like this. We have work to do, even if it's unpleasant work. We have to protect our interests here."

My children are beautiful. All my girls know, except my youngest daughter. She's eight. I'll let her play with her Barbie dolls for now. Why should I traumatize this kid?

The oldest one, I felt she was becoming too curious about the outside world. She wanted to stick her feet in the water and play around a little bit. Telling her that she was Muslim and she shouldn't do it just wasn't working. I saw her on her way to becoming sexually active, so I said to her, "Now look, if I got this and I'm married, you don't stand a chance, okay? So you got to be *real* careful."

They cried. And I let them cry for a little while. And then I said, "Okay, you got to come back now. You stay too long, nobody can pull you out. You got to want to pull yourself out, and you won't be able to. C'mon out of that little black hole you're trying to crawl into. We got things to do."

I got them tested. They thought we were going for a routine visit to the pediatrician. Everything came out just fine. None of the kids are HIV-positive. I'm so grateful that my kids don't have the virus, I haven't stopped saying *Allahu akbar!*

Deliverance

Elias Sengor

Born Edward Green, Sengor, forty-four, lives in Boston. He had a dark
childhood, then led a life of crime, and was in and out of prison. Islam, he
says, delivered him from a cycle of crime, and today he lives on the better
side of the law, working as a security guard for a large New England
corporation.

He practices Islam as best he can, but isn't a regular at the local mosque
and doesn't let the brothers know much of his personal business. Sengor in
fact is his alias; he uses it because he is estranged from the mosque, princi-
pally because he is dating, and dating is anathema to Islam.

Until I was around ten or eleven, I believed that my grandmother was my
mother. Every now and then the person who I thought was my sister would
come home. Her name was Dorothy. I remember one time I was somewhere and they showed me this guy and they said, "That's your father."
But I never talked to him or got close to him. He was walking by.

My grandmother used to drink. When she got angry with me one time,
she was going to kick me out of the house. In so many words, she said,
"I'm not your mother; your sister's your mother, so get out of the house."

I was shocked. I didn't even think my mother was a good sister. She took
me to a bar. She wanted me to dance with her. At that time, I was about
fifteen or sixteen, and she was hittin' on me. Talking about, you know,
"You're handsome; your eyes . . ." The way she was talking was not the
normal way you talk to your child.

I hated everybody in that house almost. They'd beat my brother; they'd

173

beat me. I remember being tied up to the bed and being beat with garrison belts with big fat buckles. I remember something happened with my brother and my mother. And I remember my mother used to have one of these electric irons you had to heat up on the stove and then iron clothes with. I remember her heating it up on the stove and then knocking him down, sitting on him and ironing over his arms. He had scars all over his head from them beating up on him. I've got two. [*Points to forehead.*]

I was tricked into going to the mosque. I didn't know anything about Muslims at that time. This guy asked me, "You want to go out on Sunday and have a good time?" I thought he meant partying. So when Sunday came around I didn't want to go; I was in bed sleeping. I said, "I'm not going." The guy didn't want to hear it. He said, "You *said* you were gonna come." He made me feel guilty.

I came out in regular street clothes and he said, "Brother, you ain't got a suit or anything?" And I'm thinking to myself: What the heck kind of good time is this? Where the heck are we going? I put on a suit. I went downstairs. I saw that the brothers had bow ties on and their faces were shining like light bulbs and the sisters were with these long silk gowns on and I'm saying, What have I got myself into?

So they drove me up to Roxbury to the temple, and I saw all these sisters. I was kind of leery now. And they were showing me *Muhammad Speaks* in the car. All of this is totally new to me.

I remember having déjà vu, like I've been there before. I knew it was religious but I thought it was some kind of black church.

So this woman at the door asked me if I mind being searched. When she asked me that, I knew that this was not your average black church. I remember these big FOI[6] brothers, very big, and they said if you have any guns you have to leave them outside and you can pick them up later. They explained why they were searching. They had to keep the temple safe.

The assistant minister opened up the service. He was light-skinned and this brother was really down. One thing I liked was good oratory. I knew that nobody could outspeak this guy. He was speaking about basic teachings of the Honorable Elijah Muhammad. I remember there being a blackboard on the stage. On one side it had a cross and under the cross it had "Slavery, Suffering, and Death." And on the other side of this blackboard was this red star and crescent. Under it was "Freedom, Justice, and Equal-

6 Fruit of Islam.

ity." And above it was "Who will survive the war of Armageddon? Which will survive the war of Armageddon?"

He was talking about what happened to the black man under Christianity, how Christians had brought us here and what the Christians had done in the name of Christianity, et cetera. And he was breaking down, basically, Islam. He must have spoken for an hour and a half, maybe more. And then I saw this light-skinned brother walking down the side and he got up on the stage. He shook hands with the assistant minister and the assistant minister started introducing the minister, and he was Louis X.[7] The first person had me hook, line, and sinker. Now when Louis X got up and he started speaking, this brother was super fired up and I was hooked on Islam from the very first day.

Now this was about the time there was an instance when the police entered the temple in California, shot up the temple, brought seven brothers outside the temple in handcuffs, made 'em lay down on the ground, and shot 'em in the back—all seven. That was the main thrust of his speech. He was so fired up he hit the blackboard so hard that it was about ready to fall. The FOI soldiers grabbed the blackboard before it fell on the ground. I was hooked. I was scared in a way because he was talking about that incident in California. He said this could happen to any Muslims.

It was wall-to-wall people that day. I remember going right home to my grandmother's house that day. I was talking to my brother and telling him how happy I was going to the temple and that I'm a Muslim and this is what I want to be. And I remember buying some *Muhammad Speaks* newspapers, and I was showing him about certain things Louis X was teaching on. My brother told me, "Man, you better stop talking that. Your grandmother ain't going to like this stuff."

I went to New York when I was about eighteen and I didn't have a job or anything, so I met this guy in New York and he talked me into pulling armed robbery. So at eighteen I pulled a robbery and got away with it.

We went into a women's clothing store and he had a hand underneath his coat and robbed the clothing store. That was the first robbery that I had ever pulled. We parted ways after that and then I started robbing all by myself. It was like getting up in the morning and going to work and my work was pulling robberies.

I robbed a jewelry store in Manhattan around Fifty-sixth Street. I went

[7] He later became Louis Farrakhan.

into the store and this woman didn't want to give me the money, so I had to leave the store. I had a starter's pistol. When I went outside there was a crowd of people who were aware that something was going on inside, so I started walking and then started running and the crowd of people were after me. They were screaming, "Robbery! Robbery!" I went to this cab and put the starter's pistol to the cabdriver's head. The cabdriver was sitting there having his lunch. I told him to move the cab. I had a bus ticket for Boston. I told him to go to the Port Authority. He started driving and a car pulled up on one side of the cab. I put the starter's pistol out and told the guy to take off and he took off. The second car pulled up on the other side of the cab and I did the same thing. But the second guy just pulled his gun out and put it in the window of the cab and the cabdriver stopped.

They busted me up in the jail. I ended up admitting to robberies I didn't pull. They put a paper before me and said, "You *did* this." I was ignorant at the time. I was getting some healthy good stompings.

They sent me to Elmira, then to Green Haven [Correctional Facility],[8] and from there they transferred me to almost every prison in New York.

I wrote to the Honorable Elijah Muhammad in prison. The first time I wrote to him was to get my "X." I actually got my "X" in prison around 1967. I knew Islam good. When I got my "X" I was lieutenant in the FOI in Green Haven prison. You couldn't see me without the Bible, without the Qur'an, without the *Message to the Blackman*.[9] I was always deeply studying. By 1967 I was a different person.

It was because of Islam that my stuttering left me. One time I was in Green Haven prison. I knew Islam, but I was afraid to death to speak. Because in Islam you gotta speak. You had meetings and you gotta talk about lessons. You gotta talk about the Qur'an. You gotta talk about the Bible. You gotta talk about various things. I'd be frightened to speak. All the brothers was going around the circle and speaking about some of the lessons and it came to me and I remember saying, "I-I-I-I." And I remember them saying, "Brother, we don't have that here. You gotta speak here. If you can't speak you're going to have to leave." At that moment, and this is the honest-to-God truth, I spoke so good, they were like, "Where did this come from?" There wasn't a stuttering word in it.

Now when I went to Green Haven I immediately went to the brothers

[8] In Stormville, New York.
[9] By Elijah Muhammad, published in 1965.

and began to teach. I remember the brothers telling me immediately, "They're going to test you. They're going to roll on you"—talking about the staff. "They do this with every new Muslim that comes in, so be prepared for it." So when I was in Green Haven, I became one of the squad leaders of the temple, like a sergeant. I had Qur'ans and lessons in my cell.

Early in the morning I'm in bed asleep and this guard came to the cell and he said, "Crack this cell! Come outside!" But the brothers had already prepared me that something like this might happen. So I come outside and he says, "Get across the hall!" I did what he said. He sits on my bed and I remember him going through my things. He found this notebook I had with all the Islamic lessons, prayers, and the teachings of the Honorable Elijah Muhammad. And I remember him opening it up and ripping pages out and having a good time with my book. He opens up the Qur'an, throws it on the floor—all this is to make me irritable so something will happen. So I stood across the hall and he ended up taking the Qur'an and Bible, everything that was of Islam, and locked me up for having Islamic books.

Now my punishment for having Islam is to go to the strip cell where you're naked in the cell. They throw the blanket in at six o'clock at night and take it out at eight in the morning. Just the blanket. It's a segregated cell. This one you can see out of, but there is one that you can't see anything out of. I've been in that one too. That is the box. I was sent there for having Islamic literature.

Now when I came out I was more popular than when I went in. As a matter of fact, from a squad leader I moved up immediately to a lieutenant, so that was very good for them to do. [*Laughs.*] I appreciated that. As a matter of fact, all praise due to Allah, every time they would punish me it would be good. I would come out and get a higher rank. See, Allah was always with me.

We used to eat one meal a day. The guards used to try to force Muslims to eat pork. When the brothers were passing by the pork, they used to say, "You got to at least put it on your tray." Some brothers would say no, and when they said no, there would usually be a problem. Brothers would have to go to the box for their religion.

Over the years, Islam was getting to be more acceptable in prisons. You could start having more things. But when I first went in you couldn't have things. We gave Islamic services under duress. I mean, we were out there in the prison yards when it was snowing. We would be holding regular Islamic services. I used to see white guards on the gun towers. They'd be listening to my services or Thomas 15X Johnson's and we'd be firing up the convicts. A lot of times you can hear them guards clicking them guns like they just wanted to blow our brains out.

We did that year after year. At the same time we're going into courts to try to get them legal. The prison system tried to use tricks. First they said, Okay, you can have services. And one of the first things they did was try to bring orthodox Muslim ministers into the prison, which was not the Honorable Elijah Muhammad's ministers, and say, Okay, now you got Muslim services. So we had to demand to have our minister that represents our religion come in. And that took more years.

The first religious service that was authorized by the prison system in New York State, I conducted. Sing Sing prison was the first. This was '71 or '72. I know that for a fact because, see, we would hook up with all prisons. When the brothers came from Green Haven to Clinton, they'd tell all the brothers in Clinton what's going on in Green Haven. Plus we had all the legal writs from all the prisons. We knew all the prisons that was fighting for legal services.

Most of the people who entered Islam in the '50s and '60s were criminals or were poor. Even the Honorable Elijah Muhammad admitted that. Matter of fact, he said some of his best Muslims come from the prison houses. Whether they were poor or criminals, that doesn't change anything with the Honorable Elijah Muhammad as long as you change. And eventually there's going to be a change. I haven't been in prison since '76.

The Honorable Elijah Muhammad was like a father image to me. I never had a father. When I was in prison, he used to write to me sometimes, even after I got my "X."

I knew I was going to be a Muslim for life the first day I heard the service. I'm fanatical with things like that. It might take longer. If you were a criminal most of your life and all of a sudden you hear the truth, that don't mean you're going to change real quick. It might take time for you to change. Islam is not in the extreme like that. I would prefer to have just heard Islam and be in the mosque and be a minister now and just be rosy and everything perfect. My heart and mind was Muslim from the first day, but it was a gradual step. The first day was the major thing that started it. But the best thing that could have happened to me was to be in prison for those eleven years, to go through the abuse of prison. Because I seen the white man as he really is, not the face that he puts on out here. Mr. Nice

Guy. I seen the white man make Muslims go crazy. I seen the most violent situations that got to do with people who were just believing in Allah. I seen them beating brothers.

I remember this young Five Percenter, and I remember all the brothers went to the yard this one day and I stayed in the cell. About fifteen minutes before he came in I heard one of the guards say, "We got one of them sons of Allah coming over here. We're going to really show him."

The kid came over and he had one of them stars and crescents on. I remember them telling him, "Strip down! Take that star and crescent off!" I could hear the nightsticks hitting him. This was a young brother, no more than eighteen, nineteen years old. They're hitting him on all his joints. Every time they would hit that brother, that brother would scream, *"Allahu akbar!"* They would hit him again and say, "Yeah, say it again." He would say, *"Allahu akbar!"* and they'd hit him and you'd hear him speak at the same time.

That was stuff that was good for me. A lot of people in the street ain't seen that side of the white man. They think that the Honorable Elijah Muhammad is making this stuff up.

I went to one security company to see if I could get a job and they didn't ask the right questions, so I didn't give them the right answers. What they did ask, that's what they got. In one place I carried Mace and a nightstick. I have worked a security job close to ten years now.

> *[N]ay, but man shall against himself be an eyewitness,*
> *even though he may veil himself in excuses.*
>
> Qur'an 75:14–15

Ex-Gangster for God

Nadim Sulaiman Ali

Soft-spoken Nadim, a former gang member, is now a member of the Community Mosque of Atlanta, headed by Imam Jamil Abdullah Al-Amin (formerly H. Rap Brown) and attended by about 50 families. He came through gang wars unscathed and initially was attracted to Islam because he liked the way Muslims argued: nonviolently. He literally heard the call to prayer over the airways of a local radio station. He eventually answered the call, and now he is doing the calling.

Ali is a substance-abuse counselor at Charterbrook Hospital and a part-time broadcaster at WCLK. On radio, he deals mostly in jazz and "positive" lyrics. He uses Qur'anic verses to counsel unwitting patients. In doing so, he is "dropping little things" on patients in the hope of guiding them to Islam, just as he had been "dropped on."

We were basic knuckleheads.

One day [my eighth-grade teacher] came in and said, I'm tired of this stuff, and she put on El-Hajj Malik El-Shabazz's speeches. One day she played "The Ballot or the Bullet."[10] The next day she played "Message to the Grass Roots"[11] and that opened up my head—that started it.

I was a member of several gangs, in Chester [Pennsylvania] and in Philadelphia. I wasn't a gang leader, more a follower. Basic territorial things: This is *our* turf! And have fights at parties.

[10] Recorded in Cleveland, April 3, 1964.
[11] Recorded in Detroit, November 10, 1963.

180

One part of town was at a party in another part of town. A guy was getting ready to shoot [my brother] in the head and he aimed low and shot him in the leg. They were getting ready to take off his whole leg but they had to take off his foot.

[His brother later died of a drug overdose.]

I moved to Philadelphia after that. In Philadelphia, the gang I was with, they were a little bit more precise and more serious. They would say, We're going to kill such and such. And I wasn't ready for that type of activity. In Chester you shoot into the crowd, but in Philly they'd go to somebody's house and wait for 'em. I was probably about sixteen or seventeen.

Some people came through unscathed. I was one of the blessed ones. Allah allowed me to live.

I still have shotgun pellets in my chest from being at a party and somebody shot into the party—a guy who had been beaten up earlier. He came back with his shotgun and I happened to be dancing and the young lady I was dancing with got pellets all down her back. Right where I was standing, there was a big hole in the wall. That could have been me.

When I got involved at the radio station at Temple University, I was listening to WRTI and I heard the *adhan* for the first time. I thought it was a Nina Simone song. It was Sheik Abdul Bassett blowing the *adhan*.

I said, Wow, what is that? And then [the disc jockey would] say that's the *adhan*. And so then I went down there.

I was more into fusion jazz. [The disc jockey] was into mainstream jazz. He showed me the ropes. Basically he would take me around to different Muslims and we would go meet musicians who were struggling. He taught me to respect the music to the point that you don't go and play the big names; you play the guys who are still struggling because the big names are going to get theirs.

I knew people who had gone to prison and had become Muslim, and some of them were hypocrites and we used to call them "part-time Muslims," the ones who would come back and get high with us and sell papers on the corner.

Then the people who followed the *Sunnah*, basically they were very low-key. We saw them as real religious people, even though I knew some of them who were hypocrites. And when I became Muslim I would say to myself, I'm not going to be like them.

I lived around the corner from a mosque on Fifty-second Street. I waited until my birthday to take my *shahada*. I wanted it to be my *re*-birthday. Up until that point I was calling myself an agnostic. I just came to the realization that Islam was the way.

One of the things that made a good impression on me was seeing two Muslims argue. I didn't hear one word of profanity and they didn't fight; that really impressed me to see two guys who had been in prison and had the capacity for great violence.

I probably took my first drink when I was ten years old. January '78 I took my last drink, and in between there were drugs. And I had stopped using in that January. And the way I see drug usage now is that it's a spiritual experience but it's negative spirituality. When I stopped using drugs there was a big emptiness inside of me. Had I not found Islam I probably would have gone back to drug usage.

In March I became Muslim. Basically I was going through an internal revolution before there was an external change. People said, man, he's going crazy—he stopped drinking, he stopped smoking cigarettes, he stopped chasing girls—what's up with him? They thought I was having some type of mental breakdown. Basically I was going through a purge.

I got clean and put on my best clothes. I got *shahada* in what was known as the "gangster mosque." They weren't known for illegal activity; it's just that most of the guys that have come through have come through the gangs. In Philly you have several *masajid*.[12] In some of the mosques you have more like a professional type of congregation and in some mosques you have a congregation where most of the people have come through prison.

I went down to the radio station with my *kufi* on. At that time there were probably five Muslims on the air there. We were blowing the *adhan* there every day. Basically, for two years Temple University's radio station was run by Muslims. We called it the Islamic Broadcast Network. Also we had talk shows and had people call in and ask questions about Islam.

As a result, people reaffirmed their faith and became more serious about Islam, and people came to take *shahada*.

The name of my show was "Extensions of Congo Square." Oscar

---

[12] Plural of *masjid*, meaning mosques.

Young's show was "The Young Generation." Samir's was "Journey to Mecca."

I immersed myself [in Islam] on the air and that was my ministry, my *dawah*.[13] I would do documentaries, especially on Malik El-Shabazz. I also organized a band and did poetry with this jazz band.

There's four of us in the *Dawah* Ensemble. We do a cappella and I write most of the poems and the songs. Between songs, we explain Islam and use it as a *dawah* tool. Our policy is not to perform where alcohol is served. We'll go to college campuses. We'll go to bazaars and things like that. But we want people with clear heads listening to what we're doing. We want to wash and cleanse them, not to entertain; we're there to inform in an entertaining fashion.

I would play the *adhan*, then explain it in English and say the Jews call their followers by the horn. The Christians call their followers by the bells. But the Muslims call their followers by the human voice, the *adhan*. This was a commercial station, WIGO. I did that for a year.

I graduated in '77 and I came to Atlanta in '79. Came for a week and ended up staying for a year. There were only about fourteen brothers in the community at that time. I saw the fact that they were trying to follow the *Sunnah* and they were living in the same area and consistently coming to the mosque. That impressed me because in Philly and New York the mosque is usually in a business area and you live way across town, and so you come to the mosque and you can look righteous and everything, but if you live next door to a guy you got to be more consistent.

I encourage a lot of the kids to really work the spiritual aspects of the [hospital's drug rehabilitation] program. Basically I give them *hadith* and the Qur'an and I don't necessarily tell them where it comes from. You can say that basically there's an old saying and you got to do this and do that and do this. And there's a meeting and then I'm hearing the Qur'an being spouted by kids. They don't know it.

They have birthday celebrations, and I go there and one young lady's still quoting "Be a witness against yourself." That was one of the things that changed her therapy. She was a crack addict, and one of her big problems was dishonesty, and I said, "Look, you have to be a witness even against yourself." That's a straight-up *ayat*[14] out of the Qur'an. She said

13 Propagation.
14 Verse.

that basically changed her treatment experience. She took that and ran with it.

There were some other *ayats* that I would go to meetings and hear kids say that I had told them, and they're still using them today. My whole thing is to plant seeds so that when they do get exposed to Islam, they say, "Oh, *that's* what Nadim was saying."

Chapter Four

Ecstasy

Allah is the Light of the heavens and the earth. The parable
of His Light is as if there were a Niche and within it a Lamp:
The Lamp enclosed in Glass; the glass as it were a brilliant star:
Lit from a blessed Tree, an Olive, neither of the East nor of the West,
whose Oil is well-nigh luminous, though fire scarce touched it:
Light upon Light! Allah doth set forth Parables for men:
and Allah doth know all things.

Qur'an 24:35

The great mystical tradition in Islam is called Sufism, or *tasawwuf* (purity of faith and of heart). A Sufi is one who follows a path that he hopes will bring him nearer to Allah. The path, *tariqah*, consists of many stages, some of which are repentance and avoiding the sins of the past, spiritual poverty (feeling far from perfection and seeking it in Allah), continual remembrance of Allah (*zikr*), and abstinence even from what Allah has made lawful in order to avoid distractions.

A Sufi must trust entirely in Allah and wait in hope for divine revelation. Only then will all objects in the world vanish or fuse into the oneness of Allah. The Sufi will then experience self-annihilation, taking on divine attributes and joining Allah in love.

This union with Allah, *ma'rifah*, or gnosis, transforms the soul of the Sufi, even upon his return to the everyday world.

The path is dangerous, and only masters and their trained disciples are experienced enough to walk it alone, or under guidance from a dead master or the Prophet himself, without becoming so enraptured by Allah's graces that they forsake the world and lose their way back. Novices must be guided along the route, after becoming initiated as disciples in one of the many spiritual schools, or orders, that trace themselves back to the Prophet, or at least to Ali, his cousin and the third caliph after Muhammad's death.

Sufism depends on, and exists within, the bounds of exoterism, ultimately surpassing it.

It is believed that Sufis take their name from either *soof*, wool, because the first Sufis are said to have worn ragged woolen cloth and vowed poverty, or from *suff*, a row, because these men will be honored to stand in the first row before Allah on Judgment Day.

Some historians count the first Sufis (besides the Prophet) as being forty-five men from Mecca who renounced the life of the world to devote themselves almost entirely to meditation in the Prophet's mosque.

Historically, many influential Islamic philosophers and poets were Sufis —among them al-Hallaj, ibn 'Arabi, al-Jilani, al-Ghazali, al-Junaid, and Jalaluddin Rumi, whose order is popularly known as the Whirling Dervishes.[1]

Modern-day Sufis in America often maintain their own mosques and follow the guidance of a master who lives (or lived) thousands of miles away in the Old World—Africa, the Middle East, Turkey. Some orders teach disciples to travel the path while adhering strictly to the exoteric laws, the *shari'ah,* as practiced by one of the four main schools of Islamic jurisprudence: Hanbali, Maliki, Shafi'i, and Hanafi. Other American Sufis place decidedly more emphasis on the esoteric nature of the mystical teachings. And certain "folk" Sufis take only what they want from Sufi teachings (trance dancing and chanting, for example), and get high on "spiritual gymnastics."

---

[1] Coffee lovers owe a debt of gratitude to Sufis. The earliest mention of coffee dates back to the sixteenth century, when it was drunk especially in Sufi circles to induce the wakefulness needed for nighttime devotionals.

Thy Lord hath decreed that ye worship none but Him,
and that ye be kind to parents.

Qur'an 17:23

"Does That Mean You're Not Jewish?"

Selik Baba

(a.k.a. Selik Schwartz)

Selik Baba led devotional Sufi exercises at Masjid Al-Farah in Manhattan one weekday night. But first he gave a talk to some two dozen Sufis present. It was sort of a storytelling affair. People sat and sipped tea, ate grapes and crackers and cheese, and babies cried, and everyone smiled.

Selik was bearded, looked rumpled, and smoked incessantly. He sat on a sofa next to a hafiz, *a cantor who has memorized the 6,666 Arabic verses of the Qur'an. Selik began by telling a story about a dervish in Turkey who was under pressure from religious authorities for attracting Muslims to his mosque, leaving other mosques empty. The authorities summoned the dervish and questioned him about the meaning of* zikr—*remembrances of Allah by repeating either His attributes or the central Islamic affirmation, "La illaha ill Allah," signifying "There is no god but Allah."*

According to Selik, the dervish asked his audience whether they wanted him to tell them the meaning of zikr *as they understood it or as he understood it. The grand inquisitor said, I would like to know what you know. So the dervish sheik asked for assistance from one of his followers. They sat on the floor, said a prayer, and the sheik chanted, "La illaHA!"—and the assistant beside him vanished.*

The dervish finished the phrase, "ill AlLAH!"—and his assistant reappeared. The dervish repeated the phrase and all of the people in the room vanished and then reappeared.

187

Selik's audience listened attentively but, apparently accustomed to stories of such miracles, did not react.

Selik later told the story of how he came to Islam.

When I met my wife, she was not Muslim, and I never once said to her, "You should be Muslim." I never taught her anything about Islam unless she asked. When she met our Effendi,[2] she embraced Islam that night. And then she started to make her prayers, some days, some days not. I told her the times of prayer. I told her the names. Whatever she asked. You want to make your prayers, you make your prayers. Between you and Allah. But slowly, every morning she gets up and makes her prayers.

All of a sudden she's making more and more prayers. Soon, Allah brings her to her prayers, you see. I was always joyous when I saw the prayers, but I wouldn't praise her too much and make her uncomfortable. [*Raps knuckles on table.*] I keep knocking on wood because that's a Jewish tradition. I don't know, maybe a Muslim tradition, *al-hamdulillah.*[3]

My father, God bless him, may he have a long life, he's eighty-four years old and in good health for eighty-four. He has accepted everything I've ever done. He and my mother love me because I'm their son and no matter what I do they stand by me. And because they have been so kind and gracious to me I love them and stand by them. And when I embraced Islam I never said to them, "I embraced Islam."

They knew I used to do a radio program. They knew I went all over the Middle East, and that I said, *"La illaha ill Allah."*

And one day my father said, "You're Sufi. Now, Sufi, doesn't that have something to do with Islam?"

I said, "Yes."

He said, "What does that mean?"

I said, "Well, it means it has something to do with Islam." Just like what I did with my beautiful wife.

He said, "Well, what is this, Muslim or something?"

Just as I did with my beautiful wife, I said, "Do you really want to know?"

And he said, "Yes."

I said, "Well, it means that I have embraced Islam, that I am a Muslim."

And he says [*incredulously*], "No."

---

[2] Grand sheik of the Halveti-Jerrahi order, from Istanbul.
[3] All praise is due to Allah.

And I said, "Yes, that's what I did."

He says, "Does that mean you're not Jewish?"

I said, "I didn't say that. I have not said anything about Judaism. I am a Muslim. I pray as a Muslim. I've never told you because I'm not in the business of hurting you. You're my father, but I must live my life as I see it. But I don't try to flaunt it in front of you, my Islam."

Okay, time goes on. He asks me questions about Islam. As he asks, I answer. One day I'm sitting in the house and he lives about thirty-five miles from where I live and he says to me, "You know, I would like to read the Qur'an. Do you know how to get a Qur'an?" I stayed five more minutes, had some tea. I kissed him. "Bye-bye, got to go." I drove all the way home. I got a Qur'an. I came and I brought the Qur'an all the way back. I said, "Here, here's the Qur'an."

In New Jersey, there is a section set aside in the cemetery for Muslim burial, because a Muslim is buried facing the Ka'aba.[4] You know, it has to be a certain way, and not all cemeteries will provide that because it has to be on an angle, and that means you get fewer grave sites. But we worked something out. We bought grave sites, and I went to my father and asked permission to be buried as a Muslim with my brother Jerrahis, rather than to be buried with my family in that graveyard.

My father, *al-hamdulillah*, gave me permission. Now if he said, "You'll have to be buried next to me," I would have been buried next to him—because he's my father. But he gave me permission that I can be buried with my brothers.

Now, *hamdulillah,* may my time come. May you say *Fatihahs*[5] for this poor man here. I just want to know who's going to wash me, that's what I want to know.[6]

[4] The stone, cubic building in the Grand Mosque in Mecca toward which Muslims turn in prayer.
[5] The opening chapter of the Qur'an, the *Fatihah* sura, which is said in the Islamic prayer.
[6] A Muslim ritual is to wash the dead before burial.

The Night of Power is better than a thousand months.

Qur'an 97:3

The Dream

Sheik Nur Al Jerrahi
(a.k.a. Lex Hixon)

In the back room of the Masjid Al-Farah on West Broadway in Manhattan, the sheik, leader of a Sufi order, sat in an easy chair near a photograph of his beardless leader awash in bright light. There were a few turbans on a table nearby. Sheik Nur, blond, barefoot, wore a green robe and a woolen vest. He concentrated on sharing his energy, rather than giving "informational" answers to questions, he said later.

There is only Allah's will, so that every single detail of a person's childhood is something which is known by this infinite will from before eternity. The soul in Islam doesn't just suddenly spring into being at the time of birth, it exists from pre-eternity. It contains all of the knowledge of the ages. And only a small part of this knowledge is Allah going to permit to manifest in a given lifetime. The soul is this way whether it consciously embraces Islam or not. And some souls have the destiny and the divine permission to embrace historical Islam. Others have the permission to embrace others of the great noble traditions. Others maybe have the permission to manifest truths without being part of one of the major traditions of humanity. There's not a single soul that doesn't come from Allah and that isn't bearing all this richness and pre-knowledge that is given to the soul as the crown of creation.

When one becomes a sheik one never thinks in terms of a limited personality, but sees all of one's life, one's childhood and education as just a bridge—and a very narrow bridge at that—that took one to the place where one met one's sheik and began spiritual exercise and eventually

190

where one dissolved into the affirmation *La illaha ill Allah*. The narrow bridge is a bridge going forward into the Paradise of unity. Beneath this bridge are the distractions of conventional society. One cannot fall into any of those distractions, whether they be financial distractions or even religious distractions. You can only walk on the bridge if you want the truth. Eventually you reach Paradise, which is a level of consciousness, a level of *tauhid*,[7] of unity.

The person on that bridge *was* Lex Hixon.

My first contact with Islam was when I was seventeen years old. I was visiting a friend in Washington, D.C. In the afternoons I used to walk by what was then probably the only major freestanding mosque in the United States, the Islamic Center with domes and with Islamic architecture. I had a great sense that it was something important.

Once, I knocked on the front door. There was no one there. Something drew me and I went around to the back of the building. I lifted one of the windows and I just climbed right into a classroom. I went upstairs, and there was a shoe rack there with a couple of old slippers in it. I took off my shoes and I went into the *masjid*. I was there all alone for about a half hour. I was sitting on a beautiful rug, feeling the rich spiritual atmosphere. Then I took my shoes in my hand and walked out the front door.

My conscience began bothering me: Maybe that front door didn't lock properly. Maybe that person who's in charge of this place will be blamed for something. I went back and knocked hard. I shouted. Finally a super came up from the basement. I showed him exactly what I did. I showed him where the windows were open. He wasn't upset, for some reason.

I told this story to my sheik, Muzaffer.[8] His only comment was "That was when you were taken."

While in graduate school at Columbia University studying world religions, I got involved in a radio station in New York. For fourteen years I did a weekly interview with spiritual leaders and teachers of all different orders. And on that radio station is where I met my two grand sheiks. One is Bawa Muhaiyaddeen from Sri Lanka, who has his mosque in Philadelphia and who passed away in 1986. I interviewed him eleven times over the years and became very close to him.[9]

---

[7] Belief in the oneness of God.
[8] The late Sheik Muzaffer Ozak from Istanbul, leader of the Halveti-Jerrahi order.
[9] A book, *Truth and Light,* consists of radio interviews between Hixon and Bawa Muhaiyaddeen.

Sheik Nur Al Jerrahi.

The other grand sheik was Muzaffer Ozak. I also interviewed him on radio. I didn't have a chance to meet Sheik Muzaffer before interviewing him. I just saw him sitting there very quietly. We arranged all of the microphones, and I asked for the program to begin with the call to prayer. Then the sheik sat down in front of me, and as the show was broadcast from the top of the Empire State Building (this makes the Empire State Building the world's tallest minaret)—as this call to prayer was going, I looked at the sheik. There were tears coming out of his eyes. I thought: What spiritual authenticity! He hears this call five times a day, and yet he still sheds tears when he hears it.

Later I found out that that wasn't the right interpretation, that actually he was shedding tears because he recognized me as his *califa,* as his successor, his representative. Every sheik has several. There's a real democracy in a dervish order. Nobody feels more special than anybody else. That's what makes it a precious place to be.

That was on a Sunday. And then on a Tuesday night, the sheik was giving his first *zikr*[10] at the Cathedral of St. John the Divine. Through one

[10] Remembrance of Allah in which dervishes recite His names or attributes.

of his dervishes he sent me a rose. And I decided not to enter the circle of devotees.[11] I stood at the side holding the rose, and he kept looking at me from the center of the circle. And then he invited me to come that Thursday night to Spring Valley, New York, where he was going to make a *zikr* and where he was staying. Before he left, he kissed me on the forehead. It was a very powerful form of spiritual transmission.

That night I was looking at the book of the 99 names of Allah. Two names were very attractive to me above and beyond the others. One of them was Aziz, the All-Powerful, the Beloved. And one was Nur, the Divine Light. I kept them close to my mind and heart as I went to sleep. And then on Thursday I went to his place.

As I was driving there, I was repeating, *"La illaha ill Allah"* out loud. And when I got there the first thing that Sheik Muzaffer said to me was "We heard you coming." A great sheik covers his miraculous powers. They don't flaunt them in any way. They just hint at it, and if you pick it up and if you accept it, that is something for you.

That night we did *zikr* together. The next morning, he said, "I'd like to make you my dervish. And I'd like to leave you an Arabic name. He said, "Your name is Nur." And I said, "I have a name for you: Aziz"—because of those two names that I was thinking about. And all the dervishes were shocked because Aziz was his secret name in our order.

That summer, Ramadan[12] was in August. He asked me to come to Istanbul and spend the Ramadan with him. He said that in order to prepare for that I should offer 70,000 *"La illaha ill Allah"*: 700 a day for a hundred days, which I did. (And had a lot of important experiences in that process.) And when I got to Istanbul, that was where I received the initiation in the order.

It happened in a funny way. There were no English translators that night. There were a couple of hundred Turkish men, and Turkish women were in a different part of the *tekke*.[13] They're not visible because of that particular form. In our *tekke* here, the men and women sit together and make the *zikr* together—in two separate circles but together.

The sheik just clapped his hands and called for this very old, threadbare, beautiful rug, which was brought out. He knelt on it, and his two senior *califas* took me by the arms and led me along these four steps: *shari'ah,*

---

[11] A common practice of Sufis is to worship in a circle.
[12] Ramadan, the ninth month of the lunar calendar, is the Islamic month of fasting.
[13] Sufi gathering place or lodge.

tariqah, haqiqah, and *ma'rifah,*[14] which represent the entire spiritual path. I knelt knee to knee with the sheik and we grasped right hands. All of this time, I didn't really know exactly what was happening. There was no translator. I got the impression that it was some sort of initiatory event. He gave me *shahada.* He also gave me hand in the order.[15] And he made this long prayer (he was very gifted in prayer, in *duah*—ten, fifteen minutes he could go on and on with these magnificent prayers). Everyone was weeping, and everyone wanted to kiss me.

The next day, someone came up to me who knew a little English. He said, "What does it feel like to have changed your religion?" Since I was raised as a free thinker with no religious tradition, I didn't feel I'd changed my religion. I felt that this was the affirmation of the one religion which belongs to humanity, which comes in different forms in different cultures in different times, which is based on the one truth, and which is itself unity. So the religion of unity I don't believe anyone can ever change. I think it belongs to everyone by their nature.

In Istanbul the sheik had the inspiration to make me a sheik. But it was too overwhelming a responsibility for me at that time. I was frightened by the prospect. I didn't want the responsibility. I didn't want to have anything to do with being a spiritual guide, a spiritual leader.

So I ran away from Istanbul on the Night of Power in Ramadan[16] in 1978. I remember leaving the *tekke* and not being able to find my shoes; there were just mountains of shoes there that belonged to the hundreds of dervishes who had come for the blessed Night of Power. So I had to walk out on the street barefoot. I can remember the smooth cobblestones underneath my feet that had been worn smooth by hundreds and hundreds of years of cart traffic. I was running and weeping through the streets of Istanbul in my stocking feet. I felt like a bride that ran away from the altar. And I went back to the hotel and packed my things and went to the airport. The next morning I caught a plane and came back to the United States. The Effendi was very, very shocked. He suffered a great deal.

---

[14] Exoteric law, Sufi path, intrinsic truth, and gnosis.

[15] Receiving hand is an initiatory rite in Sufism.

[16] The Night of Power (*Laylat al-Qadr*) is the night in the year 610 during which the entire Qur'an was invested into Prophet Muhammad's soul. This occurred during one of the last ten nights of Ramadan, thus the last ten days of the month are particularly holy. Although there is no Islamic source to substantiate it, common belief holds that the Night of Power is the twenty-seventh of Ramadan.

But the ostensible reason was I didn't want the responsibility. I was running away from the office rather than running toward it, which is a very good sign. Several of the members of the order were making the analogy between Jalaluddin Rumi[17] and Shamsi Tabriz, who met in Konia, and Shamsi disappeared and Rumi was in anguish.

When the sheik came to America the next fall, I met him and I embraced him. Absolutely nothing was ever said about my strange disappearance. No one ever scolded me. I was more welcome than ever.

There's love play between Allah and the soul, between the soul and its Lord, between the sheik and the dervish. There are pangs of separation, and there's the delight of the union. And those states alternate, and that alternation has a kind of alchemical effect, to purify the being and to elevate the being. So it all happens by divine permission. We don't attribute it to personality.

Anyone who has taken initiation in the order, I'm in love with them in a passionate sense, not in an abstract sense of saying, Well, I love all humanity. It's not something biological, but it's something passionate. It's like a fire inside.

One time I heard Sheik Muzaffer say to a rabbi who joined our order and was away for several months, "My blood has been boiling to see you." And this is a Sufi sheik talking to a rabbi.

The Islamic world has its conventional religious world where sheiks and rabbis are not supposed to be in love with each other. In the Sufi world all of those conventional differences fall away. The Berlin Wall has always been down in the Sufi world. And the wall between Arab and Jew, and the wall between Christian and Muslim, and the wall between other great noble traditions and Islam—all those walls in Sufism and the mystic order. It doesn't mean that we adopt other religious forms. We stay with the pillars of Islam and with the *Sunnah* of the Prophet Muhammad, upon him be peace. But we express it in a totally universal manner, in which there are no more barriers or walls.

After that first visit in '78, Sheik Effendi came about fourteen times to the United States. He was in love with America and in love with Americans in this same passionate way. He found the Medina of the heart in New York City and established the mosque here, which is called the Masjid Al-

---

[17] Persian mystic, founder of one of the oldest orders of Sufis, known in the West as the Whirling Dervishes. He lived 1207–73.

Farah, which means the *masjid* of the Eids[18] that one experiences in Paradise.

I was given the responsibility for the mosque. Spiritual leadership is something much more subtle than I ever imagined it would be. And many times, just as I ran away from Istanbul, I've tried to run away from the Masjid Al-Farah. And I realized that's also a good sign. Because someone who wants to be a spiritual leader, there's probably a greater danger that their ego will be involved than someone who doesn't really want it and who does it anyway.

Muzaffer Effendi was a rare saint, the type that comes only once in several hundred years. We're always thinking of him as our guide, and as the one who's in the center of our circle along with our founding saint, Pir Nureddin Jerrahi, who died in 1721.

At the height of the Jerrahi order in Istanbul there were as many as 60 different *tekkes* of the Jerrahi dervishes. But in the '20s Kemal Atatürk[19] took over Turkey, and in an attempt to modernize Turkey he outlawed the dervish orders. Very few of them actually survived. Our order was one of the few that did and was very much underground.

Around 1960, when Sheik Muzaffer took over the reins of the order from the previous grand sheik, he opened the doors of the *tekke* to the public for the first time since Atatürk had outlawed the orders. To this day the dervish orders are technically illegal in Turkey. But the government doesn't have any negative feeling about them. They're not engaged in any kind of political action, so there's no problem. Now the present grand sheik in Istanbul has hundreds of new dervishes coming in.

There are dervish orders in Egypt, and Sudan has some three million dervishes. In various points of Islamic civilization, the vast majorities of societies were involved with mystic orders. In Pakistan today, approximately one-third of the families have some connection with a mystic order. In Senegal at least two-thirds of the population are members of the Tijaniyya order,[20] founded in the 1800s. So we shouldn't think of Sufism or the mystic orders as sort of a small minority, necessarily. It's meant to be a guide for Islamic civilization. A mystic order is meant to be a microcosm of the whole society where people really get to know each

[18] Two Islamic festivals.
[19] Kemal Atatürk (1881–1938), first President of Turkey (1923–38).
[20] The Tijaniyya order was founded by Ahmad at-Tijani (1737–1815).

other and go beyond roles and the kind of abstract division of roles in society.

In Mexico, we have a woman who leads our *zikr* and who's the head of the community there. She has the permission from the grand sheik in Istanbul to do this. She doesn't lead the prayers. A man leads the prayers in Islam because that's the *Sunnah*. That was the way that the Holy Prophet, upon him be peace, did it. So we like to preserve those beautiful ancient ways of behaving.

The Prophet, upon him be peace, was extremely sensitive to women. He had nine wives, whom he adored and whom he attended to with more care and attention than the usual husband gives to one wife. And so that we feel that following his way, the love and courtesy of men to women, is something very essential in Islam. We don't defend various cultural patterns which have sprung up in so-called Islamic countries which might be seen to be oppressive of women. But we hold basic equality of men and women.

In the Islamic world many times women are encouraged to make their prayers at home and the men come to mosques. It's just a cultural pattern, and it's not a really good judgment about where the devotion is, where the people of prayer are. There are both men and women in great numbers.

But in the dervish orders it's quite different from a public mosque. You're going to a family in which men and women practice together so that the dervish women are encouraged to come to the *tekke* to practice the *zikr* just as much as the men are encouraged.

Allah puts one into a certain spiritual state. Sheik Nureddin Jerrahi is sitting in my heart, in my breath, in my entire nervous system as I conduct the *zikr,* and that's part of the authenticity of the *zikr.* Sheik Muzaffer said to me that I have the permission of Allah, of the Prophet of Allah, and of Nureddin Jerrahi to conduct the *zikr.* That kind of permission is absolutely necessary. It's a little bit like the mass in Christianity. The priest is ordained and the ordination comes from laying on of hands—let's say, taking hand—from bishops who became bishops because someone laid hands on them. It goes all the way back to Jesus, upon him be peace, when he laid his hands on his disciples and his apostles. So that in Roman Catholicism and in Eastern Orthodox Christianity, there is what's called apostolic succession, that the priest has been ordained by a historical process, which is unbroken. Therefore, the mass is valid and is powerful and it's not just a symbolic ceremony, but it's a place where divine reality is revealed and the communicants actually receive the divine energy in this ceremony.

I can worship along with everyone of every faith. I feel entirely comfortable with that because I don't believe that there are pluralities of faith. I don't believe that I changed my religion. I don't have the opportunity often to pray in a synagogue, but I'm sometimes with friends on their Friday-evening Shabbat meal. But I have a much more active connection with Eastern Orthodox Christianity, with Hinduism, and with Buddhism.

Islam is like a world organ. It's fourteen centuries old. It has immense subtleties and complexities, and since it's decentralized, there's no central authority who can say this is Islamic and this isn't. One can certainly speak of Islam as a totally unified expression, even though when one goes into the details, one can almost get lost. And in the apparent contradictions and disagreements between different Islamic practitioners—we consider that healthy, because it means decentralization—the truth is being worked out in the conscience of individual people and it's not being imposed from above.

Religious tradition exists to free people and to make them sense their direct connection with Allah Most High. So it's very difficult with genuine religion to control anyone or to oppress anyone. But we seek often a religion used precisely to control and oppress people. That means it's not genuine religion.

The real miracles are the change of a person's entire life when they take hand in the order and they become entirely new people. Suppose someone has a broken arm and you touch it; it's healed. How can that miracle compare with a whole life being changed? Everyone who takes hand has that experience. Everyone. True miracles are universal and democratic; they're not just isolated instances.

Many times a dervish will come to a sheik with a lot of straight questions and the sheik will respond with humorous or with mysterious responses that don't seem to mean anything. In Sufism that's the way the limited intellect is bypassed. That's why we follow dreams very much because in a dream the limited intellect is bypassed.

In our order we do everything by way of dreams. It's like the beloved Joseph, the protector of Jesus, upon him be peace. He knew by dreams when to take the holy family to Egypt in order to protect it, and when to bring it back again. We operate similarly.

Very good dervishes keep a dream book. If I have an important dream I send it to the grand sheik in Istanbul. I write it out and translate it and send it to him. He has hundreds of dervishes with hundreds of dreams.

The most memorable dream I ever had is a dream about being with the Prophet Muhammad, upon him be peace, in Paradise, and having him explain to me all the different mystical levels of being and showing me them all. And that was the dream I had about several weeks after I met the Effendi. We were together six days only, and then after that I had this dream and that was the dream that indicated I would be a sheik. The Effendi knew it already. He didn't have to wait for the dream but the dream was for my benefit.

My feeling is that the dreams don't belong to the individual dervishes. They belong to the whole mystical community, and by extension they belong to all humanity. If anyone can benefit from these dreams, then they're welcome.

One of the other most memorable dreams that I had was on the airplane coming back from Istanbul after having visited Effendi, my second visit. I dreamt that I was laying out a blanket on a dirt-floored mosque in Arabia, and on the blanket the Prophet Muhammad, upon him be peace, was going to lie down for his afternoon nap. He lay down and I took the end of the blanket and folded it over his eyes to shield him from the sun. In Islam, a dream of the *rasoolullah,* upon him be peace, is considered to be the summit of all possible experience, even more magnificent than seeing the divine light and disappearing into the divine light. The divine light actually came forth in the form of this most beautiful human being, Muhammad of Arabia, so that all of the spiritual aspirations of humanity could be sealed and brought to fruition.

When I was circumambulating the holy Ka'aba in Mecca, I really doubted whether I was even a true Muslim. What was I doing here? And at the time, I thought that that was a horrible experience to have. But then I realized it was a great blessing, because in the *hajj* everything was stripped away. Every pretension was stripped away, even the pretension of being a true Muslim, of having the right to be there. So that was a God-given experience of great blessing.

When I was in Medina—which is the pièce de résistance, you might say, of holy valleys—I had a dream that I was able to ask a question of the Prophet Muhammad. I wasn't mature enough to be able to see him in the dream. I asked him, "What does it mean in the Holy Qur'an when Allah

Most High said that every being on every plane of being is spontaneously bowing to Allah with every action, with every thought?" And he responded with the *Ikhlas*,[21] a sura from the Qur'an in which it's indicated that the entire universe is simply the attributes of Allah praising the essence of Allah—that there are no worlds, no living beings, nothing apart from the divine attributes, the divine energies. And their nature is to praise their source.

[21] Sura CXII, *Al Ikhlas,* (The Purity of Faith)
  In the name of Allah, Most Gracious, Most Merciful.
  (1) Say: He is Allah,
      The One and Only;
  (2) Allah, the Eternal, Absolute;
  (3) He begetteth not,
      Nor is He begotten;
  (4) And there is none
      Like unto Him.

  Translation: A. Yusuf Ali.

Chapter Five

The Rich and Famous

And [have We not] raised thee high in dignity?

Qur'an 94:4

Bijan Pakzad, the Iranian immigrant famous for his chic perfume ads, runs a Rodeo Drive fashion and fragrance empire, counts kings and presidents and pashas among his clientele, and is said to be among the highest-priced haberdashers on the planet. For a cool half million dollars, he flies his private jet to faraway palaces to sell his wares. But in the face of the dazzling wealth the world has come to expect from oil czars, Pakzad's fortune, no matter how many millions, pales by comparison.

The richest man in all the world is a Muslim: Sultan Haji Hassanal Bolkiah Mu'izzaddin Waddaulah, better known as the Sultan of Brunei. So stupendously wealthy is he that all of the $1, $2, $5, and $10 bills (U.S. currency) in circulation would not equal his fortune. In fact, all of the $50 U.S. bills in circulation would amount to a sum that is more than $2 billion shy of his fortune, estimated at $37 billion.[1]

The forty-six-year-old sultan and his family are joined by two other Muslims whose vast fortunes place them among the world's richest eleven: King Fahd ibn Abdul-Aziz of Saudi Arabia ($10 billion) and Kuwait's Sheik Jaber al-Ahmed al-Sabah and his family ($7.1 billion).

Their oil revenues, real estate and foreign investments, coupled with virtually unimaginable spending sprees, can inspire awe in the rest of human-

---

[1] Brunei, a small corner of the island of Borneo, has oil and gas reserves which the sultan controls. *Fortune* magazine reported that he was driven through the streets in a gilded chariot drawn by forty men on the twenty-fifth anniversary of his accession to the throne. He owns 165 Rolls-Royces.

ity. But their fame is not directly proportionate to their holdings. American Muslims, it would seem, have cornered the market on fame. Muhammad Ali and Kareem Abdul-Jabbar, each of whom has transcended his sport, claim fans in every corner of the globe, even among the richest of the rich.

Ali's and Abdul-Jabbar's appeal at home and abroad has perhaps been strengthened in part because they had the courage to declare their Islamic beliefs in spite of America's proclivity for regarding Islam as a religion of firebrands and zealots and black racists. Jimmy Breslin once called Ali a "Muslim and a bedbug," and William F. Buckley, Jr., begged someone, anyone, to knock "sense into Clay's head before he's done damaging the sport."[2] Times have changed.

Before Cassius Clay (as Ali was known then) snatched the heavyweight boxing crown from Sonny Liston on February 25, 1964, Elijah Muhammad, head of the Nation of Islam, warned that Malcolm X shouldn't get too close to Clay; if he lost the fight it would embarrass the Nation. But after Clay won, Elijah swallowed his reticence. He claimed Clay had won because he had "accepted Muhammad as the Messenger of Allah." He later gave Clay the name Muhammad Ali; Muhammad means Praiseworthy, and Ali was a cousin of the Prophet and the third caliph after the death of Prophet Muhammad.

Despite the outcry and the rejection back home, Ali was welcomed all over the Muslim world—in Pakistan, Indonesia, Turkey, Tunisia, Saudi Arabia—as a brother Muslim; ultimately he and Abdul-Jabbar after him probably gained millions more admirers and fans worldwide as a result of their conversions and their conviction.

Ali's conversion to Islam brought him membership in the Nation of Islam. It had been a repudiation of white America, Christianity, pork chops, slave names, blue-eyed devils, and "house Negroes." Abdul-Jabbar went for mainstream Islam, which was quite different and yet viewed at the time as antimainstream as anything Elijah Muhammad could have dreamed up. Ali was labeled a "Black Muslim"; Abdul-Jabbar was identified with an American Hanafi Muslim leader who is black.

Ali and Abdul-Jabbar chalked up success after success, and as their fame spread, fans took a more avid interest in what made them tick. In their own ways, they championed the cause of Islam over public airways, introducing it to millions insofar as athletes could propagate it through sports.

[2] Muhammad Ali with Richard Durham, *The Greatest: My Own Story* (New York: Random House, 1975), p. 203.

Their *jihads* were both personal strivings for self-improvement and public struggles involving Islamic ideals. The two athletes also followed Elijah Muhammad's lead, heading a wave of American-born Muslim millionaires that now includes people like Mujahid Ali (a.k.a. Clarence C. Lilley).

Over the years, Ali's and Abdul-Jabbar's Islamic practices converged, principally because Ali moved toward orthodoxy.

Still propagating, Ali moves through crowds, distributing Islamic pamphlets. His daughter May May (Maryum) writes and sings rap lyrics that are reminiscent of his "Float like a butterfly / Sting like a bee" poetry, except they include Qur'anic verses.

Malcolm's oldest daughter, Attallah, meanwhile, is a model, producer, and writer who lives in New York and maintains an office in Los Angeles.

Gift of God

Attallah Shabazz

Four of Malcolm X's six daughters witnessed almost unimaginable horror in the Audubon Ballroom on February 21, 1965, when a sawed-off double-barreled shotgun roared, at point-blank range, to rip a hole dead center in their father's chest. As one of the children wailed, asking if the assassins were about to kill everybody, their mother, Betty Shabazz, managed to shove them all under the seat and to shield them with her body.

Children and mother survived that traumatic event and the sad days to follow, their lives forever scarred, haunted by memories of flying bullets and confusion and the man they loved dearly lying lifeless on the floor of a dank ballroom.

Attallah Shabazz, Malcolm's oldest daughter, bears his complexion and facial features, his serious, straitlaced mien and regal posture. She's tall and slender and wears her hair long and braided in an elongated bun down her back. She has green eyes, at least according to her driver's license, although they look bluish or grayish, "depending on who's seeing them."

As a child, she created original "collaborations" ("music, art, dance, recitation, and tears and laughter") bridging the gap between peoples and cultures living here ("hence showing that we're related some way or another in terms of the drumbeat or the heartbeat"); majored in international law at Briar Cliff College; didn't graduate ("I had to make a living"). She writes, lectures, produces.

For lunch at one of her favorite LA haunts, a bistro, she wore a black leather jacket; with sunglasses dangling from a strap around her neck, she

cheek-kissed a Lebanese waiter and sat at a booth for an hour and a half,
talking about her life.

When you read the tenets of a lot of religions, some of them indeed have
similarities. So when my grandmother said to me, "You be a good little
Christian girl when you go to school today," and when my mother said,
"You be a good little Muslim girl," they actually meant the same thing.

I am comfortable and pleased to be of a religion that claims or grounds
itself in a sense of brotherhood, and it's not worth my altering or changing.
But I would say that I'm probably pretty reformed in comparison to others
who would have me act or function as per the suggestions of another
human being.

My parents did me either a favor or an injustice by telling me when I was
three or four that God was my friend no matter what, so that it mattered
not what another human being said in terms of how I should put one foot
in front of the other. Even if my parents were mad at me today, I knew that
God was still my friend. So I'm very comfortable Islamically. My attire and
my manner of living are probably very close to that of the culture that I
was surrounded by. But I'm not doing it simply because of that; it's just
what feels comfortable for me, Miss Shabazz.

My father was my first friend. My partner in crime. Just someone with
whom I could share things. Most people are afraid of their parents or have
to hide certain things from their parents, because they don't want to be
wrong in their eyes. I didn't feel wrong about a viewpoint, a thought—I
could share anything that came across my mind. I wasn't judged "less
than" because I didn't follow the patterns that they expected. It was okay
to be my individual self.

My father, who was so very focused and directed, really believed in
flexibility of thought and development and growth. Otherwise he wouldn't
have grown so.

Your name?

Attallah. People have to understand the autobiography[3] was written at a
time when indeed African Americans were likening themselves to warriors
to underscore our revolutionary fervor. And Attallah was close to Attila
the Hun, the warrior.[4]

[3] *The Autobiography of Malcolm X,* 1965.
[4] Lived 406?–453. King of the Huns, 433?–453. Called "the Scourge of God."

But I'm named Attallah, which in Arabic means "Gift of God." I've never been Attila.

I say more than five prayers a day. For a number of reasons. In terms of making *salat,* I say them because I'm on a plane two or three times in a day. I say it because I'm racing. My day is cluttered and I don't want to attend the next thing as if I'm carrying baggage from the old things. So I pray all day.

I think life is predestined, prewritten, and if you trust yourself and the rhythm that is preset, the answers come to you. The struggle comes through denial. Such as when you get that instinct to make a left turn and you dispute it and make a right turn, and then you have to circle around and make a U-turn to get back on track.

I've related to God closely enough, and been accompanied by Him such that as a child I thought He was in the room, knowing when a thought came to mind, when a feeling came to heart. In terms of my survival and dealing with the fact that my father was taken from me at an early age, I recognize the patterns in his life and accept the fact that we were all here for a reason. And though mortally I would rather he were alive today, I look at his heritage and messages—he was here long enough to pass on a

Attallah Shabazz.
PHOTO: ANTHONY BARBOZA

bit of something one way or another. Kahlil Gibran[5] says—we're all here to go through a passage, and as conduits.

I'm not weighted by the *jihad*. There is a *jihad*, but I don't hurt myself trying to figure it out. It comes to you, whether you're facing the east, whether you meditate, whether you say a prayer, whether you lie still at night before you go to sleep. We ache and stress ourselves trying to do things as per the pattern or the time frame that is preset. But then you go to another country, and they take two hours to eat a meal. They don't fret. They do it by the sundial. They don't get penalized for taking too long. I mean, we do everything so quickly here, and we're so shaped by judgment.

In your father's autobiography, he said, "Islam is the only religion that gives both husband and wife a true understanding of what love is. The Western 'love' concept, you take it apart, it really is lust. But love transcends just the physical. Love is disposition, behavior, attitude, thoughts, likes, dislikes—these things make a beautiful woman, a beautiful wife." Do you agree?

Uh-huh.

Do you see fundamental differences in the concept of love under Islam and in the West?

I see the fundamental differences between love and lust, and that America or the West practices lust and mistakes it for love. . . . I understand young men think that they are *supposed* to follow through, and that they are corny if they don't attempt to kiss a girl. You listen to women who have gone on a date, and the gentleman has behaved platonically, or respectfully, and then they wondered if something's wrong. And I certainly don't want to do anything that I want to have to detract or take back, so I don't act fast on things like that.

Another thing in the autobiography: Alex Haley wrote that on the spur of the moment, around Christmas, he bought two large dolls and gave them to your father to give to you and your sister.[6]

[5] 1883–1931. Poet, philosopher, artist born in Lebanon. Author of *The Prophet*, first published in 1923.
[6] Ballantine Books edition, p. 461.

It was my birthday.

And it really touched him, your father, because it says in the autobiography that he himself never bought you a gift because he was too busy.

No, he did, but he was running late, that's all. But that didn't matter to me. A child just wants you there. But when you want to give to your children, only you know what's missing. You know what you're not able to provide by the end of the week. It haunts you. But for a kid, as long as you read them that story, or they could sit on your lap, or you could slap five, or whatever that is, that's all that was really important.

There were a few warm moments when he and I were alone. If he picked me up from school and our time afterwards. You know, you'd feel like you were both riding bareback. He just made you feel like you were buddies. My first love was my mother. But my father indeed, I didn't think of him as older, because he didn't make you feel like you were "less than" because you were younger. So you kinda felt like you could share anything that was on your mind.

I had a real heartbeat crush on Frederick Douglass,[7] who I thought I was going to marry. I thought love meant that you married him. My parents loved each other, they got married. And he told me that I couldn't marry him—because he was no longer here. I remember feeling robbed. I really thought he was a wonderful person—from what I was learning of him. And [my father] went on to share more with me about who Frederick Douglass was, and actually brought a book home once, so that I could fill in the blanks and learn more about this person.

After each child in my family was born, there would be a gathering at the home, and I remember overhearing a gentleman from the Nation say to [my father], wow! implying too bad it was another girl. I asked him later did he wish that I was a boy, and he told me no, that I love you just as you are. And he went on to tell me how special I was and the rest of my sisters were; so that when gender became a question in my adolescent years and my young adult years and the struggle that many women have in this society, because *he* told me that I was special, I've been fine.

That day, February 21, 1965—you said that you remember everything. Did you see your father falling?

---

[7] 1817?–1895; abolitionist, lecturer, writer, U.S. diplomat; escaped from slavery in 1838.

Sure.

What happened after that?

Oh, everything just moved around. It was quite busy, so everybody was just down under cover. But I saw.

Did someone usher you out quickly after that?

We went backstage, but motion continued.

Did you realize right away that your father was dead?

He wasn't dead right away. I knew that he had been shot. I knew that he was gunned down. I didn't know—you know, you don't know when the last breath is until they tell you.

Any other memories of that day? Afterward someone coming up to you and explaining that your father was dead?

No. I do know that I was sitting on a woman's lap backstage, and a lot of people were crying, and my mother came back in, and she said, "You're my best friend now." But prior to her coming back, I felt old. Like something "old" happened. Something warm went right through me. I felt old and I got off of that lady's lap. I felt too old to be sitting on her lap. I remember feeling my temperature change. I remember the awareness coming to my head—that, you know, get up. It's like if you were sitting on your father's lap, you'd feel old, even though to your father you'll always be his kid, so you could sit on his lap, or your mother's lap or something.

I knew [my father's] work, I didn't know the ill—the societal ill. The initial disdain that was perpetuated toward me was from people that were around me—the standoffishness, the judgment that I first encountered after his death was from black people. I don't mean the family of people who were always around, but I just mean, standoffishness, judgment, not wanting their children around us, just in case. . . . White people can be attributed to a number of prejudices, but black folks did it too.

I never permitted any of it to be painful, because I always regarded any act like that as selfish and undue—their own shortcoming. I would only feel the pain of someone else such as a sibling or my mother. I would feel the pain on their behalf.

There was a petition signed so that we wouldn't move into [a] neighborhood after my father died. They're all like aunts and uncles now. Sure, there was a lot being done, but we survived it all, and I had a wonderful role model and metronome: my mother. And thank God for that.

What do you think of all this resurgence of interest in your father? Are you glad for the awareness?

Sure, I just hope it perpetuates continued learning not just for my father but for all subjects that have been taboo in terms of learning, touching, embracing. My father's philosophies aren't new ones. That's who he died being, so we're the late bloomers if it's only hitting us almost thirty years later, and if someone like my father has had a message that could have bonded human beings sooner, then we have to ask ourselves, who covers up that information, what is their agenda? And that if there's one person, there must be a hundred people we don't know about. So I hope that we get hip to that process, and realize that we need to spend more time in a library or file house, and know that we're entitled to it.

Do you attend a mosque here?

No, not in California.

What about the Malcolm Shabazz mosque in New York?

Which one?

116th and Lenox.

No, that's part of the Nation of Islam.

They renamed it—

I'm glad that it was renamed. I understand that Wallace Muhammad had it renamed when he was the inheritor, and he did it for understandable reasons, trying to reinstate his brother—his Islamic brother, respectfully in the Nation. But I don't have a reason to go there. There are enough mosques that I don't need to pick Temple Number 7[8] . . . At all! . . . Ever!

.   .   .

[8] In June 1954, Elijah Muhammad appointed Malcolm X minister of the Nation of Islam's Temple 7, then still a small storefront. Under Malcolm's leadership, membership multiplied, and he was able to use his position to generate national attention for the Nation. In 1964, after his split with the Nation, however, he knew he was courting disaster in establishing his own organization, Muslim Mosque, Inc., and ostensibly challenging Elijah Muhammad. In his autobiography, Malcolm X wrote: "I went few places without constant awareness that any

[My father] bridged the gap between the converted Muslim and the misconceptions of Islam as per the Nation of Islam's teaching and the East. And he made that pilgrimage and came back and then united foreign Muslims with American Muslims. He bridged that gap because most in the Nation didn't think of the origins of Islam. Wallace Muhammad, when he took over the Nation after his father's death, incorporated all kinds of people on his panel, and they didn't all look like us. The Nation's strong followers really had a problem with the range of people from the East, whose hues vary. The last years of my father's life, we had a sheik in our house—he looked like he must have been a hundred years old; he looked very rich in character, very black skin, and absolutely snow-white hair, and was wrapped in the Saudi Arabian attire, and so wonderfully spiritual; and my father was just so humbled by this man in our house, and we didn't know what his highness stood for the way my father did; he was just *really* comfortable to be around. Sheikh [Ahmed] Hassoun.[9]

I'm the third generation, on both sides of my family, of social and academic activists. My grandfather was killed. My father is what his parents were, and their parents. His life ended violently as a result of attempting to broaden an awareness. Pressure was put on my mother. She had enough examples before her, such as her mother-in-law, of how to hold on in spite of the pressure.

[My grandparents] were internationalists. They were from the Garvey movement.[10] They understood history from point go. And my grandmother, being from the Caribbean, was surrounded by Easterners, meaning North Africans, East Indians; all that had something to do with her nature. The circle of my father's life has a lot more to do with what went into it initially in the first decade of shaping his life. His commitment to people, social change, being self-sufficient. My grandmother translated four languages—to transcribe into the newspaper, which my father and his siblings shopped around. All of that social involvement—the commitment, the re-

---

number of my former brothers felt they would make heroes of themselves in the Nation of Islam if they killed me." Ballantine Books edition, p. 346.

[9] A Sudanese scholar.

[10] Marcus Garvey (1887–1940), born in Jamaica, West Indies, built the largest black nationalist organization the United States had known until his day. In 1917, nine years after he arrived in Harlem, he founded the Universal Negro Improvement Association, which aroused racial pride and an awareness of Africa as the motherland of African Americans. His empire folded in 1924 after he was convicted of mail fraud, jailed in Atlanta, and then deported from the United States. Earl Little, Malcolm X's father and Attallah's grandfather, was elected president of the Omaha branch of Garvey's UNIA. Louisa, Earl's wife, also joined.

sponsibility started early. So that when my grandfather and my grandmother were taken away, and the children separated and dispersed through the system and then my father through the streets—those were all distractions. If he did not have a strong track to begin with, he might not have found his way back. But he was nurtured from the beginning.

Interestingly enough, my grandparents were from two different religions, even though in those days you became automatically what your husband was. Neither parent invaded the other one's spiritual rearing and spirituality. My grandfather, as a result of being of the first generation born out of slavery, was exposed to Christianity. My grandmother was exposed to Islam in a nonrigid way because of the culture around her.

I live my life per the shaping, the structuring, the sculpturing that my parents set out for me, be it Islamic, be it as an American, be it as their daughter, be it as a black woman—I just live full and complete as per my instincts from the inside out. There are too many people who have expectations and if I were to jump as per their variations, I'd be a lost person.

We have indeed created man in the best of molds . . .

Qur'an 95:4

Leap of Faith

Kareem Abdul-Jabbar

He stands 86 inches tall, hardly able to fit through most doorways. You look upward toward his face as you would toward the top of some tree. And when he sits at just about any table, it's easy to imagine he's in a first-grade classroom with its tiny desks and miniature chairs.

Abdul-Jabbar is history's greatest basketball player, a six-time NBA Most Valuable Player who chalked up 1,525 NBA games and 38,028 points, and patented and perfected what Bill Russell called "the most beautiful thing in sports"—the sky hook.

As a bookish Harlemite, he led his high school team, Power Memorial, to 71 straight victories, then led UCLA to 88 wins out of 90 games, claiming three national titles. He was so good, and so tall, the NCAA temporarily changed its rulebook to outlaw his dunking.

One of his most significant moves took place off court: embracing Islam. Translated, his name means "Generous and Powerful Servant of Allah."

There was an African cultural center in Harlem, and the Muslims were on the fifth floor. I went up there, and I had on this colorful African robe. A guy says, "No, you don't want this place." I said, "Yes, I want to be Muslim." They questioned me, and I had already learned the testimony of *shahada.* We did *juma* prayers. . . .

Hamaas[11] had been a jazz drummer. My dad knew him. He basically started out okay. Hamaas was taught about Islam by a man from Bangladesh who was a mystic, and apparently knew some heavy stuff. There are a lot of very esoteric people from the Indian subcontinent that know

---

[11] Hamaas Abdul-Khaalis.

about stuff that's not easily explained. I think Hamaas got caught up in that.

As time went on, he believed that a lot of people who were trying to teach Americans to be Muslims were hypocrites and weren't worthy to teach American Muslims about anything. He wanted us to learn Islam and not get caught up in worshipping Arabs. A lot of American brothers, because they don't have any identity, end up taking on the identity of the people who taught them about Islam. We don't have the bonds that go over generations and the economic underpinnings and the ability to communicate that Muslims from the East have. Our family structure has been destroyed.

Hamaas had a lot of contempt for Arabs and people with a superior attitude that are going to show the American brothers how to be Muslim.

That is something to be aware of. Some person from the South went abroad and learned a little bit of Arabic, came back to America, said that he was some messianic person from the Sudan, and started a *jamat*[12] in Brooklyn—and this is a person from the South! Well, we'll just put on a turban and use Islam instead of Christianity and run the same stealing-in-the-name-of-the-Lord game.

But as things went on, Hamaas got into a personality cult—featuring him. It got bad, and I didn't really get into how bad it got in my book[13] because I didn't want them on my case. They were capable of violence. You saw what happened in Washington in 1977. I wanted to distance myself from them.

Hamaas Abdul-Khaalis, formerly a high official in the Nation of Islam, became openly contemptuous of Elijah Muhammad's brand of Islam, denouncing him as a false prophet in letters to Muhammad's followers. Men from the Philadelphia temple took revenge. They entered Hamaas's home while he was out and shot his wife in the head six times. They also shot his daughter, who survived, and drowned three of his other children and his nine-day-old granddaughter.

Years later, Hamaas and his followers took over Washington, D.C.'s City Hall, the Islamic Center, and the headquarters of the B'nai B'rith. Holding hostages, he demanded that the movie Mohammad, Messenger of

[12] Congregation.
[13] *Giant Steps: The Autobiography of Kareem Abdul-Jabbar* (New York: Bantam Books, 1983).

God *(which offended his religious sensibilities)* be taken from theaters and that the men convicted of killing his family members, as well as those convicted of assassinating Malcolm X, be delivered to him. A twenty-four-year-old reporter was killed during a shoot-out with police. Hamaas finally surrendered after ambassadors from Egypt, Iran, and Pakistan sat with him to read and discuss the Qur'an.

My own personal frailty, having been raised the way I was raised, made me vulnerable to somebody like that with a strong personality and very authoritarian. My parents had told me, You listen to the nuns, you listen to your coaches, and you listen to your teachers. And here was somebody that was genuinely interested in people knowing what Islam was really about. So all right, I picked him. He was another in the line of succession. I was very fortunate that he wasn't after my money.

Could he have just reached into your pocket and taken what he wanted?

Probably. As things got worse and they needed money to get people out of jail and pay lawyers, they got unreasonable. But up to that point, they never really got involved in ripping me off.

My first *shahada* basically was sufficient. You declare you believe in Allah in front of witnesses. That's sufficient.

But Hamaas had us learn five *kalimahs* and shave our heads and our pubic hair and our armpits. It's a tradition from Bangladesh. There's mention of it in some *hadiths* but he had some *hadiths* that somebody created. He said that they were "inner line"; but they were *hadiths* that nobody could substantiate.

I went to the source material and I learned Arabic. I started reading the Qur'an in Arabic. I could translate it with the dictionary. It'd take me ten hours to do three sentences but I understood what was happening grammatically.

The next summer I went to Libya and Saudi Arabia, and studied how to speak and got a little bit more into it. That was 1973. And it was that winter when the murders occurred.

I was playing [basketball]. I got a phone call from one of the brothers in D.C. He was whispering. I said, "What's going on?"

Total shock and disbelief. I couldn't conceive of somebody murdering children. Very sick behavior. Fear for my family. Fear for the other people down in D.C.

I went to D.C. and was involved in the funeral, and spent the next four to six weeks traveling around with the FBI for protection.

Then they arrested the people that did it.

Hamaas was, I think, overcome with paranoia. At that point I think he might have left the house in D.C. a dozen times in the next two or three years.

I didn't want to go through what [Muhammad Ali] went through [in his public conversion] because his got interpreted as a political statement, a statement against the war, and a racial one. I was just going to affirm my identity as an African American and as a Muslim. And I was not going to use the name Alcindor. Literally that is a slave name. There was a man named Alcindor that brought my family from West Africa to the island of Dominica. From there they went to the island of Trinidad, as slaves, and they kept his name. They were Alcindor's slaves. So the name Alcindor is the name of a slave dealer. My dad went and checked it out in the archives.

When I first took *shahada* they called me Abdul Kareem. Hamaas said, Your attribute is more Abdul-Jabbar.

Kareem Abdul-Jabbar.
PHOTO: WEN ROBERTS/PHOTOGRAPHY INK

Allah has blessed me in giving me a lot of power. That's true. So it's a lot to live up to, but I don't think I've been overwhelmed by it.

People seemed to deal with it okay. My parents were a little bit uptight about it. But they knew I was sincere. I wasn't [converting] to be a grand-stand play. It probably cost me marketability—at the time. I paid for it then, but it was an investment. Because of it, I have credibility [today]. I've been my own man, and done it my way despite the consequences.

I have never established the discipline of five prayers a day every day. I have to be out and about a lot. Especially when I was playing. I'd be too tired to wake up for *fajr*. I'd be playing ball during *maghrib* and *isha*. I'd be asleep during the middle of the day when I should be making *zuhr*, and so I never really was able to establish the discipline, but since I've stopped playing I've been better. I guess I've had to adapt to life in America. All I can hope is that Allah is pleased with it on the Day of Judgment.

I know that going to a Catholic school gave me a strong foundation. Jesus was Muslim. So I already had been turned in that direction. But with Islam you can clarify what Jesus was all about. All of a sudden it makes sense. You don't have to believe that three is one. If you ask Christians to deal with it logically, or how the Scriptures were collected and recorded, and mention that there must be human error in those Scriptures, they won't talk to you about that. It's very confusing, and if you're a Christian, it's an impossible thing to defend and it leads to a lot of frustration and anger and Crusades and all kinds of things. That's what I see from the Christian world.

In Islam, you have a very clear and untampered revelation. And if you're a person of faith and logic and you reflect as the Qur'an tells you to reflect, Allah will bless you and you can see that it is the way to live.

I just always had a very strong belief in the Supreme Being, and when I started reading the Qur'an [and] about the Prophet Muhammad, it became very clear to me that this was further revelation.

Here we don't have any cohesion as a community, and we don't have any institutions that serve us as a community; they're really fledgling. I think we have enough numbers. I just don't think we're organized as we should be. Muslims here in America are dispersed, but if we all came to-gether as one group, it would shock a lot of people.

You have to be a little bit more circumspect here, because you'll be discriminated against if you're Muslim here—not within the Muslim community [but] within the larger community. So a lot of people have to be circumspect, not too obviously Muslim.

I think a lot of that has been worn down, though. I'm happy to see that. I think the Russian invasion of Afghanistan really helped the cause of Muslims here in America. Up to that point Americans saw Muslims as these fanatical people who will not do anything but practice Islam, and fundamentalism is making them a radical force.

And then when Russia invaded Afghanistan and the Afghani Muslims had that same attitude toward Communism as they did, America said, We have to support these wonderful freedom fighters who are fighting for their religion. [*Laughs.*]

It was the same religion as those fanatics. But all of a sudden, since we were fighting Communism, the fervor and dedication and undying commitment was good for America now. People all of a sudden now can see that Muslims can be your allies, and Muslims can be your enemies. Turkey's a great example of that. Turkey is a member of NATO. Yet it would be very difficult to get them to give up Islam. I've been there the past two or three years.

Islam has an image of suppressing women's rights. You'd have to do a whole lot of talking to explain how Islam protected women's rights and advocated them. Nobody would believe that. And the conduct of the Arabs has made it almost impossible for anybody to understand, even Muslims, that women are not supposed to be oppressed.

Arabs, especially wealthy Arabs, have really given a very negative treatment of women. Their treatment of their women has permeated the whole Islamic world as far as how people view it. It wasn't what the Prophet did. The Prophet helped his wife in business. She couldn't conduct business because she was a woman. He was her advocate. He made her a fortune, because he was a shrewd businessman.

Some brothers have more than one wife and they're living on welfare. It's a travesty. Someone needs to educate these brothers that they are oppressing their wives and children, and what they're doing is irresponsible and un-Islamic. [The Qur'an] clearly states that you can have more than one wife—*if* you can afford to support all of the people involved in your care. And if you can't do that, then you shouldn't have a polygamous situation. It's very clear.

A nice thing has become evident to me. My son Amir—his mother isn't Muslim. She never was; she's Buddhist. I didn't have any idea how he was going to come out. All I could do was teach him what I could teach him, and they were having discussions in class about monotheistic religions. They said something about Islam. Amir corrected the text. He explained the pillars of Islam.

He's twelve. They asked him to do a report. They said that Islam was the newest monotheistic religion. Amir said that the Qur'an is the newest book; Islam is the *oldest* religion; it started with Adam. He had it down, just like that. He told me about it, and I was shocked that he had taken it to heart.

I was brainwashed into being a Catholic. My dad was Catholic but he wasn't into it. You know how they do in Catholic school; they couldn't make me continue with it. I can't *make* my children be Muslim. So I'm glad to see that he has taken it to heart.

When I first got traded to the Lakers, I knew these young dudes in Detroit. Basketball fans. They were all in high school. They came down to see us play. One of the brothers afterwards talked to me about Islam. He was Muslim. None of his partners were. I'd give them some tickets.

Twelve years go by. We're playing the Pistons for the world championship in 1988. The brothers give me a call, right. Five of these guys had become Muslim. Two of them came on out. Plus their kids. I felt like an uncle, like they were my younger brothers. And they had kids now. They were doing well. They're still into the religion and it's changed their lives for the better. I had told them it's worth your time and effort to check it out, and they did.

There's a Kurdish brother down in Dallas. He would bring his family to see me. One Ramadan they came and they fed me. I said, "I'm really honored, you know. Thanks."

They said, "No, we thank you. We get a lot of blessing for this."

I said, "What are you talking about?"

He said, "My dad told me that when I came to America, I would see some real Muslims."

I said, "What are you talking about? We're just struggling to open our eyes here."

He said, "No. In my country, we have a lot of knowledge, but the fire in here [*taps chest*], it's not there. When I come here, I see you people holding onto Islam with no knowledge, but with just the belief and the determination to better themselves."

I try to do what I can do. Because I couldn't fast for Ramadan, I'd always feed a family. So I'd donate money. I give brothers money and tell them what it's for. They feed people. There are people that I know that need to eat, so I'll give them a month's groceries. I *have* to do that; I have a higher income, and I have an obligation. My income doesn't exonerate me.

Everyone starts his day and is a vendor of his soul,
either freeing it or bringing about its ruin.

Prophet Muhammad, *Hadith* (Muslim)

Come to Success

A Mosque in Chicago

Before sunrise, a muezzin calls believers "to success" and "to prayer" at a modern mosque on Chicago's South Side. "Prayer," he sings in Arabic, "is better than sleep."

In the unfinished mosque, on Woodlawn Avenue, a handful of believers line up shoeless behind Jabir Muhammad, Elijah's son, for the day's first prayer. With sleepy eyes, they pray, then sit knee to knee and read the Qur'an aloud. Afterward, they mumble, "Allah speaks the truth," pray again into their cupped hands, then disappear into the day.

Jabir, a short, round man, wears a high-collared blue suit, ripped at the shoulder. The man next to him, in pinstripes, is arguably the world's best-known Muslim: Muhammad Ali. His face bloated from illness, he often makes a two-hour drive to the mosque from his 88-acre Michigan farm, once owned by Al Capone. Part of the mosque sits on the site of a gym Ali owned but never trained in.

Of the estimated 200,000 Muslims in the Chicago area, some 20,000 are African American. More of them attend Al-Faatir's Friday services than services at any other area mosque (Louis Farrakhan's group meets on Sundays).

Each Friday, about 500 males and 100 females fill Al-Faatir. Most are black Americans, but Africans, Arabs, Pakistanis, and other immigrants also pray there. Ali, a Muslim since before taking the heavyweight boxing crown from Sonny Liston in 1964, often mingles in the crowd, planting a kiss on a brother Muslim's cheek.

221

Jabir is protective of him. Ali once slept overnight on the floor of Al-Faatir, and Jabir reportedly told him, "People are going to think you've lost all your marbles or your money—and neither one is good."

Ali brought attention—and over the years donated several million dollars—to the Nation of Islam. He offered even more money, says Warith D. Mohammed, but Elijah "never wanted to be dependent on anybody," so the Messenger refused it.

Ali also provided Jabir with the means to become rich. As Ali's manager, Jabir (formerly Herbert) earned one-third of Ali's multimillion-dollar purses. In his rumpled suit and cheerless fez, Jabir does not look like a man who could afford to buy a hotel, tear it down, and build a mosque on the site. But that is what he did.

When younger, Jabir and Warith wanted to be boxers. One day while practicing on a speed bag, Jabir recalled, Elijah came up to him and said, "What are you doing?"

"I say, 'I'm developing my speed.'

"He said, 'For what?'

" 'I want to be a boxer.'

"He said, 'You better be developing your brains!' "

Both Jabir and Warith quit practicing. "But the ironic part about it is I became the manager of the heavyweight champ of the world," Jabir says.

The world is on the side of the man left standing.

Arabic proverb

The Mighty

Muhammad Ali

After breakfast in a South Side Chicago hotel, two boys recognized him, so Ali "levitated" on his way to the rest room.

"I've been fasting and praying," he told the smiling boys. "Watch my feet."

He turned to one side, his handsome profile view, and stood still. A second later, he tiptoed discreetly on his left foot, appearing to levitate when his right foot lifted off the carpet.

The boys laughed and asked for Ali's autograph. The Champ wrote his signature on an Islamic pamphlet and handed one to each boy.

Once a magnificent fighting machine who struck fear into his opponents, Ali is still a figure of fascination. He ranks among the twentieth century's greatest athletes, altering the status of the black athlete in people's consciousness. He brought the black athlete's quest for dignity to new heights, gaining respect and acceptance from the public, white and black.

Ali remained in the limelight for over two decades, claiming boxing's heavyweight crown three times in the process, while fashioning himself into a legend.

Cassius Marcellus Clay, Jr., was born January 17, 1942 in Louisville, Kentucky, to a billboard and sign painter, Cassius Marcellus Clay, Sr., and his wife, Odessa Grady Clay, a domestic. Twenty-two years later, he was reborn.

Cassius Clay was given a new name by Elijah Muhammad in 1964, when Elijah made a public announcement on a radio broadcast from Chicago on March 6: "This Clay name has no divine meaning. I hope he will accept being called by a better name. Muhammad Ali is what I will give him for as long as he believes in Allah and follows me."

For three years prior to his heavyweight championship fight with Sonny Liston, Clay had attended meetings of the Nation of Islam. His attendance was reported in the Philadelphia *Daily News* in September of 1963; but in January 1964, he spoke at a Muslim rally in New York, causing more of a sensation, and within a few weeks, his father was quoted as saying that Clay had joined the Nation.

Clay still made no public announcement of having joined the Nation of Islam. But he was busy studying Islam under Captain Sam Saxon (now Abdul Rahaman), whom Clay met in Miami in 1961, and minister Ishmael Sabakhan. Their lessons were vintage Nation of Islam: God is a black man, and yet the black man in America bears a slave master's name.

Searing lessons could be learned from traveling through the South, or simply by watching television. Jim Crow was in its heyday, and 100 years after the abolishment of slavery, blacks were being firehosed in the streets, beaten, shot, and maimed for seeking racial parity in the United States.

Clay pondered Elijah Muhammad's teachings, read the Nation's newspaper, and sought guidance and counsel from Malcolm X, whom he met in Detroit in early 1962. The message of black defiance in the face of white supremacy became embraceable.

Before Clay's bout with Liston, Malcolm visited Clay on a private basis, not as Elijah's representative. Malcolm saw Clay as a younger brother and counseled him, buoying his determination to go up against the heavily favored-to-win Liston. Remember David and Goliath, Malcolm admonished.

Malcolm left only after the promoter threatened to call off the fight if he hung around any longer. Clay for his part was afraid that he wouldn't be allowed to fight for the heavyweight title if his association with the Nation became known.

Though fearful of Liston, Clay was victorious because, he believed, it was "Allah's time." Clay literally danced out of Liston's reach and pummeled him from different angles. When at the end of the fourth round Clay's eyes were stinging and partially blinded (possibly from some ointment on Liston's body or gloves), Angelo Dundee pushed him back into the ring, and Clay used his skill and faith to avoid Liston's punches. A bewildered and wounded Liston quit on his stool before the bell for round seven rang. The world had a brand-new champ.

Muhammad Ali (left) with Louis Farrakhan in 1985.
PHOTO: ROBERT SENGSTACKE

After Clay won, Elijah Muhammad reversed his strategy. He told five thousand followers in Chicago: "I'm happy that he confessed he's a believer. Clay whipped a much tougher man and came through the bout unscarred because he has accepted Muhammad as the Messenger of Allah."

Malcolm may have tried to pull Ali into Malcolm's own corner when Malcolm was about to part from the Nation. But Ali reportedly told an associate, "That man can't convince me to go against the Messenger."

Malcolm was excommunicated and Ali remained in Elijah Muhammad's camp, snubbing Malcolm while in Ghana ("Nobody listens to Malcolm anymore") and following Elijah until the leader's death in 1975.

Today Ali says he and others in the Nation finally ended up practicing the same brand of orthodox Islam that Malcolm turned to after leaving the Nation. And Ali is more concerned with obeying and loving Allah than heeding precepts of Elijah Muhammad. Ali takes the general view that

Muhammad Ali.

Elijah played a significant role in uplifting black Americans—freeing them from drugs, alcohol, poisonous foods, and general self-destruction.

Ali never bought into the "white devils" line of thought. "Hearts and souls have no color," he now says.

He has spent several hundred thousand dollars on Islamic books and pamphlets to propagate his religion, but believes that not only Muslims but God-fearing Christians and Jews will go to heaven.

Doctors say Ali suffers from post-traumatic Parkinson's Syndrome, a result of injuries from fighting and repeated blows to the head. Of his condition, Ali says that he has had a good life before and has one now. He doesn't need sympathy; he just wants to accept Allah's will. In fact, he says there are no idols in Islam and that perhaps because he was made the idol of millions, Allah humbled him to underscore the fact that no one is greater than Allah.

Ali's main struggle now is to try to please Allah in all that he does. Conquering the world didn't bring him true happiness; true happiness, he says, is derived only from worshipping Allah.

Recite! In the name of thy Lord Who created . . .

Qur'an 96:1

May Day

May May Ali

Muhammad Ali's eldest child, born June 18, 1968; a rising rap star with a debut compact disc recording, "May May: The Introduction."[14] She says she was brushed off by record companies—rejected a hundred times because her last name is Ali and people thought she was a rich girl who had no rhyme or reason to rap. She finally landed a deal and on her disc thanked "all those who didn't have the insight" to give her a chance. "Thanks for the motivation," she says. "The Introduction," which bears no parental advisory sticker, has an air of social responsibility—positive messages for youth—as well as testimony about the ills of the world: mayhem, drive-by shootings, police brutality, stereotypical black images. The "rapumentary" "Ali" is a tribute to her father, and her idol. May May, raised by her grandparents after her parents divorced, wanted to be a boxer. She settled for doing stints as a stand-up comedienne in Los Angeles before closing her record deal. Before dinner in a Thai-Muslim restaurant in LA, she rapped one of her songs, slowly, into the cassette recorder and smiled warmly. She later posed for snapshots hugging the restaurant owner and his wife . . . then the waitress.

If I had to redo my life, I wouldn't have anyone else raise me. My daily life, and the way I think, it was Islam and my grandparents—Aminah and Sadru-Din Ali. I give them ninety percent of the credit. The worldly stuff came from my father. And I learned from my mother's mistakes. Ninety percent of my behavior I think is from Islam and my grandparents. Every-

[14] Scottie Brothers Records, 1992.

227

thing they did, they checked themselves through their religion. But they let me go places.

As a member of the Nation, did you believe as a kid that the white man was a devil?

I wasn't old enough to look at a white and go, "Oooo, there's goes the devil!" But I knew that was the whole concept. It never really stuck with me because I was too young. I was playing with my toys.

The Nation was proper in conduct but not in concept. The conduct as far as just behavior and being upright—I wish some Muslims now had that Nation conduct. They were organized. I was proud to be a little Muslim girl.

My dad's real sensitive. If he saw someone in need, and he wasn't rushing anywhere, he would just help that person, because he felt that was blessings.

One rainy night, he was out by himself driving and he brought a family home. They were in the den. It was a mother, father, and two babies and a seven-year-old. He didn't know them from Adam. His wife, Veronica, was out of the country, and his other two kids were spending the night at their friends' house and he put that family in the kids' room and let them sleep there. Fed them, and bought them a train ticket back to where they were from. My father doesn't fear a lot of things.

We traveled a lot. In airports, I observed how every single person we passed knew him. If we were on the street, they shouted out his name. I knew my dad didn't know these people, so I knew my father was like the person on TV or in the movies.

When I could talk and walk, I knew that he was famous, because I went to interviews with him. I hung out with my dad. I just wanted to be right next to him. I just liked him. He played with me a lot.

But my life wasn't sheltered at all. I saw things with my eyes I wasn't supposed to see at five, six, or seven. I was nosy when I was little. I wanted to know things that were going on, and saw things I shouldn't have seen. I mean, the world was in my house. I saw con artists begging for money, women looking dead at my mother, trying to eye my dad. I'm watching the whole thing. I knew how manipulative people could be, at a young age.

If I saw a woman approaching him and he'd give an autograph and a

May May Ali.

kiss on the cheek and be nice to her, I'd go, *"Oooo!* I'm gonna tell the Messenger on you!" Because as much as I loved my dad, I knew who the boss was, and that was Elijah Muhammad. He was very loyal to the Messenger.

Do you think that being Muhammad Ali's daughter helped you land a record deal?

No, it didn't help. This business is hard, period. You have people in the business that wait ten years to get a record deal. There are people that don't have a famous father that only wait one year.

Me being Ali's daughter, automatically, the youth know me. The first impression they get is—I wonder if she's spoiled. I wonder if she's had everything. That's the first thing my peers think—until they get to know me. So I think it's hard to prove myself in rap music. It's hard, because people are just waiting for me to just do something they don't like. I have to make sure my stuff is dead-on. I feel I have to explain my background— I wasn't raised rich. The only way they're going to buy your records [is] if they like you.

Why rap music? Your background doesn't really lend itself to becoming a rapper.

It does. Two reasons: Both of my parents were entertainers. My mother acted, she was in photography. My father was an entertainer. He was an athlete. When I was younger I never wanted to be an entertainer, but it was very much in the cards.

My dad stood up for his religion and race through boxing in a way. He was like a person with a message, all the time giving his opinion. And I'm very much like my father, and right now that medium is rap, more than any other thing.

Being in entertainment, he knew the negative influences and the mistakes he made in that limelight that he didn't want me to make, so he was just unsure. But he never argued with me.

I have lines where I say, "Take it from a Muslim sister . . ." I let them know I'm a Muslim, and I address everybody. All youth are listening to rap music right now, and that was my motivation.

My very first single that was released last year, it was called "Life's a Test." Actually, when I was reading the Qur'an and looking at the footnotes, I saw that—life's a test—and I said, wow, that's a perfect title! The first verse went:

> This life is a test
> I must confess
> 'Cause I've learnt from the very best
> Qur'anic verses say you must live to give
> Step right up
> I'm gonna tell you how it is . . .

Everyone has an idol or someone they really like. And every year, I'll experience someone that I may look up to or admire or watch on the news that's admiring my dad. Whoever it is, they love my dad. The average person never experiences that kind of attention from someone who is humbling themselves to your father. It almost is like to you in a way. I get a kick out of it. I think it's hilarious.

Unlike a lot of the other kids, I remember my father's career and being with him during his career a lot. I remember him being in training for fights. I watched him in Deer Lake and with Larry Holmes as his sparring partner. People would come in, and the gym would be packed. I remember Don King used to be in his crew and he used to walk in the kitchen. My dad used to threaten to cut his hair. The atmosphere was always nice. Just seeing his dedication, how hard he worked, I mean, you don't become the greatest in one thing and not go that extra mile. It just doesn't happen.

Was there any fight that you hoped he would lose so he could stop fighting?

Trevor Berbick. The most painful fight for me to watch was the Larry Holmes fight. I wasn't there. I watched it on closed circuit in downtown Chicago with a bunch of strangers. They had no idea his daughter was sitting right there in the back.

It was time for him to quit—before he fought Larry Holmes. He lost all this weight real fast. His crew and manager were saying, C'mon, fight, Ali, you have one more fight in you. And I knew he didn't. It was painful. I mean, he was no match for Larry Holmes at that age. It was like *I* was getting punched.

Then he fought again. We all went to that fight, and I knew Berbick wasn't as strong as Larry Holmes. Our whole family talked about it. We're like, we hope Daddy loses because he does not need to fight anymore. He had so many outside forces telling him, As long as you're winning, you keep fighting—'cause they wanted the money. They wanted that extra purse—the purse! the purse! the purse!

The family knew that was not worth his health. When he lost, I went [*sigh of relief*]. I was so happy. Not only that he didn't get hurt. He didn't get beat bad. It was really a tie fight. And I think the judges just gave it to Berbick because he didn't need to win.

Every now and then, I'll remember how he used to talk fast, but it's not painful for me now. Because when I'm with my dad, I'm happy to be with him. I'm spending time with my father. And I look at it like my dad looks at it: I did a lot of bad things in my life; I'd rather be punished now than in the hereafter. And I believe him. I believe that. As long as he's happy and healthy, doing what he wants to do, I'm happy for him.

Do you have any standard jokes in your repertoire?

I have a joke about my dad. I say, you know, he wasn't a regular dad. He didn't tell me normal nursery rhymes. He made up his own rhymes. It scared me a little bit. He'd lay me down to go to sleep and go:

> *Hush, little May May, go to bed*
> *before I get a Frazier flashback*
> *and knock you in the head.*

I address the promiscuity going on now. I say a man will walk up to me today and ask me out, and may want to get with me that same night. I say:

May May and her father at her 1986 high school graduation.

So one time this guy did that. We're at a red light; I had my little convertible top down. He looked at me. He said, "Hey, baby, how about me and you getting together tonight?" I said, "Okay, okay. I just want to let you know I'm a murderer." He said, "Cool, we got something in common." I said, "Oh, okay, I also want to let you know I tested HIV-positive." He said, "I *love* you. We got *two* things in common." Then I just drove away.

I have to be honest: I don't like the atmosphere of the comedy clubs. That's why I'm not trying to be Whoopi Goldberg or Eddie Murphy. And also I have to watch myself with comedy, because you might want to be funny so bad that if you follow someone who's gross, you don't want to even get in that trap where you think, Okay, well I can do this for comedy. But I'm not lewd and I don't talk about sex.

When I met Prince, that was after "Purple Rain." I mean, he's a star.

But Prince has always disturbed me. I don't say I don't enjoy his songs; I say as a person, I don't respect Prince. I haven't bought a Prince record since that time I met him. His lyrics, I can't listen to him. I can't listen to *"Cream—Get on top."* I can't sing that.

My outward struggle is to be an alternative and hopefully be a leader. As soon as you have a position where you're reaching millions, you're a leader whether you like it or not.

Rappers will say, Well, I am an artist; I'm not responsible for anybody. If you're saying anything to anybody, especially to millions, you're an influence on them, and that's your responsibility. That's in our religion. We believe that as Muslims.

It's for the sake of art! First Amendment! That's all you hear. It's like art is above God now.

I find that living in America, I get mad so quick. If something bothers me, I just want to focus on what should I do as a Muslim? How should I behave? Inwardly, when I bow down and pray, I pray: Behave like a Muslim as much as you possibly can—for Allah, for yourself, for others, so they can learn from that.

The Channel

Mujahid Ali

(a.k.a. Clarence C. Lilley)

Mujahid Ali, who started his career in the mailroom of the New York
Times, went on to produce more than sixty plays in New Jersey, Pennsyl-
vania, and the Caribbean, and became a co-owner of several cable televi-
sion systems. Now a film producer/director and communications entrepre-
neur, he is one of a growing number of American Muslim millionaires. But
his lifestyle is as humble as an oil czar's can be flamboyant. He lives in a
modest home and drives a company car.

I've been in the entertainment business since I was a teenager; it's been
twenty-five years now. I went from acting to directing to producing to
entrepreneurship.

Because I had such strong moral beliefs in terms of what I was doing I
knew it would be very difficult for me working for other people. When I
was an actor I had a lot of difficulty when I would get cast in things. One
director told me that if I didn't perform the part the way he was directing
me, I should go and set up my own theater company and do it the way I
wanted to. Not too long after that I did. That was Theater of Universal
Images. It's still in existence today. It's involved with everything from theater to television and educational programs.

It grew to be quite a massive operation. It started very differently than

234

most of the other theater companies that came into existence at that time. There weren't any large grants. There wasn't any massive groundswell of support. I pooled my resources, and pulled some friends together. I said, "This is something we can do." Now, it's had budgets as high as a million dollars annually and today it's a half-million-dollar operation, not for profit, tax-exempt. It's a completely charitable and social type of thing.

That theater has worked with everyone from Samuel L. Jackson, Antonio Fargas, Melvin Van Peebles, Esther Rolle, John Amos, Ella Joyce, who's on *Roc*. It's a major influence in the African American theater.

I started the cable company with a similar type of focus. I do a tremendous amount of research before I do any sort of project. I knew that cable television was coming into the urban community. I knew that unless it was controlled by African Americans it was not going to serve this community. The Newark community was 65, maybe even 70 percent African American. Too many resources have consistently come in and out that have not benefited the community.

I began the company with three other partners. We applied for and won the Newark franchise, and then won two other franchises largely because there was a large African American bloc on the Newark City Council. The African Americans voted for us; the others didn't.

[Islamic principles] I think were reflected in the character and the quality of the programming that I chose and how I conducted myself businesswise.

Mujahid Ali.
PHOTO: COPPER CUNNINGHAM

The balance of Islam helped me keep my sanity in the fact that I'm one of the few partners who is still doing fairly well. I'm one of the few who're still in the cable business.

My goals ultimately are to continue to expand the base that I have right now in the entertainment-communications area. And to do the reverse diaspora, meaning I have interests that I'm developing in the Caribbean and I have interests that I'm developing in West Africa and on the continent as a whole. Personally I feel there's a need for a connectedness between the Africans there in those two sectors of the globe and [African Americans]. There's a lot of expertise that we have that they need, and a lot of resources that they have that we need.

Islam focuses me and cleanses me of so much foolishness in life that at the moment I see negative things happening, I just excuse myself and say, Listen, I don't have to do business in this type of way or with you type of people. Islam has given me the ability to step back in the heat of the moment and look toward other recourses.

If the African American community were to focus on the fact that the majority of us, or many of us, came here as Muslims, not as Christians, that would help to connect us and strengthen ourselves to correct all the problems that we have as a people. It would stop a lot of the infighting and bickering. Not that there isn't infighting and bickering in Islam. But I think the truer and closer you are to the real religion, the less those things become an impediment to you.

My first major business was TUI. The next was a cable company, Connection Communications Corporation, in 1980, built for $12 million. It started without a lot of personal equity. We sold it to Gilbert Media for $33.5 million.

I'm very supportive of the Muslim community. The mosque I attend is a part of the American Muslim Mission. I'm a follower of Allah and the Qur'an and the *Sunnah* of the Prophet. I find Imam Warith Deen Muhammad to be one of the most learned scholars that I've come in contact with —and I've come in contact with a multitude of Middle Eastern and Islamic scholars here. He does not project himself as the leader in the sense that Farrakhan or the Honorable Elijah Muhammad did. He presents himself as a spokesperson and has developed the community in such a manner that its leadership is self-generating.

I would say there is a direct relationship between my success and the fact that I'm Muslim. There's a lot of things in terms of how I dealt with business, how I dealt with life, how I dealt with life experiences that are attributable to Islam. Everything imaginable that could be done to prevent someone like myself from achieving the successes that I've achieved has virtually been done to me. I have a basic premise in business to associate myself with the right people. But since this is not always possible, my business associates don't have to like me, but they must respect me.

So eat of [meats] on which Allah's name hath been
pronounced, if ye have faith in His Signs.

Qur'an 6:118

Over 100 Billion Served

Iqbal Musaji

"My dad said, 'Don't do anything that would embarrass
or shame your family, you or Islam.' "

*He grew up in Karachi, Pakistan, the son of an employee of the United
States Civil Services office there. His home was steeped in Islamic culture,
to the extent that when he expressed interest in studying abroad he was
admonished about the moral pitfalls he should avoid in America. He began
college in Pakistan, but completed his studies in California, where he
started working at McDonald's to make ends meet. There began his saga.
A Muslim in a fast-food joint.*

I was fortunate enough to get a mini orientation from the U.S. ambassador
at that time in Pakistan. My perception of America was formed by movies,
by what I saw in magazines. He took six of us young chaps and put us in
an auditorium and the light went dim, and what flashed on the screen was
a picture out of *Playboy* magazine. It stayed there for a minute, but it
seemed like forever. We were looking down, we were looking to the side.
We were very embarrassed, and finally he turned the light on and he looked
at us and said, "Now I want you to get it through your thick skulls that in
America this is not how all women are. They are like your sisters and your
mothers." I think all six of us learned to expect not what we saw in magazines, but to come with a much better understanding and respect for folks
in America.

238

I went to Northrop Institute of Technology in Inglewood, California. My major was electronics. Because of limited means, within six months I had to look for a job. It had to support me and my tuition. The first job I found was at a McDonald's, serving potatoes. I would go to college in the morning, then I'd go to McDonald's and work three hours. Then from there I would go to a tool shop and clean up, then to a veterinary hospital and work, do my homework, cook, and stay there, and feed the animals. That's where I slept, and then back to college the next morning.

In the first six months, while I lived in the dorm, Ramadan came—my first Ramadan away from home. We had to go to the folks and ask them to provide us with food at three-thirty in the morning. They looked at us like, You got to be kidding. We told them it was Ramadan. With so few Muslims in LA, we had to explain why we had to fast during Ramadan and get up in the morning and eat our food.

We were lucky. Northrop, which has now become a university, was very accommodating because they wanted foreign students to come. They said, We cannot provide a cook that early in the morning, but we will open the kitchen facilities for you. So me and six other brothers would get up early in the morning and go down to the kitchen, and we'd scramble our eggs on the grill and we'd eat.

It was quite difficult for people to understand. After school, I'd run over to McDonald's and cook French fries, and fast all day and serve drinks and not eat anything; and somehow people just couldn't equate the two.

It was the hardest of roads to travel. Growing up with Islam in your own country, you realize that the culture mixes in with the religion, and the result is, when you are fasting the entire country is fasting, so everybody changes their cycle. Businesses open at different hours, close at different hours; food is served at different hours; restaurants open at different hours.

But here, life goes on as usual. It's you who has to make the adjustments, and that is very different.

When you are born in Islam, you pick it up from all around you, not just the books, not just the Qur'an, but from the imam, your friends, your relatives.

I feel today I am a better Muslim with a much better understanding of my religion, and I'm much more appreciative. I am able to see my religion in its true light. I know more about what Islam is. You start seeing what is *hadith,* what is Qur'an, and what is culture. And you separate the culture out.

Iqbal Musaji and his wife, Sheila, journalist and editor.

. . .

The aerospace and electronics companies in Southern California were laying off a lot of electronic and avionic engineers when I finished school. So McDonald's offered me a position in management. I saw that as an opportunity. I've been with McDonald's now for over twenty-three years.

I went from a crew person to a shift manager to a salaried manager. Then I grew with the McDonald's Corporation, and supervised five restaurants, then moved on as a consultant for the McDonald's Corporation overseeing the operation of nine franchises in the greater Los Angeles area. Then I moved to Connecticut as a licensing manager. I covered eleven states, basically interviewing and selecting entrepreneurs who wanted to become operators of McDonald's restaurants. I put them in the training program and eventually placed them in restaurants.

After that I moved to McDonald's International headquarters in Chicago. I helped McDonald's open up restaurants in Malaysia, the Philippines, and Thailand, and made the initial trips into Indonesia and various other Pacific rim countries, including Korea.

The Muslim countries were Malaysia, Indonesia, and Singapore. In Malaysia, the McDonald's restaurants serve *halal* food. When we were opening the restaurant in Indonesia, all the headquarters people knew that this would also have to be a *halal* restaurant because it's a predominantly Muslim country, almost 98 percent. So that restaurant opened with 100 percent *halal* food. Their *halal* chicken nuggets are made in America and shipped to them. They actually stop the plant in America, have *halal* chicken come in, make nuggets, do a full *halal* line, then start over making regular chicken. This is happening both for Malaysia and for Indonesia. I encouraged it. The sausage that we use on Sausage McMuffin—we had to make a similar product out of beef, instead of the Canadian bacon, that would comply with the McDonald's standards and yet be *halal*.

I got a chance to work in Singapore also. In Singapore 30 percent of the population is Muslim. The managing director there is Chinese, and I convinced him that he was losing a portion of his population by not having *halal* food. I knew that there were Singaporeans who were going across the border into Johore Bahru,[15] which is the closest part of Malaysia, to eat McDonald's *halal* food, because they knew McDonald's around Singapore were not *halal*.

It made national news on CNN in America that the McDonald's in Singapore not only serves *halal* food but had a 19 percent increase in business. Now the Malays are coming to eat at this restaurant. That is significant.

McDonald's has been in Malaysia and Indonesia now for ten or twelve years and we have served 60 to 80 million hamburgers. There are about 42 restaurants in Singapore, no small potatoes. Malaysia has about 40 restaurants spread all over the country, and Indonesia has about four or five. I am very pleased about getting *halal* into these countries. That has opened the door for a whole lot of other countries.

McDonald's is adapting to Islam—absolutely. They know that when they are going to go into an Islamic country they are going to serve *halal* food. They have a very good understanding of what *halal* is, and have done an outstanding job.

There is work being done in the Middle East.

In each one of these countries McDonald's provides business opportunity for a lot of small entrepreneurs—farmers, bakers, and butchers. It ends up setting up the infrastructure, teaching the farmer how to grow a better crop of potatoes and how to feed the livestock to bring a quality product that McDonald's can serve.

Quite a few Saudi Arabian brothers have approached McDonald's, and one of them opened up a McDonald's-style restaurant in Saudi Arabia. At some point there will be McDonald's there.

I can think of at least ten to fifteen restaurants across the nation that are

[15] City on the southern tip of the Malay Peninsula, population 136,200.

located a stone's throw from *masajid,* and if they were to go *halal,* their business would shoot up like the 19 percent that Singapore had.

The nice thing is that the company is sensitive to where they do business. They will serve bagels and cream cheese if they're located in a predominantly Jewish area. I don't know of any restaurant that is currently serving kosher food, come to think of it.

I own three restaurants. All three are in the Missouri area.

In order to become a McDonald's operator, you need about $150,000 worth of liquid cash, just for one. From there, it's hard work, long hours, and it's tedious, but one of the things that has always attracted me is that this company operates with ethics. No dishonesty, no under-the-table dealing. And to me as a Muslim it was more important that if I associate myself with a company it was one that does not go against my principles.

Sometimes you feel that you are different or odd in the sense that you're not from the mainstream. I'll always remember what I heard a long time ago. Jesse Jackson said that excellence is the biggest deterrence against discrimination. To this day, I share that with my people. I have about 150 employees in my organization, and I challenge my people for excellence, because excellence separates everything out, even if you have a feeling that you're different.

Islam has kept me disciplined when there are temptations all around. Islam keeps me focused, keeps my priorities straight.

Chapter Six

Relations

*Let there be no compulsion in religion: Truth stands out clear
from Error: whoever rejects Evil and believes in Allah hath
grasped the most trustworthy handhold, that never breaks.
And Allah heareth and knoweth all things.*

Qur'an 2:256

Islam has many faces—the young boy struggling to follow his father at prayer in a mosque, the little girl suffering from thirst on her first day of fasting in life, the wizened old man fingering *zikr* beads, the old woman in *hijab*. These Islamic personalities are all players in a greater Islamic system, the greater Muslim community that has survived more than a millennium even in the most turbulent environments.

The key to survival has been Islam's ability to act as a sieve that can adapt or convert tension into a balancing act. If history serves as learning ground, Muslims will work to invoke a sense of religious tradition in America, while taking on certain cultural trappings of society at large and rejecting those that conflict with their Islamic ideals and beliefs.

Much of the dynamism of traditional Islam stems from Muslims' attitudes toward one another. *Hadith* stipulates that a Muslim should want for his brother or sister what he himself would want.

The Muslim family is, of course, the nucleus of the community. Ideally, individual family members shoulder clearly defined roles and responsibilities and are subject to certain rights delineated in the Qur'an. The roles are mutually complementary and reinforcing, though they can get complicated in America, particularly when family members share different religions.

243

*When a man has married, he has indeed made his religion half
perfect. Then let him fear Allah for the remaining half.*

Prophet Muhammad, *Hadith*
(al-Bukhari and Muslim)

Coming to America

Mona El-Raddaf

*She was born and educated in Cairo, where she ran a factory of 120 work-
ers. She lived in a dream world until her boss, a Christian, stunned her with
a marriage proposal. She refused to marry outside of her religion; so he
refused to retain her services. Now she lives the American Dream while
teaching her young son about the blessings of fasting during Ramadan and
refusing the pork that comes in hot dogs and pizza cherished by his friends.*

My mother and my father started praying regularly when they hit their
fifties. When they reached that age, they started thinking about the other
world. But they never forced religion on me.

The first school I attended was the Catholic school. It was run by nuns.
They taught Christianity. I used to sneak into church to watch them. I liked
it. I was six and a half. Then one day my father transferred me to a public
school. That was my first trauma. A few years later, my mother told me my
grandmother found me leaning next to the bed and praying. I knew I was a
Muslim, but I was young and I didn't know what I was doing.

I majored in Russian in Egypt. I thought that was a smart step, because
at that time, the Soviets were all over Egypt, and they were controlling
everything. I thought, If you know the language, maybe you can have a
better chance for a better job. But by the time I finished college, the Soviets
were gone. Perfect timing; I didn't even get to use it.

I used to like sewing. That was my hobby. When I finished college, I
worked in an international exhibition. I met this guy who had a lingerie

factory. He was starting a business in Egypt. He was Lebanese and Christian. I met him when I was twenty-three. I had a lot of energy and a lot of ideas, and he really liked the way I thought, and he thought he could use me in the factory. He sent me to Italy for four months, and I was trained in one of the big factories there. They taught me everything—patterns, mass production. I went to Jordan for six months to study in his factory, and then I started running his factory in Egypt.

You've heard of the Pygmalion story—this artist who made a statue and fell in love with it? That's what I think happened. He felt like he made me. He taught me everything. I worked with him for four years. I was really full of energy, and he was getting older. He was happy with my work. It was okay until I was thinking about getting married. I met somebody and I wanted to get married. And this guy went crazy. He didn't want me to go anywhere. Anyhow, he offered marriage, but it was impossible because he was Christian.

If it was up to me, I wouldn't mind, but I knew he would have to convert. If you want to marry a Christian woman, that's okay, but for a Christian man to marry a Muslim woman—that's forbidden.

He was going to convert. But my family was against it, so I just had to quit. That was the condition if I was going to marry another man.

But things didn't work. I got a divorce.

When you get divorced there, you can't live by yourself. You have to go back again to your parents' house. That's the way it is. So I went back and opened my own shop. I had four girls working for me. We made wedding dresses. That's where I met my [current] husband's sister. I met him when he went to Egypt. I didn't know he was looking for somebody. His sister's friend called me, and said there is this American and he wants to get married. I said, "No, I'm not going to go anywhere. I have five brothers, and I'm the youngest, and I don't want to leave them."

"Well, I promised him that I was going to talk to you. Please say hi, and you can give any excuse; just say you didn't like him. Don't embarrass me."

I met him. We talked, and I felt pretty good. I told him, "I can't just marry somebody that I met a couple of days ago. At least I got to make sure that you love me."

He said, "I can't love you in three days."

But that was my condition.

Anyhow, we met four or five days. I would finish my work and I would see him till two o'clock in the morning. There are a lot of places to go.

That's not normal in Egypt. I would come home and my parents would still be waiting for me. They said, "Okay, you want to get married, get married, because we can't stand it anymore. It's disgraceful for you to go out and come back so late."

After four or five days, he said, "I love you." I don't know if he was lying or not, but I got what I wanted. Then I said yes.

The girls were so excited. They said they were going to make my wedding dress, and if I didn't get married, I could save it. Every time I would go to the shop, they were working on it. . . .

We had a simple wedding.

I came here when I was thirty. My husband is Egyptian and he's been here for twenty years. He was married three times before to Americans. They were not Muslims. My husband is very Americanized, but he was afraid that when he had kids—what were they going to be? So I think he thought about getting married to a Muslim. It doesn't work out when you have two religions and the kids in the middle.

I came from a big city, and now I live in Youngstown, Ohio, so that was a shock. I felt very lonely when I came. I didn't know too many people. We didn't have a mosque until four years ago.

I used to think about God a lot. When I lived in Egypt, you could hear the *adhan* five times a day, because mosques are everywhere. It's kind of a reminder to you. You can't get it off your mind that you're a Muslim. But here: silence. Nothing. Nobody talks about religion. Yeah, they go to a church every Sunday, but I feel like it's just going to a movie. Even churches now, they compete on how they can make it easy on people so they'll come. It's business. The more people who go to a church, the more money they collect. And it's getting to be the same way in the mosques here.

In the mosques, we have Indians, Pakistanis, Arabs, and I don't know where to put myself. I'm from Egypt, but even the Arab countries always treat you different. They say either you're Egyptian or you're Arab. They don't consider us the same for some reason, I don't know why.

I didn't look for Muslims. I have all kinds of friends. I don't care if they're Christian or Jew or Muslim. I didn't think about whether I was a Muslim.

I was a sales associate in a big department store here, and I told my supervisor that I had to pray two times when I was working. She said, "No, I can't let you do that, because everybody else is going to tell me they need a break for something." It wasn't a big deal for me.

In Egypt, you have the right to go and pray, and nobody can stop you. But here, you have the freedom to wear whatever you want. Nobody's going to ask you questions.

I have a seven-year-old boy. When he was four I started praying with him, and when he started school I made him fast this year. Not the whole day. He would go without breakfast and not eat in school. When he would come home, I told him, "Every day you will have to make it a half hour more."

I didn't believe he was going to make it. I called his teacher to tell her, "When the other kids go to lunch, please give him something to do." She was so excited. That made him feel that he's special, that he was doing something different from the other kids. And all the time he's suffering. [*Laughs.*]

She sent me a note after it was over saying that she really admired his persistence. She said one time he felt pretty weak and she offered him a drink of water. He said, "No, I can't; I'm not supposed to."

I'm trying to do a better job with him than my parents did with me. I feel like you have to have something to hold on to. Because in the future he's going to see a lot of things.

(8) Have We not made for him a pair of eyes?—

(9) And a tongue, and a pair of lips?—

(10) And shown him the two highways?

Qur'an 90:8–10

Routes

Tazim Jaffer

Born in Dodoma, Tanzania, raised in Dar es Salaam, and married in Dublin, Ireland, Tazim lives today in a Midwestern city. She has been a minority wherever she has lived. Her forefathers were brought to Africa to work British railroads, and when African independence arrived, the political and economic situation became untenable for her family, forcing them to scatter around the globe. A few years back, she says, she met relatives in Kennedy, Heathrow, and Bombay airports all in the space of a single day, each living in a different country, each traveling in a different direction. She finds consolation and escape from her schizophrenic existence, she explains, in her artwork, where she creates and redefines her own boundaries.

I was raised in a traditional Ismāʿīlī family and I had a lot of pressure from my brothers to get married. I defied them because I was in love. My [future] husband had gone away to medical school while I was still in Africa. I decided that I wasn't going to marry someone else; I was going to wait until he was finished.

Finally when he finished, we got married in a registry office in Dublin. I wore a leather miniskirt.

The Ismāʿīlī Muslims follow the Aga Khan.[1] The previous Aga Khan had

[1] The Aga Khan is the spiritual leader of the Nizārī branch of Ismāʿīlīs. The title was given to Abu-l-Hasan ʿAli Shah in 1818 by the Shah of Persia. In 1841, after a failed rebellion against the Shah, Aga Khan I fled Persia to Afghanistan and then to Bombay. Aga Khan IV, Karim, the current Aga Khan, was born in 1936, educated at Harvard, and now lives near Paris. His

advised us to give up our traditional clothing and try to assimilate, so I remember all the changes we went through. Some of the elderly women when I was a child used to wear long dresses, and then overnight they gave up their shawls.

The Aga Khan has really raised the status of women in the Ismāʾīlī community. One of the things that he said was, If you have enough money to educate one person in your family, you should educate your daughter. I remember my father—he had to pick one person; he sent my sister instead of my brother to England to get an education.

The balance is now different, because the women are leaders in the community; they are more educated; they go into the rural areas to educate other people, and the men take over family businesses. The education is not equal. This creates problems in some cases.

My mother died when I was two years old. My father died when I was a teenager. I was raised by my brothers and sisters and they were young. I slept under a mosquito net. Where I was born, I have few memories, but our houses were rudimentary. They were of limestone and corrugated-metal sheets over the roof with thatch over it. There were so many kids, we would share one bed.

Sometimes I wonder if it's the same life I'm living or if I've been reborn several times, because everything changed: government, philosophy, housing, economics. And we kept moving and bettering ourselves.

My brothers ran rice and flour mills and they owned buildings, but most of it was nationalized in the 1960s and they eventually left—all of them.

Since you asked me for an interview, I tried to get some dates and some things from my family. I called my older sister who lived in Vancouver. She said all the dates were with my brother in London, but my sister in Calgary might remember. She remembered a few dates.

I found out some things that were never told to me: that my mother was a divorcée and my father married her, but she was married when she was twelve years old. It was an arranged marriage, and her husband was very abusive. He beat her and she fell and she broke her limbs. Five or six people went to get her back. It was a shock to me.

Because we were raised in traditional families and we went through a lot of changes, my husband and I thought we were very liberal. We wanted

followers believe he is the 49th Nizārī Ismāʾīlī Imam in an unbroken line of descent. There are perhaps more than two million Ismāʾīlīs today.

our children to have a liberal education, which we were deprived of. I wasn't allowed to get educated. I wanted to become a fashion artist and I remember my brothers telling me that if I had those ideas in my mind they won't even send me to England, because at that time they had just agreed to send me for a course.

We didn't have a very strict structure for our children. We gave them a very liberal education. My children are in contact with other Indians, a few Muslims. The Muslims that they meet are from Pakistan—Sunnis and other types of Shiites.

I was quite surprised that one day my friend from Washington had come and she was having a discussion with Parisa, and Parisa expressed that she wouldn't mind having an arranged marriage. I couldn't believe it!

She asked if Parisa felt pressure from us that she should get married. She said no, she had no pressure whatsoever. I went to my studio, where my husband was, and I said, "Guess what. Your daughter wants an arranged marriage."

That really baffles my mind. Especially since I defied tradition. I couldn't imagine what had caused her to think that way.

Has she told you why?

No. But I think I've decided why. Either she's too smart and she wants to hand over the responsibility, so that if the marriage fails, *we* are responsible for it, and she will not have to answer for it; or since we have given her everything, she wants to become more traditional. So she is rebelling back to tradition.

Are you going to arrange the marriage?

If I find a person that is suitable, I will arrange it, but otherwise, I have told her that if she finds somebody nice, okay. If it's an Ismā'īlī boy, that would be my first preference; if it is not, I have no objection to it. I think the genetic pool will be bigger. Also I think maybe this is one way of solving problems for peace. Because if a Jewish person marries a Muslim, and an Irish Catholic marries a Protestant, I think we might solve some of our problems.

My ideas are very liberal, but in some ways I am very conservative.

Tazim Jaffer.

Would you prefer an arranged marriage?

I am not going to advertise in papers, which some Indian people do, but just by word of mouth. I told this to my sisters. One of them said, "My gosh, don't go and tell people that you are looking for a boy!"
We're still looking.

Recently in Youngstown they have built a mosque, and in the mosque we have all the different types of Muslims. So a lot of their rituals and praying and ethics are different than I would be doing. It is more international. There are Muslims from the Middle East, Pakistan, India. When we go to the mosque, we sit on the floor but the Ismā'īlī women don't necessarily cover their heads. But in Pakistan they do cover their heads, because it's a different code of ethics for women.

When I went to the mosque here, I had my shawl on my shoulder. I had gone there for a social function. The prayers are held in the prayer hall upstairs. We were downstairs eating and I had my shawl on my shoulder. My hair was showing and I guess it was not acceptable.

One of the men got up and made an announcement: "There are some ladies that are very disrespectful and they don't have their heads covered."

I covered my head and I started to mutter to the next person, "I thought this was a social hall, not prayer."

Then she pointed out: "The whole *masjid* is considered part of the holy place."

Everybody perceives it differently.

I got out of that hall. But I still go there, because I miss not going to the mosque.

Why don't you cover your head and your legs?

The Aga Khan is trying to go along with the times, and to keep tradition in moderation and not to stand out. He interprets the Qur'an and he can change according to the times and the place. The Ismā'īlīs in Pakistan would have a different code than Ismā'īlīs, say, in England, and Ismā'īlīs in Afghanistan would have a completely different cultural aesthetic.

I think I've just gotten used to being treated like this everywhere. But I still miss the mosque, because, I mean, how much tennis can I play? There's a time and place when you want your own food, your own smells. They don't go away. You can lose everything but there are certain things that you miss.

By [the mystery of] the creation of male and female—

Qur'an 92:3

Vagabond

Tehmina Khan

Twenty-three. Student at the University of California at Berkeley. Born in America, the daughter of Indian Muslims. At odds with the cultural manifestations of Islam as practiced in her community, she established a student-initiated course on Islam in America at the university and founded a Muslim group. Many Muslim men at Berkeley didn't take well to being led by a woman, she says.

I consider myself a Muslim vagabond.

I find that I'm not completely at home here in America. I used to look at myself as being a tennis ball going back and forth on the court, trying to be like the perfect Indian Muslim girl, so to speak, or the American girl in my high school. There's strong pressures on either side trying to put you in a box.

I didn't go either way.

The Islamic community in San Jose that I grew up with was very Indian, and their sexism was very South Asian. We're brought up to be the perfect South Asian girl. There's a lot of pressure on girls within that cultural context—to learn how to cook, to dress a certain way, to serve, to do housework, to not question your parents too much, and all that.

All of this pressure, what it did as I was growing up was turn us against each other almost, because we wouldn't trust each other as sisters in the community. We would be picking at each other—well, she's not the perfect Muslim girl in this way, and she's not this and this. We would be putting the same kind of pressure that our parents put on us on each other, yet at the same time there's hypocrisy. We were only being this way around each other, but when we go to school we're different people.

To a great extent I'm really fed up with the South Asian Muslim community for all the cultural baggage and for a certain materialism. The South Asians are one of the wealthiest immigrant groups in this country—and very business-oriented, med school-oriented. The South Asian community is aspiring to work within the structure, and there's the feeling that if we are reasonable and if we talk to the power structure and let them know who we are, then we can be a part of the power structure and everything will be fine and we'll bring Islam to the power structure. In the black community, they know better. I think if we should bring the consciousness of the African American Muslim community to the South Asian Muslim community, then we can really have something.

I'm not particularly living in a Muslim community. I deal with the Muslim community when I want to, when I feel like it on my own terms as an adult. I can be myself and be Muslim at the same time. That's something that took me a long, long time to realize.

As I got older, my parents started talking about marriage. They were talking about arranged marriage, and they were talking about what are we going to do about our children, how are they going to get married? They were very worried about it. And that sort of annoyed me. My parents know me well enough to know I wouldn't deal with an arranged marriage.

In Hyderabad, India, women don't go to the mosque. I went to the mosque with my grandmother a couple of times, not during congregational prayer hours. I was fourteen years old. Eid was the next day. I said, "Great, we can all go to Eid prayers in India; this is really exciting."

And then someone told me, "Women don't go to Eid prayers here."

What! I was really disappointed.

Here I do go to Eid prayers. But even still a lot of mosques really alienate women. I get really upset. When they opened the [Berkeley] mosque last Friday it was very patriarchal. When they were speaking, that was the attitude that came across in most of the men. The men that were speaking were speaking to the brothers, you know. It was like they were talking to each other and completely ignoring our existence.

And I don't like being in a separate room. I can't hear what's going on out there, and it's assumed that I don't need to hear what's going on out there.

When people come to this country from their country, a lot of them become even more defensive and even more strict about roles, about society, about process. The Muslim men are trying to build a refuge where they're in control, so they exercise this control on the women. Also men are trying to create a situation where they're in power, a this-is-our-domain kind of attitude.

Women's liberation is possible in Islam given what the Qur'an says and given examples that we've had through history—that women can take control of their lives and have self-determination in Islam, which is key.

The idea of Islam [is] submission to God alone. It's not a woman's submission to a man; it's women and men submitting to God—I mean, that's the core of Islam.

I think [liberation] is possible but also very problematic given the fact that Islam has been interpreted by men for 1,400 years, and it's been used in many ways to the advantage of men. There's a lot of serious thinking that needs to be done, a lot of working things out, and a lot of serious education.

Most women don't know their own rights within Islam. They think it's okay for their husband to beat them. I talked to women in Egypt who think that it says in the Qur'an that they have to cook and clean for their husband. It doesn't say anything like that in the Qur'an.

What we need to do here is educate ourselves as women in what possibilities we have within Islam and organize ourselves as women so that we don't let the men overpower us.

Khadijah, the Prophet's [first] wife, is a good example.[2] She was forty years old when she married him. She ran her own business. She proposed to him. She took control of her life.

In Islam if you look at the example of Prophet Muhammad and his relationships with his wives, you see that he did housework, that he mended his clothes, that he was very kind and loving, and that his relationships with his wives were not ones of power and control but of love.

It is possible in Christianity, but I think Islam spells things out more than Christianity. Islam acknowledges the sexual rights of women and men, the right to sexual fulfillment and that a husband has to satisfy his wife sexually, emotionally, so that he just doesn't use and abuse her.

But I've always had problems with the idea of polygamy.

[2] She was the first to believe Muhammad was charged with a divine mission. He was twenty-five at the time of their marriage. She died at age sixty-five in 619.

*None of you [truly] believes until he wishes for his brother
what he wishes for himself.*

Prophet Muhammad, *Hadith*
(al-Bukhari and Muslim)

A Good Addition

Halima Touré

*She spoke in the lower level of the Mosque of Islamic Brotherhood in
Harlem. A doctoral candidate in applied linguistics at Teachers College,
Columbia University, she is on the faculty of Hostos Community College,
City University of New York. She is forty-seven.*

Sisters will confront the question of polygamy by saying, "Right."

Or they will say, "*Aaaaaaaaaaaaaaaaaaaaaaaaaaaaahhhhhhhhhhhhhh!*"

Then it starts you thinking: Well, why in the world would such a thing
like that be allowed anyway?

It made sense. First of all, there usually are more women than men.
There were very few cases in the history of humankind where polyandry
existed, a woman with more than one husband at the same time. It tended
to be polygamy.

So what is a husband anyway? And what is a wife? How do I relate to
this other woman then?

In this culture women are taught to be competitors. And what polygamy
is saying is: we're sisters. And that's a whole new concept. The women's
liberation movement talks about sisterhood. This is another way of looking
at it. That's my sister over there. She's not my enemy. She's not my competition. And supposedly a Muslim wants for her brother or sister what she
wants for herself. So if that's the case, then, I see this sister out there who's
got two children, by herself, such a good sister, struggling. If I had reached
that stage of higher development, I could say to my husband, "Why don't

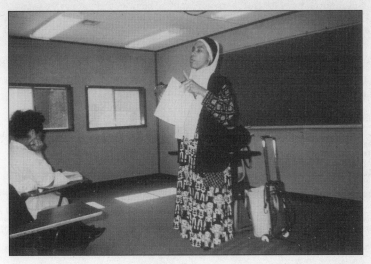

Halima Touré.

you look at her? Maybe she'd make a good addition to our family. And those children need a father figure."

You're looking at extended families then. It's not: This is my man and nobody can have him. Uh-uh. We all belong to Allah; we're all going back to Allah. We all came from Him and to Him we shall return. We don't own anybody. And the best we can do in this life is try to live this life the way Allah intended us to, and get as many blessings as we can.

You're not supposed to die in the same situation that you were born in. You somehow have to move, to grow, and I'm not talking about just physically, but spiritually. That's part of seeking Allah.

The issue of polygamy rose when I was married to my son's father and we had a situation where someone in the community was taking another wife. So all the sisters were saying: Oh my goodness, this might happen to me! How will we face this?

Well, it does say in Islam a man can have up to four wives. Why? I started thinking about that. Well, what would I do if that situation came up? And I came to the conclusion that that woman is really like my sister. I would call her sister, and well, I would care about her. So then it was this whole idea of almost enlarging yourself and seeing yourself as part of a larger family.

The issue led to a lot of ways of opening up my thinking: Oh, the concept of the extended family. Gee, that must be nice then. The children have all these women to relate to. All of these sisters in the community are his aunts. And all the brothers are his uncles.

I think it's just a wonderful way to grow up. You always know that there's somebody who's looking out for them. I just love that concept. It's not an exclusionary kind of thing; it's an inclusionary kind of thing. And so on one level polygamy could allow for that, that extended family. And it's not just this little turf.

Look at a monogamous situation. I started to see a lot of parallels. I started to see men who've had two women for a number of years. They couldn't marry both of them legally, but yet they had a girlfriend, a mistress, and had their family. The back-street situation, they used to call it.

But here, what we're saying is: Oh yes, I know what marriage is. It's a responsibility. It's not just sowing oats. It's making an honest woman of this woman. Taking care of her children. Giving psychological support. It's about responsibility.

Polygamy is not obligatory. If a man feels like he can't handle it, then he's the last person who ought to be doing it. The whole point of it, though, is intention. And you know what? If a brother says, "This is what I want," but deep down he says, "That's a fine woman. I just want to get her in bed"—he doesn't get away with it. You reap what you sow, because of the nature of law. And I'm talking about spiritual law.

Allah is the God, the All-Knowing. His law is always operating. Spiritual laws are always operating. One of my husband's favorite sayings used to be: "You know, ignorance of the law is no excuse, because you will still be affected by it."[3]

His analogy was the law of gravity. Suppose you don't know anything about the law of gravity and you jump off a building. What's going to happen to you? You fall. It has nothing to do with whether you knew about gravity or not; you are affected by it. So yes, you can be affected by your ignorance, and ma'shallah,[4] your enlightenment will come, and you'll say, Oh, that won't happen again.

Islam encompasses the totality of my life. People aren't disconnected human beings. They live in community. And in your community, you have a similar way of life, a similar way of looking at life. And I felt the only way we could live Islam in America was in communities.

If someone had told me the year before I became a Muslim that I'd be a Muslim, I'd have laughed in their face. I'd have said, "A Muslim—oh, c'mon! Wearing those long dresses!"

[3] Her second husband, Imam K. Ahmad Tawfiq, died in 1988.
[4] "Whatever is the will of Allah."

In Islam, my life changed completely. It was gradual. My first husband introduced me to Sunni Islam at a point in my life when I was seeking something. It was Islam. And I've met people after we were divorced who were shocked that I was still a Muslim. They thought that women became things because the men wanted it. I said, "But I became a Muslim for me—so why are you surprised?" It's been twenty years. I probably didn't realize how much of a change I was looking for.

Imam Tawfiq said at the time of my *shahada:* "Now this is the first step. This is the easy part—becoming a Muslim. You've just gotten on the road. Living the life of a Muslim—that's the hard part. That is the struggle. That is the *jihad*. The great *jihad*."

I don't talk about it unless somebody asks me. The only one you can change is yourself, so that's the one I'm working on.

I remember when I was doing one of those temp jobs, a woman said: "Gee, you seem so intelligent. How could you be a Muslim?" [*Laughs.*] And I said, "Oh, I like to think it's *because* I'm so intelligent."

"Like the sisters say: there's Islam,
and then there's Hislam."

Unidentified Muslim woman[5]

Three Women and a Man

And if you have reason to fear that you might not act
equitably toward orphans, then marry from among [other]
women such as are lawful to you—[even] two, or three, or four:
but if you have reason to fear that you might not be able to treat
them with equal fairness, then [only] one—or [from among] those
whom you rightfully possess. This will make it more likely that
you will not deviate from the right course.

Qur'an 4:3

[5] *The Village Voice*, May 28, 1991.

The Wives:

Shoshana Hamin

thirty-four
Wife No. 1; married 1978; mother of five

Kaliymah Hamin

thirty-nine
Wife No. 2; married 1981; mother of three

Amina Hamin

thirty-six
Wife No. 3; married 1988; mother of six

"I want her to have a happy, healthy relationship
with my husband . . ."

In a Muslim community-owned building called the Table Spread, three women sat at a large semicircular marble desk and discussed married life, sharing the same man. It felt like the Phil Donahue television show.

Amina: I was in a monogamous relationship, and I prefer a polygamous relationship. For one thing, you get time away from each other and you get time to deal with things that you have to deal with, separately and apart. And I think it makes you a stronger person. I've learned a lot of things about myself. I've learned how to be patient and giving and strong when I need to be. I don't have to be so self-reliant when I've got other people to depend on. But I don't have all that one-on-one time with my husband.

Shoshana: I was never in a monogamous relationship. What I do is look at the alternatives to [polygamy], and that's the scary part. I don't know if a woman says that she prefers it. But certainly, it's something to hold on

261

to. It's an anchor, especially in [this] society. I imagined myself being in a sound and stable relationship, and that's what this is.

Kaliymah: When you come into polygamy, you marry the man, but you also marry the sisters too, because a lot of the time, you deal with the sisters in terms of interacting with children, shopping, whatever. I'd say maybe fifty percent of your time, maybe less, you're dealing with your husband per se; you're dealing with the sisters more on a one-to-one basis in your daily living.

My parents didn't really have any problem with me embracing Islam as a way of life, religion. That was fine. But they had a problem with accepting the polygamy aspect of it. At that time it was 1980-something, like you know, women don't *do* this, and why can't you find your own husband? That was their thing. After the birth of my first child, it became a little bit easier. Then I had my second child, and the third. I went through a lot of problems. It was a struggle giving birth to her. My parents accepted polygamy more after that because there was a point where I might have left this earth, and if that happened, the sisters would have to come to some kind of agreement with my husband in order to take care of the children. I think that really kind of clinched it for my parents. They accept my co-wives; they know who they are. I call them my sisters-in-law.

Shoshana: It's really about family; that's why we're in polygamy—family in a very broad sense. And in a family you have to respect each other and be understanding and cooperative. That's the key to getting along with anyone: basic respect and fairness and consideration.

I come from a family of ten brothers and sisters.

Amina: Seven [for me].

Kaliymah: Four.

Kaliymah: *On the children:* They know who their mother is, and as a mother you know your child, but if one of their children call, as a mother you just respond. And if they're doing something wrong and I hit them, and they go, "I'm going to tell that to Mommy!"

"Oh, really? Now, you're going to get it some more!"

I don't think any one of us would abuse any other's child, and if I felt that either one of them was abusive to my children, certainly my character wouldn't allow me to let that ride. We definitely would have to deal with it. I think we all have that kind of character.

Shoshana's the first wife, and then I came in after her, and we've hit some rocky roads. We were not incompatible in our character, but we had our own personal problems, and you grow up, you get older, you mature— it's about feeling secure about yourself. You begin to develop as a woman —even though you thought you were a woman when you got into the relationship. It sort of works out. So some of the things that we went through, Amina has not dealt with and she probably will not, because we've worked out the foundations of this.

Shoshana: Polygamy can be your anchor; your family can be your anchor. But there are those times when the family is the source of your turmoil. That's when you have to reach in yourself to the root of that Oneness that is the Most High.

I would say there's probably tinges of jealousy and it kinda sorta fades away rather quickly. I won't deny any of us that human quality, jealousy.

Amina: It's very normal, very natural. I was surprised to feel it. I was surprised at how little there is of it, though. We kind of bond together, and I would feel for her, or for Kaliymah in most situations like I would feel for my sister. That kind of overpowers any type of jealous feelings you might have. I want her to have a happy, healthy relationship with my husband, because if she doesn't, some of the flak from that will fall back and I'll have to deal with it. I want him to be happy with her, with Kaliymah, so that *I* can be happy with him.

We help in subtle ways, by being there for each other and being supportive of each other, or maybe in conversation with the brother, I might mention: You know everything's okay between us, but I think you really hurt her feelings, and all it would take is a kind word, and that sort of thing, and I'm sure that if I have a problem, one of them might say, It wasn't all that bad what she did.

Shoshana: There are a lot of funny moments that would only occur under these circumstances . . .

The strangest?

I would say walking in on either one of them and there might have been a tender moment going on—and you just feel like a little bit out of place for a second. I know that has happened to me.

As women, I don't think we will really ever understand polygamy from a male point of view, just as he'll never be able to understand polygamy from our point of view.

Kaliymah: In this case the husband has three or two other options. It's not like the brother has to be with one sister all the time. If he's not at my house, then I know that he's at her house or Shoshana's house. So I think that's why it might have come into practice at the time of the Prophet—to stop all the wildness from going on.

I think there's a lot of people in polygamous situations that don't know that they are in polygamous situations. You have the wife, and then you have the other person on the side. At least I relate to these sisters every day. We know each other. We interact; it's not like I'm here, and there's somebody else down the road, and I don't know that somebody else, and maybe somebody else knows that other somebody else and they're looking at me, saying, Oh, she's a fool. If somebody sees him with her, they know that's his wife and he's supposed to be there, and that's fine.

Amina: If a person can't deal in a situation one to one, polygamy doesn't make it better. Polygamy won't save a failing marriage. There has to be the basics there first, and then you can work from there. I think I was a polygamous person even when I was married to a monogamous person. I think a polygamous person is a person who sees family in a broader sense than a monogamous person would, and I saw family in a broader sense. I saw opportunities for our families to possibly expand and for different things to be accomplished.

She was married to a Muslim in the past—monogamously.

It was so boring; the pace has stepped up so much—just life itself, things happening . . . There's so many more people involved. Things are a little more complex.

Shoshana: In sticking with any relationship you learn its quirks and you eliminate them as time goes on, and in that sense we aid each other because we're all working on eliminating the quirks.

Kaliymah: We're separate but we're together at the same time. Her anniversary is her anniversary and that's their time together; my anniversary is my time together with him. We may enjoy that day together.

Shoshana: We really live our lives together, although we don't live together. We're the friends of the family, the family, and we're the babysitters. We're in our own little world here.

Kaliymah: *On equal time spent with their husband:* Basically it varies. For the most part our husband tries to equal it out. I mean, there's times when maybe in a week, I may see him maybe once, then maybe in the following week it will balance itself out. It kinda varies. I guess it's what you require. There's times when we may not be getting along, so I may feel we don't deal, but there's nothing wrong with that.

Amina: We went to a dance once, and we were waiting for him to park the car. The people working there had to check our coats:

"Could we check your coats?"

And I said, "We're waiting for our husband."

They just kind of looked at us. I thought it was very amusing.

The Husband

Abdul Latiyf Hamin

forty-five

Not many American Muslims practice polygamy. The amir and minister of information for the African Islamic Mission,[6] headquartered in Long Island, is among a rare breed.

The Mission's full-time members wear African-inspired Islamic clothing, and work daylong at Mission-sponsored jobs—teaching, selling Mission-produced goods. Other members, working at outside jobs, donate funds.

The amir sat and listened quietly for most of the time his three wives talked.

I have about eighteen children. Something like that. In that area. It's not that I lose count, I *don't* count. Nine—no, eight boys, and about, oh, seven girls. Khadijah, Yasmin, Nuriddeen . . . I have guardianship over them, and I consider them my children. I don't treat [them] any different than I would him [*indicates his son, who's listening.*] And this is my natural son, so to speak.

Biological children?

About fifteen. I don't like to make those kinds of separations. And I could get more at any time, not so many biologically, necessarily, but because of my position, children could come and go in my life. These are permanent people in my life, *insh'allah*, if Allah wills. But say if a sister came into the community and had three children, I automatically become her guardian. Till she gets married, I watch over her like her father would. Her children become like my grandchildren.

We have what we call a religious commitment. The constitution of the United States of America says that people are allowed to have a commitment toward each other, religious, any kind of way. This is part of practic-

---

[6] It claims a membership of 8,000 Muslims, with offices in Liberia and Senegal.

ing my faith. My book sanctions it. This country is founded on religious convictions, and this is my religious conviction.

The Mormons openly practice it, but most judges don't even want to hear it. They don't want to bother with it, because of the complexities of it. But then, it sure beats adultery.

I don't operate through City Hall. I operate through City Hall like Jesus said: Give to Caesar that which belongs to Caesar; give to Allah what belongs to Allah.

Marriage is Allah's.

Presently we have three separate households. We didn't used to live like that, and we won't live like this in the future.

It's very unnatural to have three households with children and claim to be a family. A family eats, sleeps, and lives together. It's one of the basics of family. That's where all the love and everything else develops from. And it's economically ridiculous to do something like that. Islam is about pooling and sharing.

Right now we see our three dwellings as a very temporary arrangement. We will do it until our struggle manifests something different. And we work fervidly toward it every day of our lives—to combine.

When brothers come and talk to me about polygamy, I say, You should have one household if you have the space. If you don't have the space, then work on it. Don't ruin your marriage by stacking sisters on top of each other. I just don't personally think that it works for people to be stacked. And I think that it causes undue havoc in the household and confusion because it's too crowded and people tend to get on each other's nerves more, so space is a prime consideration.

The Prophet said: "Religion is sincerity."

We said: "To whom?"

*He said: "To Allah and His Book, and His Messenger, and
to the leaders of the Muslims and their common folk."*

Hadith (Muslim)

The Messenger's Kin

Ayman Muhammad

*Born in 1921, he is the eldest child of Elijah Muhammad—a slim man who
dresses like a haberdasher. He was there from the beginnings of his father's
involvement with the Nation of Islam.*

I was nine years old when I first saw Master Farad.

Master Farad was not by himself when he visited our home. He was with
one of his secretaries and his name was Eugene Ali. They had a private
conversation in the living-[room]-combination-bedroom of my father—
Master Farad, his secretary, and my father.

On Master Farad's second visit to our home, our beloved father introduced his children to Master Farad. My father had in the very beginning
taught that Master Farad was our savior. When I was incarcerated with my
father during World War II,[7] my father said to me, "Son, I want to tell you
something. When I grew into my first knowledge of Master Farad, I went
to him and asked him was he our long-awaited Jesus that the world been
looking for for the past two thousand years?" He said, "Son, Master Farad

---

[7] Elijah Muhammad enrolled his children in a Nation of Islam school in Detroit, but was
arrested in 1934 and charged with contributing to the delinquency of minors. He was released
on the condition that he return his children to public school. He refused and moved to
Chicago in September. Then in 1942 he was arrested for refusing to register for the draft, and
sentenced to five years in prison. He was paroled in 1946.

said to me, 'Yes, I am that one that the world been looking for for the last two thousand years.' "

Then he said that after he grew more and more into the knowledge of Master Farad, he went to him the second time, and asked him, "Are you the God that's supposed to come and separate the righteous from the wicked and destroy the wicked?"

He said, "Master Farad's eyes grew small and he changed to a reddish complexion and said to me, with his finger pointed in my face, 'Who would believe that but you?' "

The last time I saw Master Farad, he left our home in Detroit, Michigan, May 26, 1933. Master Farad was given twenty-four hours by the police commissioner in Detroit to leave the state of Michigan. From Detroit, Master Farad came to Chicago, and as my father said, as soon as [Farad] arrived here in Chicago, he was arrested. But he did not spend no time in jail. They turned him loose. He stayed here in Chicago for a while before he left for good. Master Farad said that he was going up in the mountains, where the cavies (he referred to the Caucasian race of people as cavies)—where they would not be able to find him. Master Farad didn't specify no particular mountain. That was in 1934.

Master Farad first made my father minister. Later he made him the supreme minister of all the temples. He also made my uncle the supreme captain of the Nation of Islam and also the head investigator. My uncle was envious of my father's position; he became an enemy of my father. He died because he began to be an alcoholic after he was expelled from the Nation of Islam under my father's leadership. [My uncle] lost his mind. Sometimes he would be out walking the street talking to himself. My father said, "Allah put him in that condition," but at that time he meant Master Farad put him in that condition.

My father had ministers teach in one place while he went someplace else and established another temple. While he was on the run for seven years, he established a temple in Washington, D.C., and other places. I was working, trying to help provide the family with food and other necessities. Due to the fact that my father during the Depression could not get a job, my mother and I are the ones who supported the family. I used to be a junker, and I would go up and down alleys with my little wagon and junk for cardboard, paper, milk bottles, brass, copper, and all these other things. My mother used to work for white folks as a maid. She cooked their food. She sewed clothes for white folks' children. She scrubbed their floor,

Ayman Muhammad.

washed dishes, washed walls. My father was out trying to find a job. He got a job in Cleveland in a foundry until he was able to save enough money to move to Detroit with his father, who was already here. And after that, he sent for his family.

He had various jobs in Detroit before the coming of Master Farad. He used to work at a Dodge plant. He used to work at the American Brass Company.

Master Farad came to us in 1930 and at that time [my father] was out of a job then.

My father used to tell his family that what is written in the Holy Qur'an concerning Prophet Muhammad is his life story—that *he* is that Muhammad that the Holy Qur'an is speaking about. One day, I said, "Dad, those books that you gave me to study on Prophet Muhammad—how can you say that you are that Muhammad that the Holy Qur'an is speaking about when you haven't suffered what Prophet Muhammad suffered thirteen hundred years ago? Prophet Muhammad was in battle. You said to me

yourself that Muslim women on the battlefield shielded Prophet Muhammad, and they [took] the arrows to save Prophet Muhammad's life. You
ain't never been on no battlefield, and ain't nobody never shot no arrows at
you. So how can you claim that that's you?"

Of course, my father got kind of angry with me and said, "Son, you will
understand one of these days." And he left it like that.

I don't believe my father deliberately led anyone astray. He was a firm
believer in what he taught.

At the last convention, Savior's Day, he said, "It is time for us to stop
calling white folks the devil because there's some black devils too—and the
white race understands who they are. We understand who they are. Why
keep on calling the man a devil?"

He was beginning to change some of his teaching and I believe it was due
to his understanding of the Holy Qur'an. He taught that whatever a
prophet of God wished for or had in mind, God accepted it. Like Prophet
Muhammad in history had many wives—and God was satisfied with that,
according to what my father believed. He taught that the Messenger had
privileges that [we] didn't have.

I believe that my father was a messenger sent by Allah to us here, the
Afro-Americans in America. But I don't want you to think that I believe
that my father was a major prophet or a messenger like Prophet Muhammad and the ones that God sent prior to Prophet Muhammad.

*Not a word does he utter but there is a sentinel
by him, ready [to note it].*

Qur'an 50:18

The Communicator

Wali Farad Muhammad

*The forty-two-year-old son of Wali and Rayya Muhammad and grandson
of Elijah Muhammad is a disc jockey at a Chicago "dusties" radio station,
WVAZ-FM. In Chicago, at least, his voice is recognizable for other reasons
too: He has done voiceovers for television commercials, cartoon voices for
"The Adventures of Muhammad Ali," color commentation for the
Muhammad Ali vs. Ken Norton heavyweight championship bout, and has
been master of ceremonies for Luther Vandross, Patti LaBelle, Ray
Charles, and Tina Turner.*

I am the Honorable Elijah Muhammad's grandson. That's a great honor
and I always felt that way. I feel even more so now. But I also tried to keep
a balance. I tried to come up as just a regular person. I didn't want to play
it up and be too arrogant about it.

My mother remembers seeing [W. D. Farad Muhammad] in the early
1930s in Detroit. This was before the Honorable Elijah Muhammad even
converted to Islam. He was still a Christian. At that time, him not having a
religion, he did a lot of drinking. My mother remembers that he had gotten
so drunk one time—he would get paid and get drunk on Friday nights—my
grandmother had to go out and look for him or he would have gambled all
his money away before he got home.

One time my uncle Ayman told me they were looking for him. They
knew that he was supposed to be coming home from work. Every time he
gets paid he goes on these binges. One of the neighbors said, "Oh, Mrs.

272

Poole! Your husband is out laying on the railroad track. You better go get him because the train is going to be coming soon."

So they went out there. Ayman was a little boy—eight, nine years old. He and his mother, they ran out there and they grabbed him off the track just in time, because the train was coming. They saved his life.

They didn't have welfare or anything like that. I remember Ayman telling me he used to go in garbage cans behind the stores and get the vegetables that people were throwing out and get the best pieces and take them home.

So that was one of the miracles of Islam coming to the Poole family at that time—how Master Farad Muhammad, with the knowledge of Islam and teachings of Islam, converted and changed Elijah Poole into Elijah Muhammad.

Many years later, my grandfather had a syndicated radio program. *Muhammad Speaks* was on about a hundred radio stations throughout the country. I did the opening and closing announcements for him. I would bring him on and whenever you heard him, I was the announcer for the national broadcast. That was my very first [radio] job.

I went to Midwestern Broadcasting School and studied broadcasting and learned techniques of announcing radio and TV and all of that. I felt— what better way to propagate the faith than to get on the mass media. We can do it in terms of reaching the people in a tenth of the time that it would take to go from door to door and see people one on one. So that was my big vision—of us one day buying a radio station, a TV station, own our own network eventually.

A lot of people would say, "You playing all that old boogety-boogety." Well, I never did really play that kind of music at first. When I first got into the industry, I was playing jazz. Even before that, I had my own radio program, which I'm still working on now. The show I did was called "The Communicator." Now, this show, it was positive thought and music with a message. It was on the air about five years. I would use The Last Poets, things like that—Nikki Giovanni, John Coltrane's "The Master Plan."

The music we play here is adult contemporary music. We don't play any rap. We don't play any house music. This music is not the kind of music that gives me a problem. We play hits and dusties. Dusties means older or gold songs of the '60s, '70s. All of our songs are pretty well screened before they go on, so we don't play any stuff that's going to be suggestive.

The only problem I used to have is that I wouldn't do—and I still don't do—any pork commercials. I don't want to do any alcohol commercials. The station plays them, but I won't go on and say, "I want you to buy Miller High Life Beer" or "I want you to buy a quarter pound of chitterlings." No, I won't do that—and they know that.

The person who really gave me the confidence to keep going was my grandfather. He was so proud of what I did, he said, "You have a voice I never heard before. You have a beautiful voice and you speak so well."

He had to okay his broadcasts. He would record the broadcast and we would edit it and then bring it back to him to approve it. Over the dinner table when all of the ministers and secretaries were there on Sundays, we would always sit and listen to the broadcast. He would make everybody be quiet at the end of it so he could hear me. He said, "Quiet! Here he comes now." That just blew me away.

I looked at him as two people. I looked at him as Elijah Muhammad, the man I see that takes his tie off at home and his slippers or whatever. The one who gave me the silver dollars or the one that sneaked me some money to go get some shoes. That's the grandfather I saw.

On the other hand, I saw Elijah Muhammad, the messenger of Almighty God. I believed that he had actually sat down with God, and talked with Him. We believed at that time that God was a flesh-and-blood person, that God's spirit was in this one man, Master Farad Muhammad.

So you looked at him with awe: "Oh, this man actually saw God!" And even my mother: "Ma, you saw God!" People that you believe that actually saw the Creator, the God Almighty, you looked at them as a whole different realm. I looked at him with fear.

I still checked out other religions. I was always weighing. It wasn't blind faith, no. I believed in God, I believed in Allah. I'd say, Well you are His messenger; you always taught me to trust and to believe in God and to pray to Him and you didn't tell me to pray to you—not to Grandfather. You were just His messenger. You were giving the message that He told you to tell us, but He was the Man to answer. Allah answers your prayers. Allah hears your cries at night. He's the One that hears your thinking. My thoughts were that if I had any problem, I'll just pray to Allah; He'll help me. And He did. I didn't have any problem where I was so hung up on my grandfather.

I said, well, I don't see anything better than this out here in the world for me. I didn't see it. I didn't see any better preachers. I didn't see any better social life.

Wali Farad Muhammad.

[My grandfather's] main thing was trying to accumulate as much assets as he could for the Nation and get as much visibility as he could for the Nation and as much progress as he could for the Nation, during those last years that he had here on earth. I know he knew he didn't have too much time, 'cause he was very sick. He had asthma. Plus he had the burden of running the whole Nation almost by himself. No decision was made unless he gave the final approval. He did everything from that dining-room table. He built the farms from the dining-room table. He bought every mosque from that dining-room table. He never went physically to see the buildings. He may have seen the farm once. He put a lot of trust in his captains and lieutenants and his secretaries.

He was very intent upon getting the Nation to be a shining star. So that means his whole idea was in the acquisition of assets of physical things, because he said, "You got to *show* black people what you got. They are very materialistic. They got to see a car. They got to see your new shoes." And even in our meetings, you would always hear, "Look how prosperous we are." All that was was bait to get more converts into the religion, because if you can't get them through religion, through Islam or through the Qur'an, then show them prosperity. What are the ministers doing now?

They show you how much you can get by you being with me. Look at [Rev. Jerry] Falwell. Look at all of them. They all were talking about getting prosperity, prosperity, prosperity. So Elijah Muhammad had schools. This man had temples all over the country. He had farms everywhere. He had businesses everywhere. He had restaurants, grocery stores. He had this, he had that.

His message was to try to save the black man's life. It was under the auspices of Islam. But he didn't teach you all the tenets of Islam. His daily lecture was survival, doing for self, becoming an upright man, knowing that you are the best, and you are not a slave anymore and you are equal to or better than anybody else. You are the Original Man. Those were basically social things.

Some of the things he taught us were wrong. It wasn't correct according to the Qur'an. But what he was doing was to get us to come out of the gutter, to get ourselves cleaned up to be Muslims, to prepare for the next teacher, which is what he always said. He said, "I'm going to prepare you for the next man, the next teacher. He will have a whole new book."

I remember as a child that the Qur'an was always on my mother and father's mantelpiece in the living room. It stayed up there. They always dusted it off and kept it clean but we never read it. I just always knew that that was a great book to respect.

I finally opened that book when the Imam [W. D. Mohammed] came in. I finally started reading it again because it was required as a Muslim during the month of Ramadan to read the whole Qur'an from cover to cover. And my first time ever reading that book was '76, when we started actually practicing Ramadan in its correct form. I was really impressed. That opened up a whole new door for me. I never knew things about the religion, about Allah, about creation. It opened my mind even more so.

There are some Muslims who had never seen the Qur'an until 1975, and they can recite it by heart now. They practice the religion better than the Muslims over in the East. We went through a lot of hell and a lot of strife just for the establishment of Islam in America. We're still going through struggles.

*And [the Unbelievers] plotted and planned, and Allah too
planned, and the best of planners is Allah.*

Qur'an 3:54

Chapter Seven

Ground Zero

As Christians and Jews pass on proud traditions, Muslims in many cases
are cut off from their past or from one another, and are sometimes not
allowed to live entirely as Muslims. Widely held stereotypes about Islam
and Muslims have become a national trait, creating a kind of blindness in
the general populace and forcing Muslims either to fade quietly into the
background or to become preoccupied with overcoming abuse. As a result,
Muslims often find themselves playing out the role of victim in America.
Unless Muslims remain vigilant, the nature of their involvement in many
major institutions—the military, schools, government—can place them in
even odder positions: as participants in their own victimization. As the
storm brews around them, Muslims find themselves constricted. But they
insist that Allah is the best of planners and defenders.

Truly Hell is as a place of ambush—

For the transgressors a place of destination.

Qur'an 78:21–22

Few Merciful Men

Samir Gustavo Jerez

According to Muslims in the Military, a Pentagon-based organization, there are Muslim military personnel in over 90 percent of the military bases worldwide. The Muslim population in the U.S. armed forces in 1993 was estimated at well over 5,000.[1]

Muslim military personnel are working toward gaining religious equality throughout the services. In the meantime, Muslim personnel in the Pentagon use the chaplain's office to hold juma *prayer services on Friday, moving aside chairs and spreading paper towels on spots where they press their foreheads to the rug. They also publish a small magazine,* Muslim Military Members, Unity in Uniform.

Samir Jerez, born in New York of Cuban and Puerto Rican ancestry, converted while an E4 at Camp Pendleton, California. A training film shown at Troop Info Day offended his religious sensibilities.

Everybody who's a sergeant or below goes to these training classes. One of them was on terrorism. It was conducted by the Navy. This class was a film called *American Exposé,*[2] produced by Jack Anderson. This film depicted Muslims, and only Muslims, as terrorists. It was supposed to be a global perspective of terrorism, and it wasn't. It concentrated on the Middle East.

It starts off with intro music and you see excerpts of people who are maimed in the street, shot, and stabbed. People bleeding and hurting and

[1] Source: U.S. Defense Department.
[2] *American Exposé: Target USA.*

278

other people crying, and, ironically, the people crying are Muslims, because they're wearing *hijab*.

They show Muslims in prayer, and they say there's a new era of fundamentalism coming around, and you see Muslims praying, and then the next scene, you'll see a person blown apart and this lady crying next to him.

It says: If they want to die for their God, then maybe we ought to go over there and help them.

The film was really boiling my blood. I was fighting myself not to just blow up. It was about forty-five minutes long. It shows a little old lady in *hijab* walking down the street, and says she could be the next terrorist. You see these Muslim kids, and it says they could be the next terrorists.

When the film was over, the first question that was asked was "Why don't we just take our super guns and blow them all away?" referring to Muslims. That really hurt me. The answer was a sarcastic response about a Presidential order which disallowed assassinations.

We're talking about Marines who just saw a bunch of pictures of their comrades, Marines who had died in the Beirut bombing. I could sense what they were feeling. I heard comments like "Man, we really need to go ahead and take care of them all, and just get rid of them. This world would be a better place." Comments like "Those nasty rag heads."

I really couldn't blame those people because that's the only exposure that they got, and to be honest with you, before I knew a lick of Islam, I myself would wear these gung-ho-type T-shirts, Marine Corps-related, and go on a plane hoping to meet a Muslim who was getting ready to attack the plane.

My question was "You said that Yasir Arafat was the originator of terrorism. What ever happened to the Mafia?"

The instructor said, "No, the United States government recognizes terrorism as being originated in 1968 by Yasir Arafat."

I challenged him. I said, "Are you sure?"

He said, "Yes, I'm sure."

Then I also asked, "Is this a global perspective of terrorism, because I would think that terrorism exists all over the world?"

He says, "This is appropriate, this is a good assessment."

He answered about seven or eight questions and there was a break, and I approached him and I said, "I'm willing to do some research. Do you mind if I get a copy of this tape? Because I really think I could use it."

Samir Gustavo Jerez.

He said, "Sure." And he gave me the tape. I gave the tape to the audiovisual department to make a copy of it.

It took me three weeks to meet with the [military] special agent, who gave me three minutes of his time, and said he would not argue religion or politics and would not take away the tape.

I couldn't find an Islamic Anti-Defamation League, so I ended up calling the American-Arab Anti-Discrimination Committee. I brought the tape to the ADC, and they sent it to the Washington chapter, which arranged for press coverage. They sent a letter to the commandant of the Marine Corps. And they sent a copy to the Secretary of Defense and to the commanding general of my base. The response that was given by the base was: We will shelve the film until further review. The media ate that up, and said the Marine Corps is finally doing something good. They have taken away the film.

But we were not the first class to see it. It was shown to our sister station, a helicopter station. The military is upset. They're upset with me for wanting to make a spectacle of it.

I file my complaint, which is about 200 pages, and I hold a press conference at the Islamic Education Center in Walnut, California. It made television news. We're still waiting for the complaint to be answered.

I hope that the tape is destroyed. And I hope that it leads to an awareness not just by Muslims but by non-Muslims. You've taken Marines who have been dispersed all around the world now, including Somalia, which is a Muslim nation, and you've taught them to hate Muslims. So I'm hoping that you have a retraining program to give people a better view of what Islam really is. I know that that's asking for a lot, but I think it's really needed. And that's what I'm hoping.

A letter from the American-Arab Anti-Discrimination Committee to General Carl E. Munday, Jr., commandant of the U.S. Marine Corps, dated February 8, 1993, highlighted the Committee's contentions, including the fact that the State Department's Bureau of Diplomatic Security reported only 8 out of 233 anti-U.S. incidents in 1990 were attributed to Near Eastern countries. The letter also says that according to the State Department's 1990 report, "Patterns of Global Terrorism," there were more international terrorism attacks in Latin America (162) and Asia (96) than in the Middle East (63), and that the distortion and inaccuracies in the film are "undeniable. The Middle East is defined as the 'cradle of terror,' Palestinian children are said to be 'tomorrow's terrorists,' and the 'millions of disciples willing to die for their [terrorist] cause' are shown to be Muslim."

Is not Allah the wisest of Judges?

Qur'an 95:8

Word at the White House

Robert Dickson Crane

Crane graduated from Harvard Law School, was a foreign policy adviser to Richard Nixon from 1963 to 1968, and for a very brief time was deputy director of the National Security Council in the Nixon administration and President Reagan's ambassador to the United Arab Emirates.

Today, Crane directs the Legal Division of the American Muslim Council, a Washington, D.C.-based organization that coordinates nationwide activities to speak out against discrimination against Muslims, to raise the political consciousness of Muslims, and to form a consensus on issues within the Muslim community. He is developing a grand strategy to "infuse Islamic thought in a systematic and professional way into the formation of current policy" in Washington.

At the root of his logic is a theological premise: that Islam does not separate the sacred or the religious from the secular. He and other Islamic traditionalists argue that Christians consider creation "fallen" and "evil" and prescribe faith as the only salvation; and likewise that Buddhists consider creation "evil" and salvation comes only through a life of self-denial. In Islam, on the contrary, creation is deemed to be good, an affirmation of Allah's glory and power, and man's role should be to rearrange this creation in an ethical way so as to serve human needs.

Crane spoke for hours about his Cherokee family tree, his roots back to seventeenth-century England, "psycho-strategic" diplomacy, the corridors of power, and a banquet in Bahrain that changed his thinking about Islam.

The Cranes came over in 1636 to New Haven, Connecticut, and some of them went down to Elizabethtown (now Elizabeth), New Jersey.

282

On my mother's side, there's European blood that came to America in 1608 aboard the second ship to go to Jamestown. It was full of prisoners. My mother's family originated from the debtors who were released from prison on condition that they work for seven years in the colonies. That was almost like a sentence of death.

I was born in Cambridge, Massachusetts. My father taught economics at Harvard for ten years. His father never went past the sixth grade. Actually, he was a hobo back in the '80s and '90s of the last century. He left home after the sixth grade and rode the rails for twelve years. He married my grandmother, from the Indian side, and she decided that their children had to get an education. The two boys got doctorates, and the two girls got college degrees—the first generation up from riding the rails and dirt farming in south-central Indiana.

My mother's family was very wealthy. My grandmother's father was one of the financial founders of Northwestern University. My mother called my father a barbarian. They couldn't survive together: two totally different views of life. With one, the only thing that mattered was money, and with the other, the only thing that mattered was living a virtuous life and being satisfied with your lot in life.

I went to Harvard and dropped out and completed a BA degree at Northwestern. My family wanted me to become president of the family's hardware company. I worked there twenty hours a week learning everything from the ground up. And then the family wanted me to go to Harvard Law School. They figured that would be better than getting a business degree. I went to Harvard Law. But I changed my mind. They wanted me to go there to get background to run the company. I went to learn about justice.

While I was in Cambridge I wrote on Soviet space strategy. The Cuban Missile Crisis broke out, and I wrote a long article about psycho-strategic warfare. It was very clear to me that the Soviets won the missile crisis. Everybody thought that the United States faced them down, but it was obvious to me that Khrushchev's aim was not to intimidate or use his missiles against the United States. His aim was to consolidate Communist power in Cuba. The way to do it was to install missiles and then withdraw them in return for an American commitment not to interfere with Fidel Castro, which is exactly what happened.

All that Khrushchev had to be sure of was that Kennedy wouldn't put his finger on the button, and that it would not get out of control. Khrushchev

Robert Dickson Crane.

did miscalculate, because Kennedy had a pathological fear of nuclear war. He figured that if he didn't get rid of these missiles down there soon, the situation would develop where there might be a nuclear war. If you're very afraid of nuclear war, you're going to take strong steps. So he was willing to risk it in order to avoid a later confrontation. If they could convince the Americans that there's a real danger, then they can manipulate us. And we just couldn't imagine a post-nuclear-war scenario. They could.

I went into the orchestration of American thinking by the Soviets, and Richard Nixon read it on a plane from California to New York. He called me as soon as he landed, in January of 1963, and asked me if I would be his adviser in foreign policy.

We divided the world up into areas and issues and then I would go through the professional periodicals to locate the best articles on each of these issues in each of these areas. Then I would put together a briefing book for him regularly, because he was a great reader.

Nixon was interested in reading about the different religions. And he wanted to know about Islam. I did read a little bit about Islam at the time, because I thought that Islam would be the strongest, most long-lasting ally of the United States against Communism—because both Nixon and I saw Communism as *the* threat in the world.

I urged Nixon at the time, from '63 to '66, to run again. I advised Gerald Ford too on various matters, and was adviser to major Republican leaders.

After the '66 elections, and 40 new congressmen were elected, there was a feeling of confidence in the Republican party. I was invited as the Republican party's official expert on defense to brief all 40 of the Republican congressmen on defense issues. We had a three-day briefing session.

Shortly after that I went into Nixon's office, and Pat Nixon was there addressing Christmas cards. Usually she sent out two or three hundred, but she had an office full of thousands of cards, and I said, "Ah, fantastic, the boss is going to run."

And she said, "Yeah, and I have a horrible premonition he's going to destroy himself."

I said, "C'mon, you've got to be kidding. That makes no sense at all."

She said, "I know, but he's going to destroy himself."

She was very upset about his wanting to run. In retrospect I think she saw the two personalities of Nixon: one, his real personality—you couldn't get a better human being than Nixon; the other was his personality when he's fighting for power—because he grew up on the wrong side of the tracks, and he wanted to make it. That's why he brought Henry Kissinger in—to get credibility with what I call the secular establishment. And that's why Watergate came about: His wrong personality came out.

When he was in a power fight, he was a street fighter, and the good Nixon just disappeared; and I think that's what Pat Nixon knew—that this would happen, as it did, when he got into the White House.

Kissinger eliminated me during the '68 campaign. My job was to write five position papers on the five key foreign policy issues. I did, at fifty pages each. This is the way Kissinger got rid of his opponents. He would keep them busy. These five position papers, I had put together in the form of a book. And Gerald Ford wrote a very nice introduction. Ford called me in, and said, "You can publish your book with my introduction, but I want to advise you: In every single-one of these major issues, you and Kissinger totally disagree. For your own good, don't publish it. Just forget your opinions. Go ahead and do what you're told."

But I still kept saying what I thought.

Nixon appointed me deputy director of planning for the National Security Council. But Kissinger was the director. So I showed up for work, they showed me where I was on the chart, and the next day, I came in and I had been eliminated. I had been fired after one day by Kissinger. Kissinger had no choice. You had to have people around you who were going to support you. So he fired me.

I never took Islam seriously, because all I knew about Islam was that good Muslims should kill Christians and the Muslim heaven is a whorehouse. I was so disgusted I never wanted to learn anything about this religion. It was just primitive. And I had advised Nixon on Islam as an ally against the Communists. I thought it was a disgusting religion, but at least it could be used against Communism.

But then in the summer of 1977, when I was in Bahrain, the temperature was well over 100 degrees and my wife wanted to see Al Muharraq, which is the old merchant town, and it's just a series of narrow alleys, like a maze, originally designed to keep the pirates out in case they should invade. We wanted to see some of the merchant princes' palaces in the middle of Al Muharraq. And we got lost in this maze, and I was about ready to pass out. I probably would have fainted in a matter of two or three minutes. This old man came walking by and he recognized that I was in trouble, so he invited us into his home, which was just across the street. We spent the rest of the day there. We had one banquet course after the other. We talked about all kinds of things, and he said he was a Muslim. I was amazed because he was such a good person. We never talked about Islam. We talked about what is good in the world, what's bad in the world, and what's important in the world. And the role of God in the world, but not about Islam.

I said, This is weird. This guy is saying everything that I believe. And yet he says he's a Muslim. Something's wrong. [*Laughs.*] I concluded I better start learning about Islam. Obviously I'd been brainwashed.

I studied the religion, and realized that everything in Islam is exactly what I had always believed. But I didn't like the idea of bowing. That to me was revolting. You only bow to a king or somebody, and I wouldn't bow to anybody.

I attended a conference on the Islamic movement in 1980 in New Hampshire. All the great intellectuals of the world Islamic movement were there. The other Americans there went down to lunch and I wanted to go with the foreign guests to lunch, because I wanted to learn as much as I could from them. And on the way down, we went into this room with sheets all over the floor. I thought we were going to lunch; what the heck's going on in here? And then I realized I should have remembered it's Friday. They're going to pray the *juma* prayer. I decided I better leave. But I figured that would insult them. So I just sat in the back of the room.

Hasan al-Turabi[3] was the imam. He was the leading Muslim in the world at that time and still is. When he made the *sujud*,[4] the thought suddenly struck me that he's bowing to Allah. That never really sank in. All I saw was bowing, but then I realized that he's bowing to Allah, and if he can bow to Allah—he's ten times the man I am, so I decided I have to make the *sujud* too. At that point. So that's when I became Muslim. It was his example.

Last Saturday I was elected president of the Muslim American Bar Association. This association is very badly needed. I want to turn it into something like the American Bar Association, addressing major issues from an Islamic perspective.

The ABA is doing everything already that Muslims should do, but Muslims are not participating in it. But there is no overall paradigm for the ABA. Muslims have an overall paradigm of thought which is exactly the paradigm that the founding fathers of America had, and our role should be to revive this original paradigm, which is that truth comes from God—it's not made by man; and that truth is the only source of justice—truth which comes from a higher source, through observation of the universe, through revelation (the three revealed religions). Since truth comes from this source, justice is an expression of this truth, and justice has been spelled out by the great scholars of Islam in the form of human rights, or human responsibilities. The six basic ones are life, community, private property, political freedom, dignity, and the freedom and duty to pursue knowledge. In each of these there's a subset of principles which should be followed, and based on these we can develop specific policies on education, crime, the role of private property, whatever the issues are that concern Americans.

We have identified more than 100 Muslim lawyers in the United States, but I believe there are several hundred more. The immigrant lawyers who are in their thirties or older do not want to defend Muslims. They don't want to tarnish their reputation. They don't want to be known as Muslim lawyers. Many of the younger generation want to become lawyers, and they want to be socially active.

[3] Hasan al-Turabi, a leading figure of the international Islamic movement and one of its most influential thinkers. He was later elected secretary-general of the Arab and Islamic Conference in April 1991 by representatives from 55 countries. He earned a law degree from the University of Khartoum in 1955, a master's in law in 1957 in London, and his doctorate from the Sorbonne in 1964. He is working toward implementing the *shari'ah* in Sudan.
[4] Prostration.

It's very clear that there's a lot of prejudice in our judicial system against Muslims. For example, up in Alaska, an imam was badly beaten up by the security guards of Anchorage airport, and they permanently injured his arm, broke his ribs. This was four years ago, and he's still in bad shape. He got a lawyer, and won his case finally after four years. They convicted the police of false arrest and exonerated him, but his lawyer was so poor the jury refused to give him any compensation for his medical costs. If he'd had any halfway good lawyer, he could have won this case within six months rather than four years, and he probably would have gotten a million dollars. And he said he would have given that to a legal defense fund. He's a typical example where Muslims just are losers in the American legal system, so we formed the American Muslim Legal Defense Association to handle individual cases.

We need a traditionalist ecumenical movement to undergird both parties to work in all the institutions in America. I don't consider myself either a Republican or a Democrat, because I think we should work within all parties.

There's basically a religious vacuum in our institutions. In the media, education, government, even the judiciary. These have been steadily secularized over the last century, in total contravention of the First Amendment, which was designed not to keep religion out of public life, but to keep government out of religion. The assumption of almost all the founding fathers was that no society can prosper unless it's based on morality and unless morality is based on a transcendent source. People argue that Jefferson was an atheist. They call him the father of secular America. It's the exact opposite. He couldn't even conceive of a secular America. He said that the key to democracy is education; the essence of education is moral education, virtue, and that must be based on a higher source than just human whim. He believed in democracy in the sense that people who govern are subject to higher morality from a higher source. Our public institutions are secular and the people are not. And this is the real problem of America, because we'll never get a consensus as long as we have this split between the people and the governing institutions.

The assumption of all the founders of America was that this was a great experiment to see whether a society can be led by people who are led by God. And right now we're failing in that experiment.

The day that the sky will be like molten brass . . .

Qur'an 70:8

Desert Storm

Ayah Hariri

Immediately after the Gulf War, there were 100 Muslim soldiers at Fort Bragg, North Carolina—and only one of them was female. Staff Sergeant Hariri, thirty, converted in Saudi Arabia, returned to the States and wore hijab *on the base.*

I promised them eight years and I gave them eleven.

I was a quartermaster, and I got deployed over to Saudi. We ended up being stationed at Dammam. The military had leased a compound that was the workers' compound. That's where we lived and that's where we also ran our warehouse operation. Some of our companies were so far out in the desert that they had no supplies. We ran the warehouse for all their food and water. The whole battalion was five companies, about a thousand troops, two hundred women.

One day, these guys were outside doing exercises. They said, "Look! A Scud!" We all thought they were joking. So I went out to correct them, because you don't joke about something like that. All of a sudden we heard this noise and we looked up, and you could see the smoke. It blew up right over our tent, and no alarms went off. It landed right across the street from where our tents were. Everyone gave verbal alarms, shouting, "Gas! Gas!" from tent to tent.

About two or three minutes later, the alarms sounded. We spent all those nights awake in the bunkers because a missile was passing *near* us, and one explodes right over our heads and there are no alarms!

We wrote a list of what we needed to buy, and got it approved through channels, and the officers went out and purchased it. And one of the people

289

that they purchased from is the man who is responsible for introducing me to Islam. He's also my husband now, Hussain Hariri. He's from Lebanon.

I asked him one day to tell us a story from the Qur'an. I wanted to see what kind of book it was—was it a book that was stern and severe? He ended up telling the story of Joseph. When he got done with that story, I said, "We got a story like that, but it's got different people in it." He just laughed. He said, "It's the same story." He said we have Moses, but we call him Musa. He told me what the biblical names were and what the Arabic names were in the Qur'an.

That just shocked me. I hadn't even heard about Islam or the Qur'an until we started having predeployment briefs about what we couldn't do and what not to say and areas to avoid.

I asked him if he could get me an English Qur'an. He got one from one of his friends. That was around December.

One night, Hussain and I were eating dinner in my room. As soon as we finished dinner, he asked me if I wanted to talk some more about Islam. I asked how much is a person supposed to know before they take *shahada*. He said you can never know everything there is about being a Muslim, and if you wait until you know everything, you'll never take it. Because there's so much to learn.

Basically, there's the five pillars. You should realize how it's going to affect your life. You should realize that from this point on, you will be held accountable for all your actions. And you need to be earnest about wanting to become a Muslim and not just—well, maybe I'll try this for a while. Sincerity and intention count for a lot.

I said, "I'll learn everything else later, but I have enough to make a decision now."

He took a deep breath, and he said, "Well, what's your decision?"

I said, "I want to become a Muslim."

He said, "You have to take *shahada*."

He said it in English and I repeated after him. Then he said, "You have to say it in Arabic." I had started learning the alphabet and conversation words, but not Qur'anic Arabic. He said it in Arabic and he told me what each word meant, and he said, "If you don't know what you're saying you're not saying anything."

I said *shahada* three times and that was it.

I told the commanding officer I worked with. He said, "Well, how does this affect your work?"

Ayah Hariri.

I said, "It wouldn't right now."

He said, "Well, all right."

There's a little store in the compound and later on that day we started talking to a Syrian guy who ran it. The guy showed me some prayer rugs and *zikr* beads. Hussain had a couple of scarves made for me. On duty time, of course, I still had to wear the desert uniforms. But off duty, I wore the black outer coat and a black scarf. I looked Saudi.

I got some strange looks. People were very surprised. I said to them, "Look, my name is Staff Sergeant Peck. Do you have a question you would like to ask me?"

They were like, "No . . ."

I was in charge of the inventory for the compound. One time a bunch of Marines came in for some supplies, and here I was dressed like this walking around with keys to the warehouse, issuing out supplies.

Tent city was just down the road from us, and that's where everybody waits till the equipment comes in. So a lot of people pass through Dammam on the way out to different cities.

I was wearing a white scarf and everyone kept saying, "What is that nun doing here?" I didn't even think about it. But when I went back to my room and looked in the mirror, I said, "Well, I do look like a nun."

Less than a month later I returned to the States. Hussain stayed there.

Hopefully this summer we will both be in the same country at the same time.

I came back to Fort Bragg. Then I took thirty days' leave to see what my rights were now that I was a Muslim and back in the States. It was peacetime. I made an appointment with the JAG,[5] the legal adviser for military people. I spoke to a captain and asked what my rights were. He said, "Well, basically you don't really have any. Talk to your commander."

In the meantime I had joined a sisters' group outside of the military. One of the sisters—her husband started the Islamic community at Fort Bragg. She mentioned it to her husband. He said, "You should be allowed some rights."

I said, "I made an appointment with the JAG. They said no."

He said, "Let me call some of my friends." He was an E8, a master sergeant. He has a little bit more clout.

He called one of his friends, who copied a command policy regulation and sent it to him from Georgia. It says there what commanders are to do with requests for accommodations and religious practices. It has the guidelines. I took a copy of that to my commander. It said any religious apparel had to be subdued. So I brought in the brown scarf that I wanted to wear.

He kept the regulation for about a week or so, and he came back and said, "There's nothing in this regulation that gives me the right to say no, so I say yes."

At lunchtime, I put my scarf on.

I'm very conspicuous. It's hard not to notice me. When I came back off leave, I worked in the battalion supply shop. Officers would come in to do their checks to make sure everything was all right, and I'd get a few strange looks from them.

Somebody said, "What are you doing with that rag on your head?" It was a lower enlisted, and I turned around and they saw the rank, and they said, "Uh-oh."

I said, "This is not a rag, this is religious apparel; I'm wearing this for religious reasons."

They said, "Sorry."

My rank has probably stopped a lot of people from saying what they wanted to say. Because most of the people in the company are E4 and

[5] Judge Advocate General.

below and I was E6. There are some people now who got permission to wear *hijab* that are E4 and below, and they're having a harder time than I had.

Last year, the command sergeant major, which is the highest enlisted person there is, wanted me to give a short talk for NCODP.[6] Every month, he'd get two or three people to give talks on different topics.

He called me up there, and when I was walking up toward the front, I overheard this E5 female say, "Do we *have* to listen to this?"

I got up there, and I said, "On my way up here, I heard the comment 'Do we have to listen to this?' And I'm here to tell you, Yes, you do. This is not about whose religion's right and whose religion's wrong. This is about your duty as NCOs and part of your duty as NCOs is to take care of your soldiers. You take care of your Christian soldiers, Lutheran soldiers, Jewish soldiers, whatever. But if you don't know about your soldiers, you won't know how to take care of them.

"If you have a soldier that's Muslim and they live in the barracks, they have the same rights as Jewish soldiers with regard to separate rations. Jewish soldiers have the right not to eat in the mess hall, because most of the food is mixed with pork. If you're married, you go to personnel and you get money every month and you go buy your own food, because you're married. Now, people in the barracks aren't authorized to get this money, but Jewish soldiers and Muslim soldiers are because they have religious dietary requirements. They can buy their own food."

The sergeant major said, "Very nice job."

---

[6] Noncommissioned Officer Development Program.

He created the heavens and the earth in true [proportions] . . .

Qur'an 39:5

Math = Jihad

Abdulalim Abdullah Shabazz

"Muslims in America are undercounted, and there's
power in numbers."

*Blacks are underrepresented among American scientists, comprising less
than 1 percent of all scientists in the U.S. In 1989, fewer than 1,200 of the
nation's more than 2,100 four-year colleges awarded even one bachelor's
degree in science or engineering to a black student.*

*Few blacks decide to take up math or science perhaps because these are
subjects one usually decides to pursue during elementary school, when, it is
said, their "logical purity and puzzle-solving seductiveness" lures the beginning scientists. But how much of that purity and seductiveness gets translated depends to a great degree on what kind of encouragement a student
has.*

*More than half of the current black mathematicians in the U.S.—109 of
200—earned their doctorates either directly or indirectly in the mathematics program that Abdulalim Abdullah Shabazz headed from 1956 to 1963.
Today, the silver-haired chairman and professor of the mathematics department at Clark Atlanta University sits in his book-filled office and explains the theory behind his success: "There's no magic potion or hocus-
pocus. It's simply believing everyone can learn if they put forth the effort."*

*Shabazz earned his bachelor's degree in 1949 from Lincoln University,
his master's in 1951 from Massachusetts Institute of Technology, and his
doctorate from Cornell University in 1955.*

Back in his early years in Atlanta, Shabazz and his students would pro-

test at public libraries where jim-crow laws wouldn't allow them to sit.
They would stand, reading books that they weren't allowed to check out.
Atlanta University's president branded him a communist, and Shabazz left.

In the 1960s, Shabazz converted to Islam, becoming a follower of Elijah
Muhammad. He studied Arabic in the Middle East and taught math at
Umm Al Qura University in Mecca, Saudi Arabia. Now he's back in At-
lanta, carrying on an educational jihad *to get more black mathematicians*
into the science pipeline.

God teaches us to seek knowledge from the cradle to the grave. That's a
hadith. In our tradition, it is a holy ordinance of Allah.

The tradition of Islam is to bring enlightenment to all people. This tradition teaches us to have reverence for the wisdom of our elders and to
transmit that which is contained in books.

In the classroom I have a mandate to teach the truth on a grander scale
and to show my students the role they had to play in the creation of mathematics. I show them that mathematics originated in Africa and then spread
to all parts of the world. If we were able to do it in days past, we could do
it again. This serves as a motivating force for students.

You find mathematics manifested in the artifacts and fossils all over Africa. One of the oldest fossils that gives knowledge that the people of this
area had a high knowledge of mathematics is in what is today known as
Zaire, a place called Ishango. Jean de Heinzelin, an archeologist from
Belgium, in the latter part of the fifties dug up a collection of artifacts and a
bone known today as the Ishango Bone. This bone had markings on it—
13, 11, 17. Every mark indicated a unit. On it were clear manifestations of
mathematical knowledge to the base 10. Heinzelin pointed out that the
oldest clue to such enumeration systems was found there at Ishango, and
this thinking was the basis upon which the later enumeration systems in
Egypt had their beginnings.

Of course there was a flowering of mathematics in Egypt, which is given
credit for being one of the oldest civilizations on earth. The presence of the
Great Pyramid and the Great Sphinx—the very existence of those struc-
tures indicates a powerful technology, a powerful science, and a powerful
mathematics. Scientists stated that when the Great Pyramid was constructed, the vertical height of it was one-billionth of the distance from the
earth to the sun. That's a distance that modern man, European man, did
not come by until around 1874.

The stones of which the Great Pyramid was constructed weighed on the average two and one-half tons and some weighed as much as fifty tons— 100,000 pounds. It is mind-boggling to think how men could move those stones and put them in place to form a perfect pyramid that rose from a square base to a height that is approximately 485 feet high. The faces of the pyramids, in terms of area, were equal to the square of the vertical height—an amazing accomplishment showing tremendous mathematical insight and knowledge.

Islam rises and sweeps across Northern Africa. Islam did not go across Africa destroying. It went across Africa restoring and building. Building schools, building institutions, and giving people direction in their lives.

In A.D. 711 a general named Tariq ibn Ziyad led a force across what is today called the Mediterranean. He conquered a mountain that was called by the Spaniards "Mons Calpe." It was renamed by the soldiers of Tariq "Jabal at-Tariq"—"Mountain of Tariq." That was contracted by the Spaniards to "Gibraltar."

Spain and Portugal—what was once called the Iberian Peninsula—were conquered and the Islamic civilization was put there by the Muslims that followed Tariq. This presence of Muslims lingered until 1492 when Granada fell. That's the same year Columbus stumbled upon America, a man who was lost.

It was during the period from 711 to 1492 that Islam preserved the knowledge of ancient Greece and Rome and Africa in books in the Arabic language. These books were translated in time into Latin and used by the scholars of Europe. Francis Bacon said, Knowledge is Arabic. If you wish to be learned, then learn the Arabic language.

Roman numerals were overthrown as soon as Arabic numerals were brought into Europe. Those clumsy numerals were outclassed by Arabic numerals that were more mobile and could not only give you a reasoning for what they represented, but also enabled you to compute without difficulty. The concept of zero is a natural concept but it had revolutionary force.

One of the books translated from Arabic to Latin was a book by a man named Muhammad ibn Musa Al-Khuwarizmi. The title of his book was *Al Jabr wa'l Muqabala,* which means "Restoration and Reduction." When it was translated to Latin they dropped *wa'l Muqabala,* and retained *Al Jabr,* which became "algebra." And from the name Al-Khuwarizmi we get "algorithm" and "logarithm."

The author was just a teacher. We never claim that what we teach is from ourselves—we get it from our teachers, and they got it from their teachers. This is why the worship of God is so important. If you worship God, you have a respect for those who came before you because you get a continual refinement of knowledge and culture and development. It continues. You don't destroy everything and start all over again and make everything start when *you* start.

Islam played a role in preparing the stage for the European Renaissance. The foundation of the Renaissance was the various pieces of civilization integrated, which gave rise to the rebirth of Europe. It was the presence of knowledge. Once knowledge is put in the soil, eventually it will cause germination. In time the explosion occurred. We can trace the movement of that knowledge by the way it was recorded by the scholars and scientists of that day.

The Muslim tradition was universal. Scholars in Córdoba and Seville and Granada corresponded with scholars in Africa in Timbuktu, in Cairo and Kairouan, Baghdad, Bukhara, Samarkand. They corresponded with one another and exchanged ideas. One of the greatest universities that existed during the twelfth, thirteenth, fourteenth centuries was Timbuktu. It was destroyed as an intellectual center. The last chancellor of the university was Ahmed Baba, who was taken away as a captive to Morocco. He was imprisoned. He was so eloquent in his sense of truth and justice that he was freed after two years. He authored more than forty books.

Muslims conserved the knowledge, spread it, and then they were kicked out of Europe. During the Inquisition, three million Moors were banished from Europe between the fall of Granada and the first decade of the seventeenth century. Many of them went back to Africa. Some went to other parts of Europe. Many of these Muslims were killed during the Inquisition.

Today we're living in what I think is the revival of the Islamic spirit, which has manifested itself throughout the world. They call it in various parts of the world fundamentalism. This is a cover to attack, to malign, to turn people against a natural phenomenon which really represents a yearning for purity of thought, for wholesomeness, for equity and for justice in the world, rather than the world continuing the way it's going now, down the road to ruin behind every conceivable debauchery and immoral type of behavior.

Islam is rising, not only in the Middle East, but in Eastern Europe. We see the slaughter of the innocent Muslims there. There are many white Muslims. It's significant to note that under Communism, which was godless, the Muslims had a better deal and a better day than they're having today under the leadership of Christians, who are murdering them by the day. And the world stands back and watches the slaughter and only says, "What a pity, what a pity."

In America the African Americans pose a key to Islamic revival. I see so many young students who are Muslims. They will not be like their elders prostrating before the almighty dollar and for position. More and more people are doing the basics—praying, sitting in circles and talking and discussing and sharing knowledge. One of the most important pieces of knowledge that any people on this earth should have is to know who they are.

I grew up in an "African" village in Alabama, and as I look back, I was in an Islamic tradition although the people did not know Islam. But the way they acted was part of that Islamic tradition that was brought from Africa—the communal spirit, respect for our elders. We respected any elder in the community, because any man, any woman in the community would be a "parent" of ours. If they were old, they would be a "grandparent" of ours. We would sit and listen to them because they had something to say to us. I learned how to be a decent teacher by growing up in a community of teachers.

That's how I teach mathematics. By doing that, it is easier to take a person who may have no knowledge today in terms of understanding and tomorrow this person can be looked upon as a genius in mathematics.

Malcolm [X] spoke at our Mathematics Club and gave talks on my invitation. These lectures were standing-room-only. He talked about the pyramids representing a high civilization. Of course he did it in his characteristic way. He was a spellbinding speaker and he had the place really rocking. Malcolm said Islam is mathematics and mathematics is Islam. They called mathematics the way we were teaching it revolutionary. Our battle cry was "Mathematics is life and life is mathematics."

Any aspect of life is mathematics—look at it from the point of view of quantity, increase, decrease, expansion, contraction. When we develop mathematical forms, however abstract and abstruse they may be, these forms came from life—these are distillations or abstractions or fractions from life. The patterns therefore are nothing more than an approximation of the life that we live.

Islam is entire submission to the will of God. If you wish to live a fruitful life and a life of meaning, if you submit, then there's harmony, there's peace. You're going in accord with the very nature of creation and that means you are bound to the will of God; you are bowing to the will of the Almighty Creator. And this makes life more livable.

Many of the scientists and scholars of math spoke in symbolic language to convey a message which could be understood only by the initiates—those who understood the code. This is one of the reasons that mathematics has gotten a bad name among our people—because it has been put into a code that they can't read and so now they have to learn the code so they can understand. We show them in my class that they already know a lot of this. We rid them of the fear of it, the dread of it. When they know how to master mathematics, then they can take their destinies back into their hands.

The only way we can free ourselves is through a greater knowledge. That comes through mathematics and that comes through our faith in Islam. Muslims cannot free themselves in the world today from oppression unless they do it themselves. They cannot look to anyone to come to their rescue, they've got to rescue themselves.

Without mathematics you can't wage *jihad*. If you have organization, that means you have mathematics; if you have insight, that's mathematics; if you have a means and a way to do something, that's mathematics. To do meaningful *jihad*, you have to understand what it is you're trying to do, you have to understand what your objective is, where you're going, what you want to establish, what you want to change.

Mathematics will teach you practical things—how to think, how to put things together, how to take things apart, how to analyze things. This is what's needed by our people today—we've got to learn how to think, how to get ourselves out of hell and put ourselves in a heavenly state; not just ourselves individually, but collectively.

The Home Front

Faris Mansour

A sixteen-year-old junior, he dreams of attending an Ivy League college and becoming a broadcast journalist. In the meantime, between family trips to the old country, he shares his views with the student body at Fenwick High School, a Catholic school in Oak Park, Illinois. (This interview took place before the PLO-Israeli peace accord was signed in September 1993.)

We traveled back to the Middle East three times: in 1978, in 1986, and in 1991. My mother's parents live in the West Bank. I have a lot of aunts and uncles and cousins there. We're always worried about the things that go on outside their door. When we were there a couple of summers ago, we saw things firsthand. The second day I was there, there was a strike. There was some big commotion. A car was trapped, and it was being struck by rocks. It was confusing. I didn't know how to feel—whether I was with the people who attacked it or against them because of the way they attacked it.

The license plates are color-coordinated, so they're easily distinguishable. This one had yellow, which was the Israeli license plate. And all of the Arab cars had blue. So they knew which ones not to touch and which ones to attack. The people in the car were Jewish.

Did your heart go out to the people in that car?

Yeah. It didn't seem right, but then after I had seen more, I'd seen that this was very little compared to what the Israelis would do to them. This is all that they could do to get their message across.

I read about instances of Israelis putting together death squads, dressing

300

up like Palestinians, running around and killing people, other instances where they've held people without charging them, in horrible conditions, and just brutalizing these people, taking away their land. In fact, my aunt lost a baby while she was carrying it because of the tear gas that they used. These are the means that they use to scare the Arabs out of their land.

The Israelis had taken away their land. They had taken away their rights. They had taken away their freedom. All they had was religion—and each other.

We left because we didn't want to get in the middle of it before the soldiers came. They were coming from a different direction. They got hit too.

When I got to high school, it was a Catholic high school, and the students and teachers didn't understand Islam. I was the only Muslim that I knew of in my class. Now there's a couple more.

Right now the student body is about 900. Actually everyone is pretty close. That's one of the things I like about it.

In terms of Islam, you can't really hide it, and I didn't want to. But there are various things that we'd be asked to do in religion classes, and we had to refrain from them, and then people would ask, and we'd have to tell them. I'm not saying it was a chore to tell them; I always liked to tell them. If they have a sincere question, I'll answer as much as they want. The problem that I've had is that there are people that don't wish to know.

Just a month ago I came close to fighting with some person because he just mocked me and never bothered to understand. He was making fun of Islam and everything about me.

We were sitting in class, and all of a sudden he turned toward me and he started going on about the PLO, the Palestinians, and he went on to all Arabs, then he went on to Muslims, making fun of their dress, their ways. He judges by what he sees in movies and shows, which may not be accurate.

I went up to him after class. I told him, "If you are going to strike at everything that is important to me, then you have to be ready to defend it and defend yourself." He didn't say anything and he just walked away.

That stuff really gets to me. You can make fun of anything else about me, but when it comes to that—that's not just me, that's a lot of people and that's something important.

During the Persian Gulf War, we were sitting in class discussing the

Iraqis and their move to try to unite the Middle East. Saddam Hussein may not have been going about it the right way, and he may be at fault, but to kill 100,000 Iraqis was not right by the United States either. So I was trying to defend them, trying to put it in a new perspective, and I was accused of being Iraqi and threatened. That never amounted to very much, but that was another incident that I didn't like.

In the summer between my freshman and my sophomore year we traveled back to Palestine. I had really followed up on my heritage and my religion. And then after spending the summer in the Middle East, I was sitting in class, and it was awkward. After seeing how those people live over there, going back to everything I used to do was a big change. When I was there I really wanted to help, to get involved and do something. I went back to school and I didn't have a cause.

There was a magazine that I had read when I came back about a person who had organized these attacks, and the Israelis had chased him for a few nights. He had been shot in the street. They picked him up. They drove around till he was dead, and then when they finally brought his body back to his parents, all of his major organs were gone. My cousins said that they knew this person; he was a friend. I couldn't believe that they would dishonor him by taking his body organs.

I've seen people walking in the streets. They would drop off soldiers, and these soldiers would just grab these people—and they didn't even do anything. They would just take them somewhere. And God knows where.

I sat in class with everyone else. I didn't feel like everyone else. I had seen things that most of these people wouldn't have ever seen except on TV. I had seen these things firsthand.

I decided that the ignorance was more widespread than a couple of people. When it came to Islam a lot of Catholics with their belief in the Father, the Son, and the Holy Spirit couldn't understand my version of Allah. The hardest thing to convince them of was that it was the same God. They all knew that the Jewish God was the same God, but because we had a different name, they thought it was a different God. They equated us with the Buddhists or the Confucianists. In a way I wish the teachers would have made it evident. I tried, but it never came up in study.

Me and a couple of friends put together a club called International Relations. It was more than just cultural; it included religion and we had a few roundtable discussions about Islam and other religions and how they're coping in the world; religions in America. To my surprise a lot of people turned out.

It was in a classroom, and about thirty people came and ten people were on the panel. It was more a discussion than it was a panel. A lot of the people came to watch. They spoke and they got involved.

The main point that some of the discussion rested on was Islam and terrorism. The point that I tried to put down the most was that Islam was a violent religion, that everyone involved in it was violent also.

When they found out that, for instance, the people who attacked the World Trade Center were Muslims, they believed that all terrorists, unless stated otherwise, were Muslim. One person brought up the Pan Am explosion.[7] He didn't even know who had blown up the Pan Am airliner, and when someone told him it was a Libyan, he assumed that it was a Muslim. He said, "Well, look, my point is clear—the Islamic religion is in fact violent."

I wasn't mad, but it struck me: How could you make such a jump to this conclusion?

He obviously knew the politics in the Middle East, I'll give him that. But he didn't know the religious aspects of it. I told him Islam was one of the most tolerant and nonviolent religions. He kept saying, "What about all these terrorists in the Middle East?" I told him that this is not true. Then I used examples—of not just the Muslims in the Middle East, but Muslims all over the world. There are Oriental Muslims, black Muslims, European Muslims, and these people aren't violent, meaning that all of Islam is not violent. I don't know if he understood right away, but he didn't say any more.

I don't think that any amount of talking is going to bring the message across. They have to see pictures; they have to actually experience to know. This is how deep the misconceptions are.

The discussions made a lot of difference to me obviously, because I knew I was doing something. I felt it was important. To do *something* was important.

The school newspaper is called *The Wick*. It's read by a lot of people. I've written three articles about Islam—one about the month of Ramadan, one about equating Islam and violence, and another about just being a

---

[7] On December 21, 1988, a Pan Am Boeing 747 exploded and crashed in Lockerbie, Scotland, resulting in 270 deaths, including 11 on the ground.

Muslim in Fenwick. That article originally started out as a paper for my English class. The teacher got it into *The Wick*.

Teachers said they liked it, that it was new and different. None of the students actually said anything.

I think I've managed to fit in more. In fact, I find it kind of neat. I like it, to be different—not a way of looking or acting, but just to have something different about me. In fact, being at Fenwick has added something more to me. I've gotten more out of it. It's given me a new perspective on how to treat people, how to get a message across, relating to other people. It's a good way of education because when I get older, I'm eventually going to have to deal with people who do not understand. And this is helping.

If I had the opportunity of changing schools and going to a Muslim school, I wouldn't. I'd rather stay here. The Christian values that they hold are very much the same. I find that there's a strong sense of tradition in Fenwick and that's how I live. That seems to fit: that sense of tradition, that sense of strength and values. And I think everyone in Fenwick has a set of values that they hold important.

If ye loan to Allah a beautiful loan, He will double it
to your [credit], and He will grant you Forgiveness: For Allah
is most Ready to appreciate [service], Most Forbearing—

Qur'an 64:17

Dress Code

Shaheera Owaynat

She is Palestinian and a spunky seventeen-year-old who lives in Alsip, Illinois, a suburb of Chicago. At Madonna Catholic High School, where she was a student for two years, she decided finally to walk into school wearing hijab. *She found herself more completely covered than the nuns. She also discovered how close-minded some people can be.*

Of course I would like to wear all the latest styles. But I want to give up everything for Allah's sake. I don't wear nail polish, I don't wear makeup. I just feel like what I'm doing is for God. I'm getting *ajr* for it—credit from God on the Day of Judgment.

When I first started wearing *hijab*, I got a lot of people following me home to pull it off. I never understood why they always wanted to bother me.

I was wearing *hijab* a long time before I went to school. The first day I went to school with it, I had a lot of questions:

"Why are you wearing it?"

"Is somebody making you?"

"Why black?"

"Do you do it because it's cold outside?"

"Don't you have any hair?"

Personally I like to wear black scarves, but here in Universal[8] they make me wear light scarves.

[8] The Muslim school she now attends.

At Brian Piccolo Elementary School, a public school, I had a seventh-grade teacher who would always refer to me as "you with the handkerchief on your head." In the morning he would say, "You probably have head-phones hidden under there." Or he would call it a rag or a towel. If I got a good grade, he would say, "Well, you got a B but you really deserve a C."

I told the principal plenty of times, and the principal said, "Oh, he's like that, can't you understand? He makes little remarks." I was like, "I can't handle these kinds of remarks." So I told my older brothers, and they all went to school, and told him, "If you don't lay off of her—" They kind of threatened him a little. He never really bothered me after that.

At Madonna High School, there was a girl who was a sophomore. During the Gulf War, she said, "You think you're all bad, you stupid Iraqi!"

I told her, "First of all, I'm not Iraqi. Second of all, I have nothing to do with the Gulf War. It's none of my business what's going on over there."

She was really disturbed because her brother was a soldier, and she acted like she wanted to take it out on somebody. The girl was a little bigger than me, so she felt like she had me, you know.

We were in gym and she pulled my scarf off. She kicked me. I jumped on top of her, and I was banging her, punching, slapping, scratching. I just went crazy. The paramedics had to come for the girl.

I never had a fight in my life. My record is clean. I never got suspended in my life. I never had detention.

The police came and the principal wanted to press charges against me. So I told her, "Why should you press charges against me when she was the one who hit me? I'm going to defend myself. What do you think I am? Do you think I'm an idiot? You think I'm going to let her hit me and I'm going to sit there and laugh with her?"

The principal says, "No, you should have come to me."

I say, "Not after she hit me. I came to you before, and I told you that I'm having problems with this girl, and this girl just wants to fight with some-body, and you've done nothing about it. So I'm not going to sit there and take it."

The policemen talked to the other girls and they all said that the girl hit me first. The principal couldn't press charges because she would have to press charges on both of us. And it's not fair just because she's the one who got hurt more. So the police officer said, "You look like a nice girl, and I'm sure all these girls wouldn't be lying for you." So that was the end of it.

The next week in school, the girl apologized. But we never really got along.

During religious classes, I participated, because it's good to participate and learn about their religion. The teacher was a nun, and her skirt was short, and she would wear sleeveless shirts. She let us pick any religion and make a report about it. I used to always pick Islam. I would read the report and their main questions were: in Islam why are men allowed to beat their wives up, and why are they allowed to make their wives slaves, and why does the wife have to obey the man so much?

I explained to them that a woman has equal rights with a man, and I told them that a lot of Christian people have fights, but we don't blame it on the Bible. We don't say that the Bible says a man can beat his wife.

I always had a lot of questions. One time I asked the teacher, Why do people say Jesus is God and the Son of God. Sometimes you say he's God, and sometimes you say, "In the name of the Father and of the son . . ." I asked her, "Who's the Father, who's the Son?"

She said, "That's a good question, and I really don't know the answer."

I told her that Mary never showed her hair. She never wore sleeveless shirts. She never wore skirts to her knees. Her dress used to drag on the floor, it was so long. It's written in the Qur'an *and* the Bible. It's in their Bible too.

Or the drinking. When Jesus drank wine, it didn't have alcohol in it like you guys drink and say, Well, Jesus used to drink. I said, Everything you guys want, you make a good excuse for it and say it's from the Bible. And then when you tell me, Well, it's in the Bible, I don't know which Bible to look at. I don't even know what's the real Bible. It's really confusing because they have so many Bibles. And they say, Well, that's what's good about it.

I said, "You're wrong. When you've got seventy-two books and you got one book, I'd rather look in the one book than in the seventy-two books to find something."

She said, "Well, it's true, but I can't do anything about it. People changed words."

So I said, "So you know?"

She said, "Of course I know."

That's what went on in class.

I transferred. Now I'm president of the student council in Universal

School. It's a Muslim school in Bridgeview, Illinois. There are about 300 students.

In the Catholic school I got along with everybody—except with that girl that I fought with. They didn't feel like I was different after they got to know me. But Universal School feels different, like I'm in a whole different world. I'm in a world that I belong in, I feel. In a Muslim school, my feeling comfortable around everybody is enough.

Catholic school teaches me how to deal with other kinds of people. But when I go to a Muslim school and my friend goes to a Muslim school and her friend goes to a Muslim school, and so on, before you know it you got a whole school. And that's what we're trying to do; we're trying to build our Muslim community so when we need something from the government or from each other, we'll be strong enough as a community or as a Muslim body to give help or get what we want.

Chapter Eight

Pilgrim's Progress

To each is a goal to which Allah turns him; then strive
together [as in a race] toward all that is good. Wheresoever
ye are, Allah will bring you together. For Allah
has power over all things.

Qur'an 2:148

The pilgrim is not necessarily en route to Mecca for *hajj*. He or she continually moves toward self-purification through faith, prayer, fasting, and *zakat*. For this Muslim, Islam is as much a state of mind as a way of life, and a *jihad*, or striving, can take place anywhere—even on the trip toward embracing Islam. Often a journey of self-discovery, this spiritual odyssey can involve lessons learned on the streets, years spent in prison, trips to the Old World, life among Berbers in the Sahara, or a jaunt to the local bookstore.

"Just Take Me!"

Idris M. Diaz

Raised in Jamaica, Queens, Idris Diaz graduated from Wesleyan University, then earned a master's degree from Columbia Journalism School in 1983. He worked as a reporter for the Louisville Courier-Journal *for three and a half years before joining the staff of the Philadelphia* Inquirer, *where he worked for five years. He is now a student at Howard University Law School.*

Diaz found himself the sole representative of his faith wherever he has worked. As the staff expert, reporters and editors alike would call his home at all hours to ask for advice when covering news about Islam. The experience enlightened him about the media's shortcomings in treating Islam knowledgeably and fairly. "I think there's just not the sensitivity in the portrayal of Muslims. Look at the World Trade Center bombing," he says. "You see a spate of stories talking about Muslims as a threat. You don't get a picture that there's another side to the religion."

Diaz himself ended up writing the piece of his lifetime: covering his own hajj *experience. He painted a picture of the scope of the annual* hajj *event for readers by asking them to imagine the entire population of Philadelphia descending on the city of Allentown for a few weeks' stay. Entitled "For the Love of Allah," the piece made the cover of* The Philadelphia Inquirer Magazine *on April 2, 1989.*

He spoke about his eye-opening pilgrimage and what led up to it. (Indented paragraphs are excerpts from his article.)

My father was black Honduran, and my mother was from New Orleans. I was an altar boy, that whole bit, yet the whole notion of Jesus never made sense to me. The Holy Trinity is something I never bought into. I don't think it was a conscious intellectual thing so much as it was a gut thing: Why should I talk to the middleman? I want to go straight to the Big Guy. [*Laughs.*]

In Catholic school, I was disillusioned by the time I was fourteen, and I met a brother who was about ten years older than me who had become Muslim. He was very intense. He always wore the garb and his wife used to walk ten paces behind him. There were aspects of him that scared me.

I was fifteen when I became Muslim, and I can't say that I completely knew what I was doing. I really didn't want to be like this guy. For me, there's been this constant searching, trying to find a place within Islam. You have to rely on what you find in the Qur'an and not on what people tell you. You have to come to terms with it for yourself. I'm still struggling with this thing.

Because the religion is so new, there's a tendency to make everything an issue: Do you send me a card at Christmas because I'm Muslim? That's an issue. Some people get really upset over things that really need not be issues. I like Christmas cards.

I changed my name to Idris Abdul-Ghani about 1983, and then I moved down South. I was in Kentucky, using this name, and people automatically assumed I was Arab. Somebody wrote a letter to the editor complaining that we had this foreigner on the staff—why couldn't we get any good Americans to work for the newspaper? And when Indira Gandhi got shot, I had a couple of people come up and ask me if she had been my mother or relative.

I guess that focused me on the issue of yes, I want to assert my Islamic identity, but that is not totally inconsistent with my black American identity, and I did not want to lose my Latin identity. After much reflection, I finally became a hybrid. I changed my name again to Idris Diaz. It created peace in my family—my mother had a hard time when I became Muslim; it was a difficult thing for her to accept.

At the Philadelphia *Inquirer,* I nagged them to send me overseas. In 1987, they had the big rioting in Mecca. It was a clash between the Iranians and the Saudis, and about 400 people died. There weren't any good news accounts of what happened because it was a closed city, and you don't get anything other than what the Saudis put out.

In '88 the Saudis and the Iranians were at it again, and there was a big war of words. Basically the Saudis were trying to limit the number of

Idris M. Diaz at a joint press conference for the governors of Pennsylvania and New Jersey in 1988.

Iranian pilgrims. There was concern that something like what happened in '87 would happen again, so the foreign editor came down to my desk and said, Would you have a problem going? I looked at him like he was crazy. Let's go tomorrow! Although I had to stop and think about it. I didn't know if having someone else pay for my *hajj* would tarnish it.

I asked an Islamic scholar at Howard University, and he looked at me like *I* was crazy. He said it's perfectly legitimate for people to do trading or conduct business while on *hajj*. When you get to Mecca, you will see people who come and sell things. They're conducting their trade and you're conducting yours. That worked for me.

The goal of going was initially to cover whatever might happen politically, but what happens if I go and it's quiet? Come hell or high water, I had to come back with some kind of story.

I went and it was very calm, but it was really a strange scene—religion and militia. There were soldiers everywhere. I walked into the Prophet's Mosque in Medina, which is the number two shrine in Islam, and inside there's Muhammad's tomb. There's a lot of blessings to be gotten from visiting that place. There's a gate around the tomb, and it's completely surrounded by soldiers carrying big submachine guns.

The air was tense with anticipation; people were eager to be the first inside so they could get as close as possible to the front of the mosque. Nearby, a group of West African Muslims chatted in their Hausa language as they played with thick black zikr beads. Women stood off to one side waiting to enter the mosque through a separate door. Some were covered head to foot in black. Others, African women in particular, were adorned with bright dresses and sparkling gold bracelets, their hair only partially covered with thin scarves. After a few minutes,

the adhan, *call to prayer, roared from loudspeakers in the mosque:*
"Allahu akbar." *Allah is the Greatest. The huge wooden doors of the*
mosque swung open, and the pilgrims snatched off their shoes, accord-
ing to the custom, and rushed forward in one swift motion. After a
cursory frisk by one of the guards, I rushed inside and grabbed a spot
near a white marble column. Within minutes the mosque was packed.

You had to get frisked every time you went in the mosque. *Fajr* prayer
would be at about five, but you had to get there at three just to get in. You
show up, and okay, let's go, frisk me.

After a couple of days, I blocked the soldiers out. I realized that the
whole political subtext was irrelevant to what I was really there to do. The
soldiers became invisible.

I went with a group of mostly Egyptians. It brought back a lot of flash-
backs from that chapter in *The Autobiography of Malcolm X* in which
Malcolm talks about going on *hajj* and how people took him in as a
brother.[1] That was really what it was like: Everywhere I went, it was constant kindness. People invited me out to eat with them or sit with them.

Like millions of other pilgrims before us, the group I was traveling
with spent the day in a tent of white-and-black-striped canvas. Middle
Eastern rugs covered the soil beneath our feet. During the day, on
Arafat, pilgrims prayed, chanted and read from their Qur'ans. Out-
side, the heat hovered near 110 degrees, and those who dared to ven-
ture out covered their heads with white umbrellas. Inside my tent,
pilgrims shared fruit, cheese and dates and took sips of bottled water,
which was in short supply.

I felt almost a kind of guilt. I saw people who had saved all their lives
and really struggled to go, and yet Allah just dropped this thing on me. I
had a feeling of being unworthy. What was I supposed to get out of this?

One of the lessons it taught me is that the Lord works in mysterious
ways. At breakfast in the morning, we'd have a lot of discussions about

[1] In the chapter entitled "Mecca," Malcolm X recalls a letter he wrote to his associates in
New York: "During the past eleven days here in the Muslim world, I have eaten from the
same plate, drunk from the same glass, and slept in the same bed (or on the same rug)—while
praying to the *same* God—with fellow Muslims, whose eyes were the bluest of blue, whose
hair was the blondest of blond, and whose skin was the whitest of white. And in the *words*
and in the *actions* and in the *deeds* of the 'white' Muslims, I felt the same sincerity that I felt
among the black African Muslims of Nigeria, Sudan, and Ghana.

"We were *truly* all the same (brothers)—because their belief in one God had removed the
'white' from their minds, the 'white' from their behavior, and the 'white' from their attitude."

politics. Some people were really anti-Jewish. I said, "Well, gee, it was a Jewish guy who footed the bill for my *hajj*; how can I have any problem with Jews? In fact, isn't that what the Qur'an teaches—there are good people of every faith?"

These people were actually much more knowledgeable about Islam than I was, but I think they realized I was right. It was a real lesson of tolerance for them, and what *hajj* is really supposed to be about.

You had to be certain places by certain times, take certain routes to get to certain places. It was very, very detailed, and often the details were a little contradictory. I remember being with groups of people who were arguing over the details of how we're going to accomplish this next piece of it. My attitude was: "Look, I'm here for my *hajj*; you're really messing with my head. I've got a nice head going here. I'm going to in good faith do whatever you tell me, and I'm going to hope Allah accepts it, but I'm not going to sit here and argue over these fine points."

That didn't change anything for them. They went on and argued about it anyway.

For pilgrims, the stoning of pillars at Mina represents a modern-day rejection of Satan and a reaffirmation of faith in Allah . . . As I waded into the crowd that had gathered near the pillars, I thought about passages in the Qur'an that describe the Day of Judgment as a terrible event, a time when the heavens will be torn asunder and mankind will be driven to a frenzy of terror. It seemed that with every stone they threw, the pilgrims in Mina were trying to put as much distance as they possibly could between themselves and the horror of the Last Day. As I moved close to the first pillar, pebbles flew wildly, and I was struck on the back of my head and the side of my face. The expressions of people in the crowd ranged from elation to terror, and women held tightly to their children, some of whom were screaming with fright.

When I came back [to the States], both of my parents died. The *hajj* really focuses your mind on dying. One of the things the Sufis say is you should think of your death every moment of your life.

I don't have a grand strategy. I have a few ideas, but it's not like there's this big plan, because when you need to know something, Allah will reveal it.

I was in the Grand Mosque in Mecca. The Ka'aba was about 200 yards away, and I was praying. There's a *hadith* which says when you're on *hajj* every prayer you make makes up for a thousand missed prayers. So I was making them *hard*. [*Laughs.*]

This place was packed! You could hardly move. You're praying in about a body's width of space, trying to get down on your knees.

At one point I stood up and I was just looking at the Ka'aba, and it just came over me. I just said to Allah, "This life is Yours! Just *take* it. Wherever You want it to go, I'll be. This is Yours! C'mon! *Just come get me!*"

People pressed against me from all sides, and I was pushed helplessly back and forth. There was no point in resisting. Pilgrims are often warned to forget anything they might drop during the tawaf *[the rite of walking around the Ka'aba seven times] because to bend over in the crowd is to risk being trampled. As I walked barefoot around the Ka'aba, I stepped over sandals, bags and other items that had been lost by pilgrims.*

When I got back, I was assigned to an older editor on the magazine. He was Christian. He was very sensitive to the project, and he really helped me get the piece on paper. He talked me through the piece.

After it was published, I got tons of letters from Muslims and from non-Muslims. I got letters from people telling me they didn't have much of a clear sense of what the religion was about until they read that. Muslims told me they were glad that my piece was out there. And I got a couple of letters from people telling me that I should burn in hell for putting out propaganda.

And He sends down from the sky mountain masses [of clouds]
wherein is hail: He strikes therewith whom He pleases and He
turns it away from whom He pleases. The vivid flash of His
lightning well-nigh blinds the sight.

Qur'an 24:43

From the Watchtower
to the Minaret

Raphael Narbaez, Jr.

A forty-two-year-old Latino, Raphael is a Los Angeles-based comic and lecturer. He was born in Texas, where he attended his first Jehovah's Witness meeting at age six, gave his first Bible sermon at eight, tended his own congregation at twenty, and was headed for a position of leadership among the 904,000 Jehovah's Witnesses in the United States.[2] But he traded in his Bible for a Qur'an after having braved a visit to a local mosque.

On November 1, 1991, he embraced Islam, bringing to the Muslim community the organizational and speaking skills he developed among Jehovah's Witnesses. He speaks with the urgency of a new convert, but one who can make immigrant Muslims laugh at themselves.

He told his story mimicking a cast of characters.

I remember vividly being in a discussion where we were all sitting in my parents' living room and there were some other Jehovah's Witnesses there. They were talking about: "It's Armageddon! The time of the end! And Christ is coming! And you know the hailstones are going to be out here as big as cars! God is going to use all kinds of things to destroy this wicked system and remove the governments! And the Bible talks about the earth opening up! It's going to swallow whole city blocks!"

[2] Reportedly, there are 4.5 million Jehovah's Witnesses worldwide.

I'm scared to death! And then my mother turned around: "See what's going to happen to you if you don't get baptized, and if you don't do God's will? The earth is going to swallow you up, or one of these huge hailstones is going to hit you on the head [*klonk*], knock you out, and you will not exist ever again. I'll have to make another child."

I wasn't going to take a chance being hit by one of those big hailstones. So I got baptized. And of course Jehovah's Witnesses don't believe in the sprinkling of the water. They submerge you completely, hold you there for a second, and then bring you back up.

I did that at the age of thirteen, September 7, 1963, in Pasadena, California, at the Rose Bowl. It was a big international assembly. We had 100,000 people.[3] We drove all the way from Lubbock, Texas.

Eventually I started giving bigger talks—ten minutes in front of the congregation. And a circuit servant[4] recommended me to give the hour lectures that are done on Sunday when they invite the general public. They usually reserved those [sermons] for the elders of the congregation.

[*In an authoritarian voice:*] "Sure he's young. But he can handle it. He's a good Christian boy. He has no vices, and he's obedient to his parents and seems to have pretty good Bible knowledge."

So at the age of sixteen I started giving hour lectures in front of whole congregations. I was assigned first a group in Sweetwater, Texas, and then eventually in Brownfield, Texas, I got my first congregation. At age twenty, I had become what they call a pioneer minister.

Jehovah's Witnesses have a very sophisticated training program, and they also have kind of a quota system. You had to devote ten to twelve hours a month to door-to-door preaching. It's like sales management. IBM has nothing on these guys.

So when I became a pioneer minister, I devoted most of my full time to doing the door-to-door ministry. I had to do like 100 hours a month, and I had to have seven Bible studies. I started lecturing other congregations. I began to get a lot of responsibility, and I was accepted at a school in Brooklyn, New York, a very elite school that Jehovah's Witnesses have for the crème de la crème, the top one percent. But I didn't go.

A few things no longer made sense to me. For example, the quota system. It seemed like every time I wanted to turn a corner and get into

---

[3] 118,447 people attended the public talks; 2,496 people were baptized.
[4] Traveling minister.

Raphael Narbaez, Jr.

another position of responsibility I had to do these secular material things to prove my godliness. It's like if you meet your quotas this month, God loves you. If you don't meet your quotas next month, God doesn't love you. That didn't make very much sense. One month God loves me and one month He doesn't?

The other thing I started noticing is tunnel vision. Jehovah's Witnesses are the only ones who are going to be saved in God's new order, nobody else, because all of them are practicing false religions. Well, I thought, Mother Teresa's a Catholic. That's our dire enemy. So I said, Wait a minute, Mother Teresa has spent her entire life doing things that Jesus said: take care of the poor, the sick, the orphans. But she's not going to have God's favor because she's a Catholic?

We criticized the Catholic Church because they had a man, a priest, whom they had to confess to. And we'd say, "You shouldn't have to go to a man to confess your sins! Your sin is against God!" And yet we went to a Body of Elders. You confessed your sin to them, and they put you on hold, and said [*Elder as telephone operator:*] "Hold on just a minute . . . What do you think, Lord? No? . . . Okay, I'm sorry, we tried our best but you're not repentant enough. Your sin is too big, so you either lose your fellowship in the church or you're going to be on probation."

If the sin is against God, shouldn't I directly go to God and beg for mercy?

Probably the nail that hit the coffin was that I noticed that they started reading their Bible less. Jehovah's Witnesses have books for everything that are put out by the Watchtower Bible and Tract Society.[5] The *only* people on the entire planet who know how to interpret Bible Scripture correctly are that group of men, that committee in Brooklyn, who tell Jehovah's Witnesses worldwide how to dress, how to talk, what to say, what not to say, how to apply Scripture and what the future is going to be like. God told them, so they can tell us. I appreciated the books. But if the Bible is the book of knowledge and if it's God's instructions, well, shouldn't we get our answers out of the Bible? Paul himself said find out for yourself what is a true and acceptable word of God. Don't let men tickle your ears.

I started saying, "Don't worry so much about what the Watchtower says —read the Bible for yourself." Ears started to prick up.

[*Old Southerner's drawl:*] "I think we got us an apostate here, Judge. Yup. I think this old boy's one taco short of something."

Even my father said, "You better watch it, young man, that's the demons talking right there. That's the demons trying to get in and cause division."

I said, "Dad, it's not the demons. People don't need to read so much of these other publications. They can find their answers with prayer and in the Bible."

Spiritually I no longer felt at ease. So in 1979, knowing that I could not make headway, I left, disgruntled and with a bad taste in my mouth, because all my life I had put my soul, my heart, my mind into the church. That was the problem. I didn't put it in God. I put it in a man-made organization.

I can't go to other religions. As a Jehovah's Witness, I had been trained, through the Scriptures, to show that they are all wrong. That idolatry is bad. Trinity doesn't exist.

I'm like a man without a religion. I was not a man without a God. But where could I go?

In 1985, I decided to come to Los Angeles and get on the Johnny Carson show and make my mark as a great comedian and actor. I have always felt like I was born for something. I didn't know whether it was going to be

---

[5] The publishing arm of the organization. *The Watchtower*, its bimonthly magazine, has perhaps the highest circulation of any religious periodical—16,400,000 copies, printed in 112 languages.

finding the cure to cancer or becoming an actor. I kept praying and it got frustrating after a while.

So I just went to the Catholic church close to my house, and I tried it. I remember on Ash Wednesday I had that ash cross on my forehead. I was trying anything I could. I went for about two or three months, and I just couldn't do it anymore, man. It was:

Stand up.

Sit down.

Stand up.

Sit down.

Okay, stick your tongue out.

You got a lot of exercise. I think I lost about five pounds. But that's about it. So now I'm more lost than ever.

But it never passed through my mind that there is not a Creator. I have His phone number, but the line's always busy.

I'm doing my little movie shots. A film called *Deadly Intent*. A telephone commercial in Chicago. An Exxon commercial. A couple of bank commercials. In the meantime I'm doing construction work on the side.

We're working on this mall. It's the holiday season, and they put these extra booths in the hallways. There was a gal at one, and we had to pass right in front of her. I'd say, "Good morning, how are you?" If she said anything, it was "Hi." And that was it.

Finally, I said, "Miss, you never say anything. I just wanted to apologize if there was something I said wrong."

She said, "No, you see, I'm a Muslim."

"You're what?"

"I'm a Muslim, and Muslim women, we don't talk to men unless we have something specific to talk about; otherwise we don't have anything to do with men."

"Ohhhhh. Muslim."

She said, "Yes, we practice the religion of Islam."

"Islam—how do you spell that?"

"I-s-l-a-m."

At the time, I knew that Muslims were all terrorists. She doesn't even have a beard. How could she possibly be Muslim?

"How did this religion get started?"

"Well, there was a prophet."

"A prophet?"

"Muhammad."

I started some research. But I just came from one religion. I had no intention of becoming Muslim.

The holidays are over. The booth moves. She's gone.

I continued to pray, and asked why my prayers weren't being answered. In November of 1991, I was going to bring my uncle Rockie home from the hospital. I started to empty his drawers to pack his stuff and there was a Gideon Bible. I said, God has answered my prayers. This Gideon Bible. (Of course, they put it in every hotel room.) This is a sign from God that He's ready to teach me.

So I stole the Bible.

I went home and I started praying: O God, teach me to be a Christian. Don't teach me the Jehovah's Witness way. Don't teach me the Catholic way. Teach me *Your* way! You would not have made this Bible so hard that ordinary people sincere in prayer could not understand it.

I got all the way through the New Testament. I started the Old Testament. Well, eventually there's a part in the Bible about the prophets.

Bing!

I said, Wait a minute, that Muslim lady said they had a prophet. How come he's not in here?

I started thinking, Muslims—one billion in the world. Man, one out of every five people on the street theoretically could be a Muslim. And I thought: One billion people! C'mon now, Satan is good. But he's not *that* good.

So then I said, I'll read their book, the Qur'an, and I'll see what kind of pack of lies this thing is. It probably has an illustration on how to disassemble an AK-47. So I went to an Arabic bookstore.

They asked, "What can I help you with?"

"I'm looking for a Qur'an."

"Okay, we have some over here."

They had some very nice ones—thirty dollars, forty dollars.

"Look, I just want to read it, I don't want to become one, okay?"

"Okay, we have this little five-dollar paperback edition."

I went home, and started reading my Qur'an from the beginning, with *Al-Fatihah*. And I could not get my eyes off of it.

Hey, look at this. It talks about a Noah in here. We have Noah in our Bible too. Hey, it talks Lot and Abraham. I can't believe it. I never knew Satan's name was Iblis. Hey, how about that.

When you get that picture on your TV set and it's got a little bit of static and you push that button [*klop*]—fine-tune. That's exactly what happened with the Qur'an.

I went through the whole thing. So I said, Okay, I've done this, now what's the next thing you got to do? Well, you gotta go to their meeting place. I looked in the yellow pages, and I finally found it: Islamic Center of Southern California, on Vermont. I called and they said, "Come on Friday."

Now I really start getting nervous, 'cause now I know I'm going to have to confront Habib and his AK-47.

I want people to understand what it's like for an American Christian coming into Islam. I'm kidding about the AK-47, but I don't know if these guys have daggers under their coats, you know. So I come up to the front, and sure enough, there's this six-foot-three, 240-pound brother, beard and everything, and I'm just in awe.

I walked up and said, "Excuse me, sir."

[*Arabic accent:*] "Go to the back!"

He thought I was already a brother.

I said, "Yessir, yessir" [*meekly*].

I didn't know what I was going back for, but I went back anyway. They had the tent and the rugs were out. I'm standing there, kind of shy, and people are sitting down listening to the lecture. And people are saying, Go ahead, brother, sit down. And I'm going, No, thanks, no, thanks, I'm just visiting.

So finally the lecture's over. They're all lined up for prayer and they go into *sajdah*. I was really taken aback.

It started making sense intellectually, in my muscles, in my bones, in my heart and my soul.

So prayers are over. I say, hey, who's going to recognize me? So I start to mingle like I'm one of the brothers, and I'm walking into the mosque and a brother says, *"Assalaamu alaikum."* And I thought, Did he say "salt and bacon"?

"Assalaamu alaikum."

There's another guy who said "salt and bacon" to me.

I didn't know what in the world they were saying, but they all smiled.

Before one of these guys noticed that I was not supposed to be there and took me to the torture chamber, or beheaded me, I wanted to see as much as I could. So eventually I went to the library, and there was a young Egyptian brother; his name was Omar. God sent him to me.

Omar comes up to me, and he says, "Excuse me. This your first time here?" He has a real strong accent.

And I said, Yeah, it is.

"Oh, very good. You are Muslim?"

"No, I'm just reading a little."

"Oh, you are studying? This is your first visit to a mosque?"

"Yes."

"Come, let me show you around." And he grabs me by the hand, and I'm walking with another man—holding hands. I said, These Muslims are friendly.

So he shows me around.

"First of all, this is our prayer hall, and you take your shoes off right here."

"What are these things?"

"These are little cubicles. That's where you put your shoes."

"Why?"

"Well, because you're approaching the prayer area, and it's very holy. You don't go in there with your shoes on; it's kept real clean."

So he takes me to the men's room.

"And right here, this is where we do *wudu.*"

"Voodoo! I didn't read anything about voodoo!"

"No, not voodoo. *Wudu!*"

"Okay, because I saw that stuff with the dolls and the pins, and I'm just not ready for that kind of commitment yet."

He says, "No, *wudu,* that's when we clean ourselves."

"Why do you do that?"

"Well, when you pray to God, you have to be clean, so we wash our hands and feet."

So I learned all these things. He let me go, and said, Come back again.

I went back and asked the librarian for a booklet on prayer, and I went home and practiced. I felt that if I was trying to do it right, God would accept it. I just continued to read and read and visit the mosque.

I had a commitment to go on a tour of the Midwest on a comedy circuit. Well, I took a prayer rug with me. I knew that I was supposed to pray at certain times, but there are certain places where you are not supposed to pray, one of which is in the bathroom. I went into a men's room on a tourist stop and I laid out my carpet and I started doing my prayers.

I came back, and when Ramadan was over, I started getting calls from different parts of the country to go and lecture as a Jehovah's Witness minister who embraced Islam. People find me a novelty.

[*Two immigrants converse:*]

"This guy likes apple pie and he drives a Chevy truck. He is a red-blooded American boy. He was a Jehovah's Witness."

"Those people that come in the morning?"

"Yeah, those."

"That never let us sleep on Sundays?"

"Yeah, this guy was one of them. Now he's one of us."

Eventually somebody would come up to me and say [*Pakistani accent*], "Oh, brother, your talk was so good. But you know, in the Shafi'i school of thought—"

The only thing I could do was turn to them and say, "Gee, brother, I'm so sorry, I wish I knew about that, but I don't know anything about Islam except what's in the Qur'an and *Sunnah*.

Some of them are taken aback and say, "*Ha-ha!* Poor brother. He doesn't know anything. He only knows the Qur'an."

Well, that's what I'm supposed to know. And it's been a very loving protection. I think it's all in God's hands.

Raphael performed hajj *in 1993.*

*Whosoever of you sees an evil action, let him change
it with his hand; and if he is not able to do so, then with his
tongue; and if he is not able to do so, then with his heart—
and that is the weakest of faith.*

—Prophet Muhammad, *Hadith* (Muslim)

By Hand or By Heart

Hassan Sulaiman

His journey toward Islam started with a call to 911. He has since tried to correct evil actions with at least his heart, if not his hands. One major struggle, however, is right at home. His wife is a churchgoer, and he worries about his children's Islam. He also worries about Muslims idolizing Malcolm X. "They're into this hero-worshipping thing," he says. Islam forbids it.

I was standing in front of my house talking with my friends and the drunk that lives next door came out. He was a nice drunk. He didn't bother nobody, but we always made jokes about him. He went across the street to the bodega to get his beer or his wine. When he came out of the store, one of the neighborhood hard-rock guys seen him. He must have stepped on his foot or something. The guy took exception. He took a long cardboard box and started hitting the drunk guy with it. So I ran upstairs and I called 911. When I came back downstairs the guy had left and the drunk was dead. Somebody had pulled out a gun and shot him.

My friends who had remained downstairs witnessed it. The shot rang out and everybody ran. But I stayed downstairs and when the cops came I told them what I had saw and what I had done. So I stood there and I gave my statement to the police 'cause I knew who it was that had did the hitting.

So they called me down to the precinct. I told my parents and they were both upset that I had got involved. Eventually I had to testify in front of the grand jury.

Because of that incident, my parents felt that it wasn't safe for me to live there anymore. We eventually moved to Coney Island. But that's something that I will never forget. Until this day I know I was right, and I believe they should have supported me in that matter. They kept preaching to me how you can't save the world. There's certain things that you can't do because you put yourself and other people in jeopardy. My response was "Dad, if somebody had killed you and my friends had saw it I would want them to testify to the police so that guy could get put away."

Good argument, logic. But when you're seventeen, eighteen, it didn't work with them.

When you look in Jewish neighborhoods, like Williamsburg, you don't see cops, but you don't see crime. You look in our neighborhood, you see all these cops but you see numbers, prostitution, drugs, crime. So it's not the cops that's going to stop the crime; it's going to be the people in the community. If I try to sell drugs on the corner in Williamsburg, it won't be the cops that will arrest me; it will be the community that will come after me with bats and sticks and guns, chasing me out of there. And after they beat me up, then they will call the cops to take my body out of there.

In our neighborhood, it doesn't work that way because we African Americans purchase the drugs, play the numbers, go to the prostitutes. We're not the ones that want it out of the community.

There's a *hadith* that says when you see a negative action you must correct it with your hand. If you can't, speak out about it. If you can't speak out about it, feel bad about it in your heart. That *hadith* stays in my mind as well as another:

There were two sets of people in a boat, the good and the bad. The bad were on the lower portion and the good people were on the upper portion. The bad people had to come up to the top to get water from the good people. They got tired of doing it, so they said, If we drill a hole in the bottom of the boat, we won't have to bother you to get water. So the Prophet said, If the good people on top do not stop the bad people on the bottom from drilling a hole, then they will all drown.

I vowed to myself that regardless of who got upset or felt bad about it, if there was something negative that I saw, I will go out and try to correct it with my hand or speak out against it, or at least feel bad about it in my heart.

. . .

The people that I admired the most—Muhammad Ali, Malcolm X, and Kareem Abdul-Jabbar—were all Muslims. All the men, even my grandfather, were followers of Noble Drew Ali. Sammie Travis Bey, my mother's father. He didn't make *salat*[6] five times. He was more like the Nation of Islam. He believed the black man was the Original Man and some other foolishness.

He never stole. He didn't drink. He didn't smoke. He didn't lie. He treated everybody fairly. Everybody loved him because of these qualities that he had. His wife died and he finished raising two boys and six girls while working for the railroad during the Depression. He never missed a day of work in over thirty years. If he said to be ready by seven o'clock, that he was coming to get you, you better believe that by six-thirty he was going to be there.

He died in '87 at the age of eighty-six. And he had a taste of Islam.

I guess I had read as much as I could read on my own. I wasn't going to church. I didn't feel Christian. I was torn between two worlds. I knew eventually I was going to get into Islam. I didn't know how or what role I had to play in it, but one day I got up enough nerve to do it.

There were Nubian Hebrews right there where I lived, within walking distance. There were many days when I walked up to the door and couldn't open it. The State Street Mosque had literature that struck a nerve. I gave them a call and they said, "Come on down."

I took *shahada* August 27, 1974, at 143 State Street. Shaikh Dauod was the brother.[7] I stayed in there for about an hour. When I walked out of there I was on cloud nine. I was really excited; I had taken a big step, accepted Islam. I filled out some paperwork. He gave me an ID card, very formal. I called him back that Friday because the last thing he said was I have to come back and get some instruction. He picked up the phone and he was ranting at me: "How come you haven't come back? Where you been? You gotta learn more. You know, you just can't leave like this."

That turned me off. I left feeling great that one day and the next day when I called back to find out when I could get an appointment to learn how to make *wudu,* he was attacking me. I didn't know why. So I didn't go back.

I didn't have a group of Muslims that I could learn from, so I did what

[6] Islamic prayer.
[7] Shaikh Dauod Ahmad Faisal (1891–1980).

I've always done, that is, go to bookstores and buy *hadith* books. I bought the Qur'an and I tried to learn on my own. I had my own perception of Islam. I thought I could live Islam privately.

I was gaining more knowledge but I wasn't interacting with Muslims. I was doing my own thing. I didn't know how to pray. I was fairly satisfied. I was different. I didn't drink, smoke, and do other things. But then again I wasn't making *salat*. I didn't know it was as important as it was.

In 1985, I started going to *juma,* and this is what motivated me to get more into the religion. What really struck me was a brother from the post office who had his bag on his shoulder, dropping his bag and taking off his shoes and coming onto the carpet and making *salat*. What a contrast. You think about the Middle East and camels and what have you. And you talk about 1985 in America, in Manhattan, somebody in the post office doing that? And then seeing court officers, people from banks, Wall Street, you name it. The full mosaic had an influence. The brothers were so dedicated. People had answers to questions. I didn't feel that any of the answers were tainted with racism or black supremacy or anything like that. That hooked me hook, line, and sinker.

Later on, '86, '87, a brother brought the son of a preacher to the *masjid* on a Friday. When that brother left, he came out and he said he hadn't seen so many black men in any one place like that in all his life. That's when I first really reflected on the fact that they were all men. But I looked at the positive aspect. When you think about the Christian church, it's predominantly women. There are no men there. This is a positive step, to see all these black men in the same place—no weapons, not trying to kill each other, all trying to worship the same God. I mean, this is beautiful. We need to get more black men in here.

We have Islam and we have Christianity. My children come to me and they ask me, "When is Mommy gonna be a Muslim?" There's no answer. In some ways it would be better if she just came out and said, "I've got no intention of being a Muslim, you hear? I hate you guys. Take a flying leap." It would be a little bit easier to deal with. But I've been told by her that she will accept Islam. I've offered: "What can I do to speed it up?" Nothing. I can't do anything to speed it up. She will at whatever time when the spirit hits her.

Although she says she will accept Islam, she's going to church now. And I know from what I've learned, you can't learn anything good there.

They're only deceiving you, because who are you praying to? You're praying to Jesus, which is *shirk*.[8] So the more I learn about the religion, the more frustrating it is when I go home. As I go to Masjid Medina and listen to the brothers speak on Fridays, I feel great. I'm learning. I'm getting closer to Allah. But then when I come home, I'm depressed.

I see that as a problem in our community, my life being a microcosm of the African American community. Our churches are filled with women, and our mosques are filled with men.

Look at all the brothers that aren't married because the women aren't coming here. They're in church, okay? So if we can find a way for the women to get the *deen*,[9] we'd take care of a lot of problems.

I've gotten out of the hero-worship thing. Eventually when you follow someone's career or admire them, you'll find some character flaws in them that will bring you back down to earth. And I think that what makes Malcolm so popular with so many people is the fact that he's dead and we can't find his flaws, whatever they may have been. If he was alive today and he made certain statements and he did certain things, then people would be criticizing him like they were doing in the '60s.

I believe that Malcolm actually believed that what he was teaching was correct. And Malcolm did not profit other than to gain exposure. Financially he had no money, no large car, the house that he lived in was not his. So you could see he was driven by something different than financial gain.

I have his albums. I have maybe ten books on his life. I have cassette tapes. I have videotapes. For my wedding present I had someone paint a picture of Malcolm. I had an obsession about him for a period of time.

I struggle with Malcolm now. I still love him. Malcolm was the tool that Allah used to bring me into Islam. But I listen to other African American brothers talk about Malcolm and how great he was and it worries me. Muslims are not supposed to love anybody more than the Prophet. But I hear some brothers talking about Malcolm in the same ways they should be talking about the Prophet. And we must remember, as great as he was, he was only Muslim for about a year and a half. All that other stuff was right out of the Nation of Islam, where he believed that the white man was the devil. He believed that Farad Muhammad was Allah incarnate, which is *shirk*. So it's hard for me to come to grips with this reality.

[8] Polytheism.
[9] The divine code of life.

The big contradiction is people say Malcolm was great, and while they're saying that, they're drinking a wine cooler and eating a ham sandwich, so they really don't understand what he was about. They don't know what Islam is. But that's what made Malcolm Malcolm. Even though he didn't have the whole truth of Islam, what little bit of the truth of Islam he had helped catapult him to that position, and people don't understand that. They just see somebody who talked bad about whitey. But they don't see what made him great, the moral strength that he had.

I cannot deny his contributions and the fact that I'm still living in America. His observations were accurate. So I have to incorporate Islam from the Prophet's time with Malcolm's vision and try to mesh the two. I can't totally disregard Malcolm but he has a [more] subservient part in my vision than before.

[T]umult and oppression are worse than slaughter . . .

Qur'an 2:191

The Last Poet

Suliaman El Hadi

"The war with words is as important as, if not more important
than, the war with guns, because propaganda is what sets the tone
for the relationship that you have with your enemy, you understand,
or even your potential with friends."

*A member of the Last Poets, a group of poet/musicians whose albums of
New York street poetry were popular in the late '60s and '70s and whose
verse of protest has been rediscovered by rap musicians of the '90s.*

*Suliaman, a Sunni Muslim, found Islam as a saving grace from a world
of crime, drugs, poverty, and prison. He made protest poetry, tempering
his anger with lyrics that espouse Islamic values.*

*Despite the acclaim his poetry brought him, he never changed. He lives
in the projects in Brooklyn, where economic conditions have in many ways
deteriorated since the days when he first started reciting. He walks the
streets like an elder statesman, wearing a* kufi *and chatting with teenagers, who treat him deferentially—he was, after all, one of the original
rappers.*

*El Hadi ("the Guide") has two wives. He has been married to the first
for twenty-nine years; the second has been a partnership of seventeen
years. On marriage, he says, "Well, it's difficult, because, as you know,
Muslims can have more than one wife, but the test comes in maintaining
them and treating them equal. It don't mean if you buy one a skirt you
gotta buy the other one a skirt, but it means you don't discriminate against
them and you try not to consciously show any difference between them.*

331

You try your best to be as just as possible. It's hard because of your feel-
ings, because Allah created but one heart for you, not two hearts. It's even
more difficult to maintain on the physical tip. You be working your butt
off!"

Suliaman now counts 70 Muslims in his family. He was the first to con-
vert from Christianity.

He still writes and recites and travels the globe to spread the word of
Islam in verse. His personal jihad *is to combat ignorance. "You could say*
that we are like parrots that imitate what the prophets say. . . . Our jihad
against ignorance is first and foremost, because before you can have a
revolution physically, you have to have an evolution mentally and spiritu-
ally. You have to evolve before you can revolve."

We call our art form "spoetgraphics"—"spoetry," or speaking poetry rapidly. And that's where rap comes in. The meter is fast and slow, with a
slow lead and fast background, or fast lead with slow background, or a
mixture of the two simultaneously.

I got involved in the Last Poets in 1970. The group started in 1968. It
was a group that started spontaneously at a rally for El-Hajj Malik El-
Shabazz at Mount Morris Park. They had artists from the community performing. At the finale, some of the poets decided to recite together and the
people liked it. They wound up naming themselves the Last Poets for a
verse from a poem by a South African poet in exile. He wrote a poem
saying, "This is the last day for poems and essays, guns and rifles will take
the places of . . . essays in the future."

He really was talking about South Africa, but it fitted us too. So consequently we are the last poets of this age.

The very first album recorded was called just plain *The Last Poets*. It
was a two-album contract. The third album was *Chastisement*, made in
1971. It was released in '72. That's the first album I'm on.

Our concepts are based on Islamic concepts. For instance, the poem:

> *Blessed are those who struggle*
> *Oppression is worse than the grave*
> *Better to die for a noble cause*
> *Than to live and die a slave*

That is really Qur'anic. I wrote it, but it is Allah Who says in the Qur'an,
Surely oppression is worse than slaughter, so fight against oppression
wherever you may find it. Therefore in speaking about our struggle and

our oppression, we also mention what Allah has said, and consequently all of our work is influenced primarily by the Qur'an and the traditions of the Prophet Muhammad.

We dress like Muslims when we come onstage. We greet the crowd. We first go *Assalaamu alaikum,* peace be upon you. We remind them of Allah, you understand. First we'd like to thank Allah for being here, thank Allah for creating us, creating you all, so that you all could be here. Before we could give anything up to anybody else, we have to give it up to Allah.

I think that *Niggers Is Scared of Revolution* is famous. We have an album called *Delights of the Garden.* The whole B side is about the Last Day, the destruction of the earth.

> *Put your words and actions in accord*
> *Keep your obligations to your Lord*
> *The time is much too late*
> *To procrastinate*
> *Your actions will determine your reward*

Prophet Muhammad used to say, Speak to the people in the language they understand, so this is the language they understand. So I'm calling my people to Islam. At most of the shows we have somebody call us later on and tell us that they accepted Islam.

Suliaman El Hadi backstage at a Paris jazz concert in the summer of 1993.

The revolutionary government invited us to Iran and paid for our stay there. We stayed for two weeks in 1984 for the celebration of Al Fajr, the anniversary of the revolution. We were invited as honored guests. There were only eight people invited from the United States.

It was one of the best experiences that I ever had. Only other trip that I could compare it to was the *hajj*, to Mecca. That was just as heavy—because Allah had prescribed that.

In Iran I saw guys riding around on motorcycles, the sin squad. They were looking for anybody in violation of the law of Allah. They had signs on the doors of public buildings that said no women permitted in here without [a veil]. They had turned the liquor stores into classrooms and everybody was vibed up! They was vibed up on the *jihad* tip too. From the young ones to the old ones. I enjoyed myself and they treated us like royalty.

There's no comparison between poetry and the Qur'an. Allah speaks to men through inspiration. He speaks to men through His messengers, through His signs. You could say that we are like parrots that imitate what the prophets say. Yeah, Polly wants a cracker.

It's the same because we read the Qur'an, we read the traditions, we know the mystery. We study ourselves, and we research. When you speak about the past—our relationship to the ex-slave master and our relationship to the Indians—so far most of the story that we have heard has been related by the perpetrator. So the story has been slanted to favor him. Consequently when we talk about history, we wind up talking about *his-story*—the perpetrator's story. *His*-story is history; but *my* story is *mystery!* Because my story is missing—by design. So we do a lot of things that are historical. But none of our stuff do we do haphazard. Everything that we do, we research.

We was rapping when the kids was napping. When I see the kids that are doing this today, it makes me feel good, it makes me feel that somebody was listening, and even though they haven't developed the message yet, they will in time, as they grow and mature and learn and their life experiences are greater. They will, I'm sure, become more positive in what they say.

[Right now] it's all about content—it ain't about message. They can't talk about what they don't know about. You put down a beat [*demonstrates, pounding on a table*] and then they put words to a copy of the beat. That's backwards [from] the way we do it.

When we add music to our thing, it's music to enhance the message, as opposed to the message to enhance the music—because we're not the Last Rappers, we're the Last Poets; we're *real* poets. So we're not going to just say anything; we have to say something that has content and worth. When we put together a poem it will be *about* something.

[He is] Lord of the two Easts and Lord of the two Wests . . .

Qur'an 55:17

This Old World

Davud Abdul Hakim

The interview took place in a study room at New York University, which he attends. Formerly named David Hunsicker, he had closely cropped hair, fingered prayer beads, wore stonewashed jeans and a lumberjack-like flannel shirt, and slouched in his chair.

He says his parents "considered Islam to be a religion for black people because of the impressions they had gotten of Farrakhan and Malcolm X in the past. So when I decided I wanted to become a Muslim they didn't see how I could. If I went to the mosque, my mother would say, 'So were you the only white person there?' " [Laughs.]

Davud tried other religions before settling on Islam. His visit to Turkey as an exchange student hastened his decision.

I was born in Allentown, Pennsylvania, October 23, 1971. I lived in a village on the outskirts. Germansville. I'd say right now about 80 percent of the people are Pennsylvania Dutch and everybody has German ancestors.

There's probably 500 people in the town, spread out over a lot of square miles. Until I was five years old I lived right on the family farm. After that we moved a quarter mile away and built our own house on what used to be a field. An old man in the neighborhood used to complain to my father that he built a house on the best potato field in the area.

What made me decide to become an exchange student is that I wasn't much of an American patriot. I didn't believe in the American Dream. I don't think I ever did. I was looking to find somewhere else I could call home and I started looking at other religions.

I studied Buddhism. Nothing seemed to satisfy me. I was looking for some kind of a sacred guru-type text. I bought a translation of the Qur'an. As I was reading through it, it just hit me. It spoke to me. It told me I must become a Muslim. I could see no other way but to become a Muslim. The Qur'an explained things to me. I recognized the truth.

I declared myself to people around me—that I am Muslim. This is before taking *shahada*. I'd never met a Muslim. I just felt that I was a Muslim.

I tried to find more books. Since I wanted to become a Muslim and wanted to go to Germany because it was my ethnic homeland, at the same time I knew there were a lot of ethnic Turks in Germany who were Muslims. I was hoping that maybe I would meet them and they would teach me some more about Islam. Turkey was the only Muslim country that was offered through the program. Turkey was my eighth choice on the list. By chance I was sent there.

When I got to Turkey more books were available. Muslims everywhere around me. I could hear the *adhan* five times a day. So I began to mature as a Muslim. I was there for a year and it was a slow process.

Most people didn't think twice about it. A lot of them declared themselves atheists: "Oh, we don't believe that. We're too good for that. We want to be Western. We want to be like Europe." So they pretty much abandoned Islam. But I still had friends who were good practicing Muslims. I was caught between them because the atheists wanted an American lifestyle. I didn't want to get homesick, so I tended to stick with the atheists a lot of times. But the Muslims said, "Well, you know, you should start coming to *juma* prayers,"[10] and eventually I started going. They helped me to learn more about how to do my prayers and they stuck with me and helped me out.

The first time I went to *juma,* it was the night of *Mi'raj.*[11] I was with my [host] family and we were fasting.

Istanbul has pseudo holy places all around it. We went to one. I have no idea who's buried there. It's on a military base. No foreigners are allowed. We made *duah*[12] at the grave. It was a Friday. I was scared 'cause I was afraid of making a mistake. There was a Turkish boy with us. I don't think he had ever been to prayer before. The two of us were both lost. I remem-

---

[10] Friday congregational prayers.
[11] The night of the ascension of the Prophet through the "seven heavens," when he was enjoined to direct Muslims to pray five times each day.
[12] Supplication.

ber sitting there, trying to get something out of the ceremony. I just went through the motions as best I could.

In 1988 I was with some Mevlevi dervishes. The Mevlevis are the Whirling Dervishes that are famous in Turkey. It was a spiritual feeling for me too to see them. I decided I wanted to be a dervish. I didn't want to be just a Muslim. Ironically an aunt of my host family belonged to this Mevlevi order. They had little clandestine meetings in Istanbul, because while the Mevlevis were allowed pretty much to practice freely, all dervish orders were forbidden inside Turkey.

My aunt took me to their meeting and they took me to their sheik. They did a little bit of the whirling and then *zikr* and the sheik said to me, "Okay, you want to be a dervish?" I said, "Yeah," and he said, "Have you taken *shahada* yet?" and I said, "No," and so he gave me *shahada* and he inducted me into their order.

It was a sort of pseudo induction. I had to kiss his knee and his hand. I was wearing a conical cap. I laid my head down on his knee, and he put his hand down over my head and said some *duahs* over me. I'm kneeling and he's sitting on a chair.

That was the first step toward becoming a Mevlevi. I tried whirling at home but I really didn't stick with it.

I'm grateful that I didn't go to more meetings because now I don't see Sufism as being correct Islam. Instead I'm glad I got to be better friends with Muslims at school, traditional Muslims, Sunni Muslims. They taught me more than the Mevlevis ever could have, because a lot of [Mevlevis] don't pray five times a day. They're Mevlevis first, Muslims second a lot of the times.

In school on Fridays we had to sneak to go to *juma* prayer, because it was illegal for students to get out of school for *juma*. But there was one principal who was sympathetic toward Muslims. He couldn't leave to go to *juma* because he was an official, but he could allow us to go. He wrote a little note in Arabic saying, "These people can go out of the gate and go to *juma*." We'd give it to the doorman, who could read the old Arabic script. He'd say, "Okay, you, you, and you go out; you can go to *juma*."

A block and a half away there was a *masjid*. But sometimes we would go to the principal and he'd say, "I'm sorry, but there's too much pressure. I can't let you out this week." So then what we'd do is we'd go out back and we'd jump the gate and go around so we could get to *juma*.

I still didn't understand too much but it was a very spiritual experience. I enjoyed going. At this point I was going every week. In some senses it helped my host family get back into their roots. The host father had always prayed off and on, but when I came and I said I wanted to be a Muslim, he made a point of praying. I don't think it was to humor me. It kind of made him feel guilty.

In Ramadan we would pray the *fajr* prayer.[13] Sometimes the mother would also join. They had some prayer rugs, and they would lay them out in the living room.

About two weeks after I had taken the *shahada* with the Mevlevis, I went to the mufti of the *masjid* that was close to my host father's place of business and I took *shahada* there also. I wanted to make it official. I wanted papers that said I was Muslim. I didn't get them because I was under age to change my religion. He spoke elegant Turkish, which I didn't understand.

One day me and one of my friends from school went inside this huge *masjid*. It was time for *asr* prayer.[14] This was a city of 8 million people, and there were ten people praying in this *masjid* with all this historical significance. That was incredible to me. The *masjid* was built by this sultan who was declared the *califa* and his tomb is next door and nobody was there. I mean, people were sightseeing and there were tourists everywhere, but nobody was praying in *jamat*.[15] I prayed in *jamat* and I said to my friend afterward that this is really sad because there's nobody here. But another time with the same friend, we met at the Blue Mosque. This was a Saturday. It was time for the *zuhr* prayer.[16] This huge mosque was packed with people. That was inspiring. It was big and gorgeous. Bright blue arabesques. Huge columns.

My parents came the last three weeks while I was there. They got to see some of the things I was talking about, and they got to learn a little bit more about Islam because I had written them and said, "Hi, I am now a Muslim."

Even before I went to Turkey, when I had just declared that I was a Muslim, my mother said to me, "As long as you worship the same God that we do, I have nothing against whatever you do." That's pretty much the way it stands today.

. . .

[13] The morning prayer, completed before sunrise.
[14] The midafternoon prayer.
[15] Congregation.
[16] Noon prayer.

When I was in Turkey, everybody's a Turk—complete uniformity. But coming to New York and going to a mosque, it's incredible to see different races and different nationalities all together. I grew up in a rural community. Like I said, there were no blacks in my community, no Asians. Islam has really made me mature in that sense.

When I returned [from Turkey], I had another year in high school. I had chosen a new first name, I went from David to Davud, but I didn't really tell people, because I've known these people all of my life. Some people thought it was just another phase. But the people who know me closely know that I'm a Muslim and pretty much know what that means.

I had just turned sixteen and I just started driving. I knew that there was a Shiite *masjid* nearby, but I was prejudiced against the Shiites. I didn't want to go there, and I didn't know about the other mosque because it was listed in the phone book under "religious organizations," not under "Islamic churches" like the Shiite *masjid* was.

Ironically, there was a prominent Muslim from Allentown killed in an accident, and the newspaper listed where his funeral was going to be, in a *masjid*. I said, "Wow, where's this?" I didn't know this place existed.

A couple of weeks after that I went to my first *juma*. I had sort of Islamic dress, Turkish Islamic dress—baggy pants, with the low crotch. I had a turban on, in addition to my *kufi*. I went in and asked where can I make *wudu,* and they directed me. Then I sat and went through the prayer. Afterward people came up to me and said, Hi, I'm so-and-so; nice to meet you, and friendships came up from there.

My goal is to study Islamic jurisprudence and become a *faquih*. That's my goal, *insh'allah*.[17] That's why I want to learn Arabic—so I can have a vehicle to study Islamic jurisprudence. I've applied to the American University in Cairo, which is an accredited American university. They specialize in Arabic and Middle Eastern studies. I'm waiting for a letter of acceptance. If I get accepted, I'm definitely going.

---

[17] God willing.

(6) Show us the straight way,

*(7) The way of those on whom Thou has bestowed Thy Grace,
those whose [portion] is not wrath, and who go not astray.*

Qur'an 1:6–7

Red Road

Lois Stands-Raheem

*Lois Stands-Raheem's original name is Wenya Chante Wishaka Uha—
"Woman Who Has a Strong Heart." The name was given to her at birth by
her grandmother, a member of the Lakota tribe of Native Americans
whose best-known battle was fought in 1876 at the Little Bighorn, where
General George Custer and most of his 200 men died. In 1890, in the last
major battle of the Indian Wars, nearly 200 Lakota were killed by the U.S.
Army at Wounded Knee. While today many Lakota still live on reservations, Lois moved from reservations to big cities and settled in Euclid,
Ohio, with her new husband. As soon as she left the reservation, she said,
her spiritual journey through life went into high gear.*

We call ourselves Lakota. That means "the people." In the white man's
world, most people know us as the Sioux. We don't call ourselves that.

I was born on the Pine Ridge Reservation in South Dakota, in one of the
communities called Oglala. My grandmother and grandfather lived in a log
house. It was very primitive there. I was there till I was five with them, and
then when my grandmother died, my earth father and my earth mother
came and got me. They took me out to my mother's reservation, Standing
Rock, right around the North Dakota border. I was there for a year. At
that time, there was what they called the King Alfred Act. It allowed them
to take Indian children and teach them to assimilate to white culture. The
government had taken one child out of every home and sent us away to
boarding schools.

I was in the boarding school for nine years. It was run by the govern-ment and the mission schools were run by churches. They were very mean. I was real glad I didn't go to the mission school.

When I went to the boarding school, all we knew was our native tongue, and we couldn't speak our language. We couldn't practice the traditions we were raised with, and those of us raised by our grandparents had a lot of the traditions instilled in us, and we were more stubborn than the other kids who were raised by their parents.

The more they abused me, the tougher my spirit got. There was some-thing inside me that just would not submit to these people. We were taught to respect our elders, but these people were not respectful, so we didn't respect them.

We would have to sneak and pray, they wouldn't even let us practice our own prayers. They took us to church, and that was my first exposure to Christianity. But every Sunday they took us in busloads to different churches, and we could barely understand English, let alone speak it. We were listening to these white preachers talking and all the white people (we called them *Washechus*) sat up front. They made us sit in the back. We were the last ones in and the first ones to leave, and when they said, Love thy neighbor, they didn't show us love. They didn't show us no kind of kindness. Even as children we knew. In our culture the children were re-spected. We were fed first. In the white man's society, it was totally the opposite of how we were raised. It was confusing. And we didn't have elders or parents to rescue us.

After I left the boarding school I went to Idaho Falls, Idaho, with these Mormons. I was twelve or so, and I lived there two years. I asked them why black people could not hold the priesthood. They really didn't want to answer me except to say that black people were cursed with black skin, and I instantly rejected that religion, because my spirit taught me that all my relations, anything the Creator created, we were related to. And that included black people. So I couldn't bear witness that it was the true church. I listened to them preach but when they asked me to bear witness that Joseph Smith was a prophet, my spirit spoke out: "He's *your* prophet, not mine. I believe the White Buffalo Calf Woman was sent to my people. I can't go against my beliefs."

They kicked me out of there. They just sent me back to Pine Ridge and my uncles took me up north to Bismarck, North Dakota.

Then I was married. I was sixteen. I was considered an old maid. My

Lois Stands-Raheem with her husband, Ismail.

father was the one that told me who I was going to marry. It was what we called tradition.

There was another tradition: My grandmother told me when your earth father dies, you only listen to the Great Holy One. Nobody could tell me nothing. My earth father died in '77.

I left my husband in 1983, and I went to Rapid City, South Dakota, for one year, and from there I went to Denver. That was the big, big city, and while I was in Denver, I only associated with other Lakotas. We had a Sweat Lodge[18] and our prayer ceremonies.

I went to Portland, Oregon, for two years, and I was away from my people, and there was no Sweat Lodge, no spiritual leader. Some call him Medicine Man.

Then I went to Atlanta, Georgia. I went to this big convention center, where a black minister was going to be speaking. I was standing in line waiting to buy my ticket, and I heard the loudspeakers come on, and then

---

[18] The Sweat Lodge, a dome-shaped structure about four feet high, is constructed of bent willow saplings covered with canvas or blankets. The door faces east, the direction of the morning star and the rising sun, symbols of renewal. During ceremonies in the Sweat Lodge, cold water is poured over hot rocks in a central hole, producing heat. The ceremony is a means of purification during which prayers are offered while suffering intense heat.

this man started singing in a language I never heard. And then all of a sudden my spirit got still, and it was like lightning was coming up from the ground, up through my legs, my back, and on top of my head. I had goose bumps.

I didn't understand the language; all I knew is it was like a prayer and it was feeding my spirit. I hadn't experienced that in a long long time. It was that same feeling in the Sweat Lodge—the purification lodge—or at the Sun Dance.[19] These are things I hadn't experienced in the city.

I asked the woman in front of me, "What's that? What are they saying?"

She said, "Oh, that's Arabic."

"But what is it?"

"It's the *adhan,* the call to prayer," she said.

"Wow. Hurry up, let me in there. I wanna know more."

It was just like with the spiritual leaders in the Sweat Lodge singing with the drums. It was the voice—how they sang. I didn't know what they were saying, but it's like I heard it before. It was like my spirit that calls the *adhan.* So I went in and listened to this Muslim minister, and the quotes he quoted from the Qur'an.

As a Lakota, we've always had the book of truth built in within us. But I had never read it in no book. But anyway, when I first got a Qur'an this grin came over my face: Here's the book! There is actually a book that has things that I've known but I've never seen written in a book before.

There's a difference between religion and spirituality. In this society, where we have urban industrial values, religion is a segment of life. With that, you don't get spirituality from religion, whereas traditional value is that religion is the way of life. And then when Islam came along and Muslims said Islam is the way of life, I said, Hey I'm familiar with religion being a way of life, not a *segment* of life.

The minister was Louis Farrakhan. He was saying things my human will wanted to hear.

I was able to go to their mosque, but there was something inside me that still wasn't right. I felt like I was oppressed among the oppressed. My second husband was half black, and a lot of my people oppressed me because of that. It was socially acceptable to be married with a white man

---

[19] During Sun Dance ceremonies, displays of tribal unity and renewal, dancers fulfill personal vows of thanksgiving. Male dancers are pierced either in their chests and tied to cottonwood trees, or in the back so they can drag buffalo skulls.

but not a black man. Among my own people, I felt discriminated against, so I turned from them.

I felt the same thing when I went among Louis Farrakhan's people. They said the white man was the devil and they wouldn't allow white people in their mosque. But my heart was thinking about the Creator. I knew in the physical world they were judging people, and I knew my spirit didn't want to take part in it.

At one time, when I was told Islam was a black man's religion, I didn't believe that for a second. My spirit said this is a way of life. Even in Islam I found African Americans being discriminated against by other so-called Muslims. They weren't really welcomed in certain *masjids,* and that hurt me to see this happen.

In our culture, it's like the Two-Legged—that's what we were, whether you're Lakota, black, white, Hispanic, Asian. Two-Legged is Two-Legged: man. Everything the Creator created, we're related to. *Tunkashila wakan tanka*—the Creator—created tribes, nations. I didn't really know a lot of white people, but I knew some were good, just like in any race.

To me, the truth was the truth, wherever I heard it. For me, religion is a way. Islam taught a way of life; and the Creator had a purpose for the Nation of Islam—to be here for a group of people whose minds needed the kind of discipline that this religion brought. It brought them out of the kind of world that they were imprisoned in, in their mind.

I read the Qur'an and I found out about sects; that there are going to be a lot of sects. The Qur'an said not to be a part of those sects. So I wouldn't join. And if I was to go to *juma* prayer it would be in a mosque where I felt they thought universally. The followers of Warith D. Mohammed were the ones that I felt thought universally—people with a train of thought like Malik Shabazz, as they call Malcolm X—that was where I felt most comfortable.

My Creator was putting people in my life that were righteous Muslims—and close-minded ones.

It was real enlightening to learn that Islam had a lot of similarities. The Lakotas pray to the East, and *umpa* was the most important prayer. That was at daybreak. That's like *fajr*. We were supposed to pray all day too.

There are over 510 [Native American] tribes. They have languages and traditions that are different, but pretty much we all believe in one Creator. The spiritual leaders—some are men, some are women.

The Lakota call religion "the red road." In Islam it's the "straight path." It means being righteous, good-hearted, kind, generous, thoughtful, giving, being real, helping others, sacrificing, not lying. At one time it was just called the "straight road," but after whites came with their language, they changed it to the "red road," because people called us Indians red.

People walked on this straight path and were basically good. And sometimes they'd get off it and go on the black road, the crooked road. It had a lot to do with race. When the missionaries came, anything crooked or bad was black, and then we were to look at the black people like that. I knew that was part of why they changed it to the black road.

In the spring when the thunder bands came, there was a ceremony called the *Hamblecha,* which was a Vision Quest.[20] And those who made a commitment to sun-dance that year had to seek a Vision before they sun-danced. Now, at some point in time, we were to commit ourselves to do this. This would help guide us throughout life, yearly. That was usually June, and then July was a Sun Dance, it's four days of fasting and dancing and giving praise.

The Vision Quest—you sit in one place and you just seek a vision. The Sun Dance was on what they called sacred ground—the Medicine Men blessed this ground with this willow tree or cedar in the middle. We gave the sun-dancers our strength to dance for four days, from sunup and the very first prayer till sundown. And then they went into the Sweat Lodge that night and slept a little. Early the next morning before sunup, we started again. Then the men gave flesh offering on the third and the fourth day, when they were pierced in their chest. And this is part of sacrifice in the physical world. They were considered holy people by the fourth day.

I've seen a lot of signs. Some people call them miracles. I went to one Sun Dance. The fourth day just before they were winding down, these gray clouds opened up, and the sun was shining down only on the dancers, and there was no sun where we were. They were facing the east, and it was around noon, then about five eagles came and circled above them. It just took your breath away. It was like the Creator let them know He was pleased. And it was kind of chilly by that time, so the sun warmed them up. And it was just on that spot, that holy ground. Old women started crying.

[20] During a Vision Quest, The Lakota seek a vision on a hill in a sacred place marked off by colored flags for the four directions and a string of tobacco pouches stretched out between the flags. Visions are considered the source of power to perform ceremonies with a pipe.

It was after the Sun Dance that they made another commitment for the next year to dance. So during that year they had to stay on the red road. They had to be righteous, not lie, cheat, steal, manipulate, con, fornicate, or commit adultery. You commit yourself for four years and then after four years, you commit yourself on behalf of your father, and after that, on behalf of your mother. And it's supposed to be a lifetime thing.

I've left that circle, the tradition of the Lakota ways, because it stopped me from growing and becoming universal. I had to stay within my race. As long as I associated with black people I could not participate in certain ceremonies. I remember telling the Medicine Man, "I don't need you, and I don't need this. My Creator is with me wherever I go." And I left. It was in a Sweat Lodge. This was when I married my second husband. The Medicine Man told me as long as I associate with a black man, I could not participate.

And nobody defended me. All of my cousins and relatives that were there, going to the Sweat Lodge—nobody spoke up. And I looked at the Medicine Man like: You're just a man. You're not my Creator. I don't need to listen to you. You're wrong. And I left. All I knew was when I leave this earth, my spirit's going to account for what it did and how it grew.

In the city, my main purpose was looking for a group of people who thought the way I did: universally. I knew among my own people, the traditions themselves would stop me from thinking like that, so I had to leave the circle.

I had this idea in my head: I'm going to look for a husband.

One day I got just tired of being independent. I wanted companionship. So when I mentioned marriage, I remember one sister said, "Why don't you look for a Native American Muslim?"

I said, "Where? Please tell me where!"

A Muslim sister gave me a copy of The American Muslim, and I sent my story in, and it was printed. I wrote about marriage. In the physical world, I just wanted to be called Muslim, one who submits. But I felt separated.

I believed that Allah would lead a good righteous man to me. But if it wasn't for my letter, I wouldn't have met my husband.

My letter was printed last spring, just before Ramadan. I got letters from around the country. His letter came from Cleveland, Ohio. I was in Denver, Colorado.

Everybody else asked me about my race or nationality, age. Can you have children? How much money do you make a year? What do you do? What kind of car do you own? This is the physical, material world. My current husband—he never asked me questions about my race. That came later, but his first thought was about Islam, about my spirit. I didn't feel I was being separated or dissected or classified. He read that I was strong spiritually, and he was happy to meet a strong spirit.

All the other letters, I answered nicely, and I answered his letter and gave my phone number and just waited, but I didn't call him right away.

There was a brother before him that asked me about my culture and my spirit. I wrote to him for maybe six weeks, and we talked on the phone. It sounded like we were compatible in some areas. But one day, he wanted me to fly to meet him. He would pay for the ticket for me to come and stay at his house. I said, No, I would stay at a motel. He said, Why, when I have this three-bedroom house? I said, Because Islamically that isn't something I will do.

He told me that he's making all the arrangements and if I didn't like it . . . So I just said no. It would be setting up to fornicate. I wouldn't do that. He got upset, so I knew he wasn't the person.

I never did meet him. As a matter of fact, I told him that I didn't want to correspond with him anymore.

And then the next letter was from my [current] husband. He didn't ask me about my culture. Islam was the culture that he was mainly concerned about, and that's what he practiced.

I got his letter four days after Ramadan was over. That was May. We were married June 13, six weeks later. There were many letters, many calls, like a courtship. I just knew by his spirit. I just knew that he was the soul mate that I was to have.

I married him in June, and I didn't meet him until the third week in August.

You got married over the phone?

There was an imam that married us over the phone. Spiritually we got to know each other first. That was the most important thing to us.

In this society, there's the physical realm, the chemistry, then the communication, and then the commitment. This was opposite. It was the spirit first. So I just knew him. It seemed like we've always been to-gether.

How did you get married on the phone? They sent the contract, and then he called you on a party line?

Uh-huh. And we were married. But first he sent me a contract, and I answered that and then it was set up.

But I married him sight unseen. I didn't care if he was tall, fat, bald-headed, one-eyed, one-legged. It was that kind of thing. It was the spirit.

Then I moved from Denver. I saved up my money. I rented a U-Haul and towed my car and moved to Cleveland.

What happened when you met for the first time?

The door was open and he was standing right there. He was wearing a light blue shirt, blue jeans, and he had a *kufi* on, and I didn't know he was bald. I really didn't care. He looks mean, to most people. He's got this deep voice, like he intimidates people. He's tall, and I'm short.

We just sat down and visited, and then there were prayers. We talked and talked and talked. We were in the present, not in the future or the past. He knew so much about me already and I knew so much about him.

We said this was something that only our Creator could give us—such a gift of His love.

Ye shall surely travel from stage to stage.

Qur'an 84:19

Nomad

Hamza Hanson

Born: Walla Walla, Washington. His Arabic translation of the name of his hometown: "O Allah, O Allah!"

Young, gleamy-eyed, well versed in Arabic, he told of a burial of a young Muslim boy who had died of a brain tumor. The corpse, wrapped in cloth for burial, had to be rewashed according to Islamic ritual. Once unwrapped—on the corpse's face: a smile that wasn't there earlier: the sign of a sin-forgiven martyr in the cause of Islam, Hamza explained, consoling the boy's father.

Hamza's journey toward Islam stretched from California to Timbuktu to the Arabian Peninsula. His jihad *may eventually take him to Africa once again.*

My grandfather was one of the publishers of the New York *Herald Tribune.* My father came out West after he finished Columbia University. He was teaching. I grew up in Marin County. My mother was very ecumenical even though she was Greek Orthodox and I was baptized Greek Orthodox.

I went to a Jesuit school when I was thirteen, back East, Georgetown Preparatory School. I was around Jesuits. I thought there was something very strange. A lot of them were alcoholics. I lived in dorms and I definitely saw them staggering down the halls and there was some homosexuality and they just seemed like real odd fishes to me. I spent almost two years there and then I came back out West.

I was in a used-book store and I saw on the bottom shelf a little Qur'an and I thought that's the one religion I don't know anything about. So I bought the Qur'an and the introduction said the Muslims believe in a very simple creed—*La illaha ill Allah* and Muhammad is His messenger, and I looked in the Contents and saw the chapter of Mary and I was amazed that they believed in Mary. I saw all these names of prophets that I recognized, like Joseph and Moses. So I read the chapter of Mary and there's a verse where God says, The likeness of Jesus is the likeness of Adam. That God only says to a thing: Be, and it is. And it was kind of negating the Son of God thing that I'd always had a hard time with. And all the Christians that I'd met that have converted to Islam—they'd always said that.

I became Muslim about a week later.

A girlfriend that I was dating at that time—I told her that I was reading about Islam. She'd met a Muslim from Mecca at the University of California at Santa Barbara. I was eighteen, and I said I really want to meet this person. He invited us to dinner with him and his wife. So we went and I started asking about Islam, and after that I'd met them a few other times.

I took *shahada* with him and then the journey began.

He was a member of a group of Muslims that was based in England. They were Sufis. I was in college at the time. I left. I ended up staying in Monterey for a few months and learned just the basics about how to pray, how to fast.

At a certain point I was in Bradford, England, and there was a Kuwaiti man. I was telling him how hard it was to call English people to Islam because they're just not interested, and he said, Well, don't forget the words of Noah when he said, I called my people by night and by day, and it hasn't increased them except in distancing themselves from me. He told me that Noah was doing that for 950 years, so I shouldn't get discouraged.

When he said those *ayats* in Arabic, suddenly Arabic had a relevancy that it didn't have before. And I just saw him applying something to everyday life, and the Qur'an hadn't had that effect on me yet. I told him that I really wanted to learn Arabic, and so I visited these Kuwaitis in London. One night there was a man giving a talk, and before long most of the people in the room were in tears. I was really impressed with this language.

I traveled a lot. I visited Timbuktu. Timbuktu is an ancient trading center in the middle of the Sahara on the Niger River. Very beautiful oasis town. It's where the nomads bring the salt tablets still to this day from mines in the desert by caravan. There was just a simplicity and beauty that I hadn't seen before, because most of the Muslim world has been turned upside down since colonialism—and it's like the post-Renaissance period.

Anyway, I got very sick and I had to go back. I went to Switzerland and I was in the hospital for a while. And then I went to the Emirates and lived there for four years. In the Emirates, I became an imam and was a muezzin in a mosque. I used to climb the minaret and call the *adhan*.

And then I studied in the deep desert. No cars. You had to travel by camel or walk.

I went first to Morocco, and then to Algeria for three months. I was studying in a mosque and the Algerian government at the time was very paranoid about Muslim fundamentalists. I was thrown out. So I took a train to Tunis and went to the Mauritanian embassy and the ambassador arranged for me to go to his country. I went into the desert. They sent messages over the radio to the Bedouin camp of the teacher I was going to: "Hamza is arriving on camel" on such and such a date. It took about a day and a half. I lived in a little hut that was made for me by students out of tree branches, thatch, covered with burlap sacks from rice. And I lived there for ten months. They've had drought for almost twenty years and their livestock has been devastated.

Those people live half in the unseen world. They're deeply spiritual. I was once riding. We were going from one place to another, about a day's journey, and there was a Bedouin encampment. The person I was riding with said, "Let's go and get something to eat and rest." It was about noon. And so we headed toward this encampment. When we arrived, all the people came out of the tents. I was wearing a blue robe with a black turban. We sat down. They brought us a bowl of milk, and there was a very old woman. When she saw me she said, *"La illaha ill Allah."*

She told one of the men, who told me, that she had had a dream the night before that a very white man with a black turban would come on a camel and have lunch with them, and that we should honor him because he's come a long way.

I realized that it's the illusion of choice. It had taken place in the unseen. We just needed to complete the event in the seen world.

Mauritanians—really, West Africans—still have an incredible pride of culture, of language, of religion, whereas most of the Arabs have had their pride taken away from them, because they're a defeated people. They co-opted the conquerors' culture.

When we think of Islam we automatically think of the Arab, and there is some validity to that, even though Islam is not an Arab religion. It has an Arab flavor because the Prophet was Arab, just as Judaism has a Semitic flavor. Original Christianity had a Semitic flavor. You can't get away from that.

In Europe, literacy was for priests and aristocrats, and common people were kept illiterate, ignorant. The Protestant Reformation, in part, was a result of a man reading the Bible and saying, Wait a second; there are a lot of things that aren't jibing with what the Church is telling us. And all of a sudden you have people translating the Bible out of Latin and into the vernacular.

Galileo was crucified metaphorically by the Church not so much because of his heretical stances, but one of the major things that disturbed the Church was that he wrote in Italian, not in Latin. He wrote in the vernacular of the people and was putting out scientific ideas in a language that people could understand, and that was very frightening.

Islam has never had that fear of educating people. It wasn't built on a structure of exploitation. It was built on a structure of liberation—liberation through education, through critical understanding.

The Qur'an demands that you question things. There are constant rhetorical questions in it: Where then are you going? What speech are you going to believe in after this if not the Qur'an? Abraham says, Do you worship what you make with your hands? And we can apply that to the consumer society.

Muslims are accused of being fatalists. It's not so much that Muslims are fatalists; the Muslims understand that life has very powerful tragic elements and within that tragedy there are moments in our life that we are given to sustain us through our tragedy. The Qur'an came at a time when Arab poetry had reached a pinnacle. The Qur'an tells us that this life is tribulation, but look at all the blessings that come during the time of trial and tribulation.

I've taken a three-year diversion here in the States to study homeopathy. I want to go back to Mauritania and offer them something in return.

There is slavery there. Slavery is allowed under Islam, but under very strict, humane standards. The last thing that the Prophet said on his deathbed was: Those under you—what your right hand possesses—treat them well.

We have to see him in his historical context. He didn't come out of a vacuum. Freeing a slave is one of the highest things that you can do in Islam. He freed all of his slaves.

Slavery is all about war, and war is a part of Islam; it's a part of life. So in Islam, we don't have an altruistic picture of man. Islam accepts the hormone of aggression—that man is aggressive against his neighbor. Allah says, Allah does not love those who are aggressive. And there's no aggression except on those who are oppressed, so all of a sudden war is put into a spiritual context. The only time you are allowed to fight is against oppressors. And that's something that Malcolm X was acutely aware of. When you're being beaten to a pulp, you can't remain a pacifist. You have to defend yourself.

Christ says, I have not come to bring peace to the world. He says that. When he went into the temple, he went in turning over tables—that's not turning the other cheek. He saw that those people were oppressing the rights of God in the temple of God.

The Europeans used their own form of Christianity as a way of controlling people. What you do is send in missionaries, teach people to turn the other cheek, and then follow with a wave of conquistadors who are going to open up new markets and take all of the resources of pacifistic people, because the only people who followed "turn the other cheek" are people in the Third World. The African Christians are always turning the other cheek. You never see a European turning the other cheek.

Part of reconstruction in Islam is incorporating people into the society through slavery. Slavery in Islam is seen as a transitory period where a people—who would otherwise have a refugee status and would be without any rights, without any home, without any nourishment, and live life destitute—are incorporated into homes and brought into the homes of wealthy people and educated. The Prophet said, The best of you are those who take a slave and educate them. Many of the greatest scholars in Islam were slaves. And Muslims liberated their slaves traditionally.

Slavery in Mauritania didn't shock me. Our understanding of slavery comes from the nineteenth century. There in Mauritania slaves live in their own encampments next to the encampments of their owners, and they have their own lives. They have their own children. They marry. They give a portion of their food to their owners.

In Islam, if you ask for your freedom, then the Qur'an demands that the master must give the freedom to the slave, if he sees in him good. But it's done through indentured servitude. You make an arrangement. The government officially freed all the slaves, several years back,[21] and now they can go if they want to.

The injunctions that were put into the Qur'an were radical at that time—like giving women the right to inherit. That was a very radical departure from the norm. Women didn't get the right to inherit in Western civilization until the 19th century.

There's a story that the people of Mecca said to one of the companions of the Prophet, "We heard that he's giving your women rights. Next he's going to be giving your animals rights." This companion retorted, "He has. We can't give them a burden more than they can bear on their backs."

The Prophet is described in the Qur'an as the mercy for all the worlds, which includes the animal kingdom and the vegetable kingdom. In the rules of war, the Prophet forbade people to tear up fruit-bearing trees as an act of aggression against their enemy. They did that traditionally. Look at how Agent Orange was used in Vietnam.

But I think that there's a lot of sickness in the Muslim world. There's a lot of fighting, disunity, most of it coming from ignorance. An Egyptian Muslim is somebody whose father perhaps became Westernized and oftentimes left Islam. So an eighteen-year-old who's rediscovering Islam is rediscovering his roots.

The immigrants here have brought all these "diseases" over here—factionalism and cultural Islam. To become a Muslim doesn't mean to become Pakistani or Moroccan or Syrian. It means to embrace a universal teaching that transcends cultural boundaries.

In the Muslim world it's like I'm suspect. Like: Why would an American want to go to a backward country to learn all these things about the Bedouin way of life? He's coming from the most advanced culture in the world. So they think there must be something suspect. I've had that a lot in the Muslim world. And then in America I get the opposite, it's kind of like I'm a traitor. I've become one of "them."

I've made *hajj* twice and *umrah* several times, the lesser *hajj*.

The first time I made *hajj* was overwhelming. I saw it ultimately as an intimate experience with the human race, because all of a sudden you see the commonality of mankind.

Mankind is in desperation. Thoreau said most men live lives of quiet desperation. The Muslim lives a life of vociferous desperation. It's like I

[21] Mauritania abolished slavery in 1981; Saudi Arabia abolished it in 1962.

have to get through this with my soul. I have to obtain the mercy of God, and in a sense because of that reason, it's not a dismal despair but it's an intense desire to free oneself of the chains of the self. We're imprisoned.

The Prophet said that this world is a prison for the believer, and it's the paradise of the one who rejects the truth. So for the Muslim—that's his despair. He's chained in this body and this ego, this self that is constantly calling him to the lowest aspects of himself. And the *nafs*—I love that term. The *nafs*, the lower self, is taking us down and the spirit is journeying to break free of that bondage of the *nafs*. And so *hajj* is kind of the ultimate manifestation of that intense desire to free oneself of this world and enter a state of purity.

There's no spiritual place that equals the Ka'aba—and Medina, where the Prophet is buried. It's like a place of light. One man said, "I feel like I'm wading through light like one wades through water; I feel it's so thick here, the spiritual light."

The *hajj* strips away all that cultural garb. Everybody's dressed the same. You strip away that cultural garb, jettison all that baggage, and there you are with two sheets of cloth, unsewn, the women dressed in white, before God, and you see the man next to you is no different from you, no matter what his color.

Islam

Islam (which means "submission" and is derived from the word for "peace") is the religion of Muslims. They believe that Allah (or God) revealed His will to Muhammad, who was born of the Quraish tribe in Mecca in A.D. 570 and was commissioned to prophethood one night at age forty, when the archangel Gabriel visited him and ordered him to "recite."

A series of revelations, continued until Muhammad's death at age sixty-three.

During his life, decadent Mecca was steeped in idolatry, and Muhammad and other Muslims suffered persecution. After thirteen years of patiently preaching, Muhammad, in 622, fled north to the city of Yathrib, escaping a plot to murder him. His 260-mile journey is known as the *Hijra* (migration), and marks the first year of the Muslim calendar.

Eight years later, he returned to Mecca in conquest without shedding blood. He entered the Ka'aba, the sacred house that Muslims believe was founded by Adam and rebuilt by Abraham and Ishmael, breaking into pieces the 360 idols placed there, and purifying the house for worshipping Allah. Muhammad died on June 8, 632, acknowledged by Meccans as a prophet.[1]

---

[1] Muhammad was both legislator and prophet. Of him, the French poet Lamartine (1790–1869) wrote in a work entitled *A History of Turkey,* published in 1854:

"Never has a man proposed, either of his own free will or upon orders from above, so noble a goal . . . If a man's genius is measured according to the greatness of his design, the limited nature of the means at his disposal, and the immensity of the results achieved, then Muhammad was great in a way that no modern figure can hope to emulate. The most celebrated among them have done no more than win a few victories, pass a few laws, or create an empire. When and if they actually accomplished something, it was usually swept away after their death. Muhammad's ideas set whole armies in motion, affected legislation, empires, peoples, dynasties, millions of people in an area covering one-third of the inhabited surface of the globe. But he accomplished more than that: he also stirred up new ideas, beliefs, and souls.

Allah's revelations to Muhammad are preserved in the Qur'an in 114 chapters (suras). Muslims consider the words to be holy and unchanged since the Prophet's day. They add that the Qur'an is the only divinely revealed Scripture to remain unchanged. Earlier revelations to Allah's messengers (segments of the Torah given to Moses, the Psalms revealed to David, and the Evangel revealed to Jesus) have been altered by man to such a degree that the original messages have been adulterated.

Muslims believe the Qu'ran is Allah's final message to His final messenger, the "seal of the prophets" in a long line that includes Adam, Noah, Enoch, Abraham, Ishmael, Isaac, Jacob, David, Solomon, Job, Joseph, Moses, Aaron, Elijah, Elisha, Jonah, Lot, Ezekiel, Zechariah, John, and Jesus. Some Muslim scholars say the total number is 124,000 prophets, each chosen by Allah to convey His message to mankind to all regions on earth.

Muslims do not worship Muhammad, nor any of the prophets; they worship only Allah and love each of the prophets equally, including Moses and Jesus, and while the Qur'an states that Jesus was born to a virgin mother by the power of Allah, it rejects the concept of Jesus as the Son of God. Jesus' birth is considered miraculous but his nature was no more divine than was Adam's, who was born without parents. The *hadith* are a voluminous collection of well-documented reports of the sayings and traditions of Prophet Muhammad. Muslims use these traditions as a secondary source of guidance. The primary source is Allah's Qur'an. As the word of Allah, it is to be recited in the original Arabic at prayer time and on other occasions by Muslims, helping to inscribe the word of Allah in their hearts and minds.

The Qur'an informs us that Allah is just, and goodness and piety will be rewarded, and evil deeds will be met with punishment. It contains injunctions and outlines Allah's complete guidance in life for all humanity, focusing on pure monotheism, enjoining social reforms, and including the concept of the Last Judgment. On Judgment Day, Allah, Creator of the universe, will destroy creation and resurrect the dead, and everlasting life in Paradise or hell will begin. Humankind will stand before Allah, who will

---

On the basis of one book, whose every word has become a law, he created a spiritual nationality that embraces people of every color and language. The indelible character of this Muslim faith resides in a hatred of false idols and a passion for the one and only, immaterial deity . . . Philosopher, orator, apostle, legislator, warrior, conqueror of ideas, restorer of rational dogma, of a cult without images, founder of twenty worldly empires and one spiritual empire, such is Muhammad. According to every standard by which human greatness can be measured, what man was ever greater?"

decide the fate of each soul, according to his or her deeds, recorded by angels. Until death, when the fate of a soul is sealed, humans can absolve themselves from sins through worship of Allah and sincere repentance, availing themselves of Allah's mercy and forgiveness.

More so than Christianity and Judaism, Islam entails a complete code for living, with guidance for every aspect of community and individual life —religion, politics, social systems, economics. Humans are considered equal before their Lord, except in piety, and there is no hierarchy of authority and no priesthood in Islam.

Muslims believe in articles of faith—belief in Allah as the One and Only God, the angels, the revealed Scriptures, Allah's messengers, the hereafter, and the divine decree that all creation is governed by Allah.

Muslims practice the five pillars of Islam, which are obligatory acts of worship (*ibadat*). These are:

Faith. Translated, the declaration of faith (*shahada*) is: "I bear witness that there is no god but God, and I bear witness that Muhammad is the messenger of God."

Prayer. *Salat* is the name of the obligatory prayers Muslims are enjoined to perform five times daily—at dawn, noon, midafternoon, sunset, and nightfall. It serves as a direct link to Allah.

Fasting. Each year during Ramadan, the ninth lunar month of the Islamic calendar, Muslims fast from before sunrise until sunset, abstaining from not only food but drink and sexual relations. The fast is an act of self-purification, and a way to gain sympathy for those who are hungry.

Zakat. The word means both purification and growth. The act reminds Muslims that Allah is the true owner of everything, not man, and that He bestows wealth out of His beneficence. To purify their remaining possessions, Muslims yearly pay *zakat,* a poor-due assessed at 2.5 percent on cash or capital beyond one's immediate needs.

Pilgrimage. The *hajj* to Mecca in Saudi Arabia during the lunar month of Dhul-Hijja commemorates total submission and obedience to Allah. Forsaking ordinary comforts and conveniences, as well as the benefits of status and individuality, Muslims must complete this act of worship once in their life, if they are able.

Glossary

adhan Call to prayer.

aisha Third wife of Prophet Muhammad and daughter of Abu Bakr, the first man outside of the Prophet Muhammad's family to accept Islam.

ajr Recompense.

Allah God, the Deity (Arab Christians use the same term to refer to God).

Allahu akbar "Allah is great" or "Allah is the greatest."

asr The midafternoon prayer; title of the 103rd Sura of the Holy Qur'an. Also means time through the ages.

Assalaamu alaikum "Peace be unto you." Used upon greeting and leaving a Muslim.

Astaghfirullah "God forgive me."

ayat Signs, proofs, clear evidence of miracles; also verses of the Qur'an.

bid'ah An innovation in religion.

Bismillah "In the name of Allah." Used to commence any prayer, action, meal, etc.

califa (Also *khalifah;* Anglicized version: *caliph*) Successor, vicar, lieutenant.

dawah Call, appeal, invocation, invitation, missionary activity, supplication, propagation of Islam.

deen Divine code of life.

dervish Islamic devotee dedicated to a life of poverty and chastity, some of whom practice whirling as part of their religious experience.

duah Individual or spontaneous prayer.

Effendi Master, a Turkish title of respect.

Eid al-Adha "Feast of Sacrifice" at the culmination of *hajj*.

Eid al-Fitr "Feast of Breaking Fast," held on the first day of the month of Shawwal to mark the end of the month of fasting (Ramadan).

fajr Dawn. First prayer of the day.

faquih Someone who is versed in *fiqh,* Islamic jurisprudence.

Fatihah "The Opening One," the first sura of the Holy Qur'an.

Fatimah Daughter of the Prophet Muhammad.

fatwa A religious opinion or decision pronounced by a recognized authority, often called a *mufti.*

fez Conical hat that tapers to a flat crown.

fiqh Jurisprudence.

fitnah Confusion, trial, revolt, seduction, discord, riot, war, civil war.

ghusl Taking a bath in a religious, ceremonial way.

hadith The traditions of the Prophet Muhammad; i.e., his sayings.

hafiz One who has committed the complete Qur'an to memory. One of the ninety-nine attributes of Allah, meaning "the Guardian."

hajj A pilgrimage to Mecca which is obligatory for every Muslim who can afford it; a pilgrim to Mecca; title of the 22nd Sura of the Qur'an.

halal Lawful, permissible, legal, sacrificed with the name of Allah.

al-hamdulillah "All praise is due to Allah alone."

Hanafi School of law founded by Abu Hanifah (d. 767). This school is dominant in many countries that formed part of the Turkish Empire, and in India.

Hanbali School of law founded by Ahmad ibn Hanbal (d. 855). This school is observed in Saudi Arabia and Qatar.

haqiqah Esoteric truth which transcends human and theological limitations.

al-Haram The sacred, inviolable sanctuary of Mecca.

hijab Veiling or concealing.

hijra Prophet Muhammad's migration from Mecca to Medina, marking year one of the Muslim calendar.

ihram The state entered in order to perform *hajj* or umrah pilgrimages; the name of the costume that the pilgrim wears.

ijtihad Independent judgment in a legal or theological question.

ijtimah An assembly held to formulate a consensus on a point of Islamic jurisprudence.

imam A responsible, knowledgeable leader who leads others in prayer.

insh'allah "If it pleases Allah"; "God willing."

isha The night prayer, performed about one and a half hours after sunset.

al-Jahiliyyah The "time of ignorance" or period of Arab paganism preceding the revelation of Islam.

jamat Congregation.

jihad An effort or strife.

jinn Unseen and seen beings created of "smokeless fire."

juma (also *jumu'a*) Friday. Day of reunion or gathering.

Ka'aba The sacred house in Mecca around which pilgrims circumambulate during *hajj*. The building is not worshipped by Muslims, but regarded as a spiritual center.

kalimah "Word." The creed of the Muslim, meaning "None has the right to be worshipped but Allah and Muhammad is His Apostle."

keemahs Head-covering.

khutbah The sermon delivered on Friday before the prayer, Eid prayers, engagement, betrothal.

kufi Skullcap.

La illaha ill Allah "There is no god but Allah," the first pillar in declaring the faith of Islam.

madrasah A traditional school of higher study; students entering a madrasah were presumed to have already committed the entire Qur'an to memory.

maghrib The sunset prayer.

Maliki School of law founded by Malik ibn Anas (d. 795). This school predominates in the Arab West and West Africa.

ma'rifah Knowledge in general, especially in modern Arabic usage. In religious literature it means esoteric or mystical knowledge of God, gnosis.

ma'shallah "Whatever is the will of Allah."

masjid (plural: *masajid*) Place of prayer, mosque.

Mevlevi A Sufi order founded by Mevlana Jalal ad-Din ar-Rumi. Members are sometimes called "whirling dervishes" because of their revolving dance done for spiritual realization.

mihrab Niche in the wall of a mosque, indicating the *qiblah,* the direction of Mecca.

minaret Tower from which the muezzin performs the call to prayer.

minbar A pulpit, in the form of a movable staircase, from which the *imam* preaches the Friday sermon, *khutbah*.

Mi'raj Ascent; Prophet Muhammad's journey to the Seven Heavens.

mosque from the Arabic *masjid,* "a place of prostration." Mosques are customarily uncluttered sacred spaces where worshippers perform Islamic prayers. A *mihrab* indicates the direction of Mecca, toward which Muslims face in prayer. To the right of the *mihrab* is the *minbar* (pulpit).

Muhammad (also *Mohamed, Mohammed*)   The Prophet of Islam (570–632).

Muhammadan   A name often used incorrectly by non-Muslims in referring to followers of Islam (Muslims). The term is unacceptable to Muslims, for it implies that their worship and religion revolve around the man Muhammad.

muezzin   One who performs the call to prayer.

mufti   A learned Islamic leader who gives or is qualified to give Islamic verdicts.

nafs   Breath, soul, conscience.

prayer   There are three types in Islam: *duah, salat,* and *zikr.*

Prophet(s)   There are two classes: *rasool* (messenger or envoy), who brings a new religion or major revelation, and *nabi* (prophet), whose mission lies within the framework of an existing religion.

qiblah   The direction toward Mecca, to which Muslims face when performing *salat.*

Quraish   The tribe of Mecca. Prophet Muhammad was born into this tribe.

Qur'an (Also *Koran*)   The holy book of Islam. It was revealed by Allah in Arabic. Its language became the basis of formal and classical Arabic, written and spoken. Revelation of the Qur'an began during the month of Ramadan in A.D. 610, when the Prophet was in the cave of Hira near the summit of Jabal Nur mountain. The angel Gabriel appeared with the first revelation, the beginning of Surah 96. The Qur'an contains laws, warnings, descriptions of Judgment Day, heaven and hell, stories of Biblical figures, metaphysical passages, and sacred history. Unchanged since revelation, and considered eternal and uncreated in its essence, the Qur'an is revered as the divine word of Allah, and is recited in prayer.

rahmatullah wa barakatuh   Mercy and blessings of Allah.

raka'at (also *raka'ah*)   prayer unit made up primarily of standing, bowing, prostration, and sitting.

Ramadan   The ninth month of the Islamic calendar, in which began the revelation of the Qur'an to Prophet Muhammad. (The revelation continued for twenty-three years until his death.)

rasool A messenger of God who is entrusted with a divinely revealed scripture.

rosary The Islamic rosary consists of ninety-nine beads, corresponding to the ninety-nine names of Allah. Typically, the string of beads is divided into three sections of thirty-three beads. After *salat,* Muslims finger to recite various litanies, each thirty-three times. The Prophet used his fingers to count the litanies, moving his thumb across the finger joints of both hands.

ruh Spirit.

ruku The bow in the canonical prayer, *salat.*

sajdah Touching the forehead on the ground during prayer, *salat.*

salat Canonical or ritual prayer; the obligatory five daily prayers to be performed at stated times, after ablution is made.

Seal of Prophecy A title of Muhammad, considered the last prophet and messenger of Allah; also the large lump of flesh ("the size of a pigeon's egg") in the small of the back of Muhammad, interpreted as a physical sign of his prophecy.

Shafi'i School of law founded by Muhammad ibn Idris ash-Shafi'i (d. 820). This school is dominant in Indonesia, Malaysia, and the Philippines. Along with the Hanafi and Maliki schools, it is also observed in Egypt, and is followed in Central Asia and the Caucasus.

shahada Declaration of faith in Islam.

shari'ah Islamic law based on the Qur'an and *hadith,* and as elaborated by the analytical principles of the four schools of jurisprudence.

Shaytan Satan.

Shi'a Doctrine of the legitimacy which holds that Ali ibn Abi Talib, the fourth of the Orthodox caliphs, was the true spiritual and political heir of the Prophet Muhammad.

Shiite One who follows the *Shi'a* doctrine. Ten percent, or less, of the total number of Muslims are Shiite.

shirk Polytheism, idolatry, paganism: to worship or associate others along with Allah.

Sufi One who gives up all worldly things to seek the pleasure or nearness of Allah.

Sufism Islamic mysticism or esoterism.

sujud   The touching of the forehead to the ground during *salat*.

Sunnah   A path, a way of life, all the traditions and practices of the Prophet Muhammad that have become models to be followed by Muslims.

Sunni   One who follows the *Sunnah* in all spheres of life.

sura (also *surah*)   A row or series; strictly refers to the chapters of the Qur'an.

Sura Ikhlas   The "Verse of Sincerity." It proclaims the unity or absoluteness of the Divine Essence.

tabligh   Spreading, delivering, preaching the teachings of Islam.

tariqah (also *tarikah*)   Spiritual doctrines and methods of mystic union; mystical path of Sufis.

tauhid   Monotheism, the unity of Allah.

tekka   Sufi gathering place or lodge.

thobe   One-piece, long-sleeved robe.

ummah   A community or nation that transcends ethnic or political definition.

umrah   An individual pilgrimage to Mecca at some time other than the *hajj* season.

Wahhabi   Sect dominant in Saudi Arabia and Qatar. Founded by Muhammad ibn 'Abd al-Wahhab (1703–87). Wahhabi, said to be followers of the Hanbali school, see themselves as belonging to no school, just as the first generations of Muslims did not follow schools of jurisprudence.

Walaikum salaam   "And unto you be peace." Used as a response in greeting or bidding farewell.

wudu   Ablution, prescribed washing done before saying prayers.

zakat   Obligatory, prescribed alms to be given by Muslims in order to "purify" what they retain.

zikr   Remembrance of Allah as an act of worship, invocation. For Sufis, *zikr* is a spiritual exercise involving the invocation of Allah's divine names or a sacred formula under the direction of a spiritual master. The Prophet said, "For everything there is a polish that takes away rust, and the polish of the heart is remembrance of Allah."

zuhr   Noon prayer.

Ninety-nine Names of Allah

The most beautiful names belong to Allah . . .

Qur'an 7:180

"There are 99 names that are Allah's alone. Whoever learns, understands and enumerates them enters Paradise and achieves eternal salvation."

Hadith (Abu Hurayrah)

1.	al-Awwal	The First	(Qur'an 57:3)
2.	al-Akhir	The Last	(57:3)
3.	al-Ahad	The One	(112:1)
4.	al-Badi	The Originator	(2:117)
5.	al-Bari'	The Producer	(59:24)
6.	al-Barr	The Beneficent	(52:28)
7.	al-Basir	The Seeing	(57:3)
8.	al-Basit	The Expander (a derived Name)	(13:26)
9.	al-Batin	The Inner	(57:3)
10.	al-Ba'ith	The Raiser	(16:89)
11.	al-Baqi	The Enduring	(20:73)
12.	at-Tawwab	The Relenting	(2:37)
13.	al-Jabbar	The Irresistible	(59:23)

367

14.	al-Jalil	The Majestic (a derived Name)	
15.	al-Jami'	The Gatherer	(3:9)
16.	al-Hasib	The Accounter	(4:6)
17.	al-Hafiz	The Guardian	(11:57)
18.	al-Haqq	The Truth	(20:114)
19.	al-Hakim	The Wise	(6:18)
20.	al-Hakam	The Judge	(40:48)
21.	al-Halim	The Kindly	(2:235)
22.	al-Hamid	The Praiseworthy	(2:269)
23.	al-Hayy	The Living	(20:111)
24.	al-Khabir	The Well-Informed	(6:18)
25.	al-Khafid	The Abaser (a derived Name)	
26.	al-Khaliq	The Creator	(13:16)
27.	Dhu-l-Jalal wa-l-Ikram	Full of Majesty & Generosity	(55:27)
28.	ar-Ra'uf	The Gentle	(2:143)
29.	ar-Rahman	The Merciful	(55:1)
30.	ar-Rahim	The Compassionate	(2:143)
31.	ar-Razzaq	The Provider	(51:57)
32.	ar-Rashid	The Guide (a traditional Name)	
33.	ar-Rafi	The Exalter (a derived Name)	(6:83)
34.	ar-Raqib	The Vigilant	(5:117)
35.	as-Salaam	The Peace	(59:23)
36.	as-Sami	The Hearer	(17:1)
37.	ash-Shakur	The Grateful	(64:17)
38.	ash-Shahid	The Witness	(5:117)
39.	as-Sabur	The Forebearing (a traditional Name)	
40.	as-Samad	The Eternal	(112:2)
41.	ad-Darr	The Afflicter (a derived Name)	(48:11)
42.	az-Zahir	The Outer	(57:3)
43.	al-Adl	The Just	(6:115)
44.	al-Aziz	The Mighty/The Precious	(59:23)
45.	al-Azim	The Great	(2:255)
46.	al-Afuw	The Pardoner	(4:99)

47.	al-Alim	The Knowing	(2:29)
48.	al-Ali	The High One	(2:255)
49.	al-Ghafur	The Forgiver	(2:235)
50.	al-Ghaffar	The Forgiving	(2:235)
51.	al-Ghani	The Rich	(2:267)
52.	al-Fattah	The Opener	(34:26)
53.	al-Qabid	The Seizer	(2:245)
		(a derived Name)	
54.	al-Qadir	The Capable	(17:99)
55.	al-Quddus	The Holy	(62:1)
56.	al-Qahhar	The Victorious	(13:16)
57.	al-Qawi	The Strong	(22:40)
58.	al-Qayyum	The Self-Subsistent	(3:2)
59.	al-Kabir	The Great	(22:62)
60.	al-Karim	The Magnanimous/	(27:40)
		Generous/Noble	
61.	al-Latif	The Gracious	(42:19)
62.	al-Muta'akhkhir	The Deferrer	(14:42)
63.	al-Mu'min	The Believer	(59:23)
64.	al-Muta'ali	The Self-Exalted	(13:9)
65.	al-Mutakkabir	The Superb	(59:23)
66.	al-Matin	The Firm	(51:58)
67.	al-Mubdi'	The Founder	(85:13)
68.	al-Mujib	The Responsive	(11:61)
69.	al-Majid	The Glorious	(11:73)
70.	al-Muhsi	The Counter	(19:94)
71.	al-Muhyi	The Giver of Life	(30:50)
72.	al-Mudhill	The Abaser	(3:26)
		(a derived Name)	
73.	al-Muzil	The Separator	(10:28)
74.	al-Musawwir	The Shaper	(59:24)
75.	al-Mu'id	The Restorer	(85:13)
76.	al-Mu'izz	The Honorer	(3:26)
		(a derived Name)	
77.	al-Mu'ti	The Giver	(20:50)
78.	al-Mughni	The Enricher	(9:74)
79.	al-Muqit	The Maintainer/	(4:85)
		Determiner	

80.	al-Muqtadir	The Prevailer	(54:42)
81.	al-Muqaddim	The Bringer Forward	(50:28)
82.	al-Muqsit	The Equitable	(21:47)
83.	al-Malik	The King	(59:23)
84.	Malik al-Mulk	Possessor of the Kingdom	(3:26)
85.	al-Mumit	The Slayer	(15:23)
86.	al-Muntaqim	The Avenger	(30:47)
87.	al-Muhamin	The Vigilant/Guardian	(59:23)
88.	an-Nafi	The Propitious (a derived Name)	(48:11)
89.	an-Nasir	The Helper	(4:45)
90.	an-Nur	The Light	(24:35)
91.	al-Hadi	The Guide	(22:54)
92.	al-Wahid	The Unique	(74:11)
93.	al-Wadud	The Loving	(11:90)
94.	al-Warith	The Inheritor	(19:40)
95.	al-Wasi	The Vast	(2:268)
96.	al-Wakil	The Steward	(6:102)
97.	al-Waliy	The Patron	(4:45)
98.	al-Wali	The Protector	(13:11)
99.	al-Wahhab	The Bestower	(3:8)